Copyright 2019
All rights reserved.
Printed in the United States of America

First Edition

The contents of this book are the property of Brown Technical Publications, Inc. All rights reserved. No part of this book covered by the copyright hereon may be reproduced, transmitted, stored or used in any form or by any means, graphic, electronic or mechanical, including, but not limited to, photocopying, recording, scanning, digitizing, Web distribution, information networks or by any information storage and retrieval systems, except as permitted under Section 107 or 108 of the 1976 United States Copyright Act, without the prior written permission of the publisher.

While every precaution has been taken in preparation of this book, the author and publisher assumes no responsibility for errors or omissions. Neither is any liability assumed from the use of the information contained herein. The reader is expressly warned to consider and adopt all safety precautions and to avoid all potential hazards. The publisher and author make no representations or warranties of any kind, nor are any such representations implied with respect to the material set forth here. The publisher and author shall not be liable for any special, consequently, or exemplary damages resulting, in whole or part, from the reader's use of, or reliance upon, this material.

Author: One Exam Prep (1-877-804-3959)
www.1examprep.com

ABOUT 1 EXAM PREP

1 EXAM PREP TAKES PRIDE IN BEING THE MOST EFFECTIVE AND EFFICIENT EXAM PREPARATION SCHOOL IN THE INDUSTRY.

All of our Classes and Exam Prep Material is available 24 Hours a Day online when you purchase a online course at www.1examprep.com or call 1-877-804-3959 Access the information whenever and as often as you need.

No Classrooms
No Time Schedules
No Pressure

We provide the TOOLS for YOU to be SUCCESSFUL on YOUR schedule, not ours!
ALL of the Information you need is available at ONE LOW PRICE!

We provide you with exactly what you need to be successful. We are up to date with ALL of our Textbooks. No Bait and switch. No hidden upsells. We invite you to compare......

WE HAVE THE LOWEST TEXT BOOK PRICES IN THE INDUSTRY!!!!!

1 Exam Prep takes pride in our students and in their success. We want you to pass your exam the first time, every time in the most cost efficient way. We offer the most comprehensive, easy to follow, **easy** to use **exam preparation** techniques in the industry. We offer both State and County Licensing Exam Prep Courses throughout the United States. We have helped thousands of students successfully pass State and County Licensing Exams and we are seriously committed in helping you!

ALL OF OUR COURSES INCLUDE OUR PROVEN 4 POINT LEARNING SYSTEM UNRIVALED IN THE INDUSTRY YOU WILL **RECEIVE**:

TABBING AND HIGHLIGHTING INSTRUCTIONS
The most comprehensive, up to date Tabbing and Highlighting instructions found anywhere in the industry. Our experienced instructors will provide you with more tabs, more highlights than any other exam prep school in the country. We know the material cover to cover. We show you what you need to know and where you will find it, when the pressure is on and the clock is moving.

TEST TAKING TECHNIQUES
Learn the strategy on how to be the most efficient and effective on exam day. Learn how to manage the exam, the questions and the clock and make it work to your advantage

PRACTICE QUESTIONS AND ANSWERS
We provide our students with 1000's of Questions and Answers to help you prepare for your exam. We are continually updating and adding relevant questions with answers to prepare for the current exams. Our years of experience and thorough knowledge of the subject matter and testing formats allow us to provide you with the skills needed to address each question on the exam.

TEXTBOOK OVERVIEW
You will receive a high level summary on each textbook you receive and is required for your exam. The summary will outline the topics covered in the textbook, where these topics can be in the textbook and the types of questions most likely to be answered in each textbook. You will also learn which parts of the textbook and which questions are aimed at a particular trade(s). Being thorough, efficient and confident is a huge advantage on exam day. Our Textbook Overview will help you manage your time and efficiency when the pressure is on and you need to stay focused.

TABLE OF CONTENTS

TESTING INFORMATION & SCOPE OF EXAM
TESTTAKING TECHNIQUES
    Test Taking 101
    Time Management
Highlights & Tabs

    Roofing Construction and Estimating
    Architectural Metal Flashing, Condensation and Air Leakage Control, 2018
    NRCA Architectural Metal Flashing, Condensation, Control, and Reroofing, 2014
    NRCA Membrane Roof Systems 2019
        NRCA Metal Panel and SPF Roof System 2016
        NRCA Steep-Slope Roof Systems, 2017

PRACTICE EXAMS

    The N.R.C.A. Roofing Manual: Membrane Roof Systems, 2011 and 2015
    The N.R.C.A. Roofing Manual: Metal Panel and SPF Roof Systems, 2016
    The N.R.C.A. Roofing Manual: Steep-slope Roof Systems, 2017
    The N.R.C.A. Roofing Manual: Architectural Metal Flashing, Condensation Control and Reroofing, 2018
    The N.R.C.A. Waterproofing Manual, 2005
    Roofing Construction and Estimating Questions and Answers Pt.1
    Roofing Construction and Estimating Questions and Answers Pt. 2
    Roofing Contractors Questions and Answers
    OSHA Questions and Answers for Roofing Contractors Pt.1
        OSHA Questions and Answers for Roofing Contractors Pt. 2
        Roofing Math Questions

Illinois Residential Roofing Exam Prep

Continental Testing Services

Closed Book

    The NRCA Roofing Manual Box set
    Repair Manual for Low-slope Membrane Roof Systems
    The NRCA Safety Manual, Third Edition
    NRCA Pocket Guide to Safety
    Roofing Construction and Estimating

Test Taking 101

Read each question carefully and read all the answers before you make a selection. Once you choose the answer to a question, look it up in the reference books. This is especially important even if you believe you know the answer without looking it up. Examination questions are validated by state codes and reference books, not merely according to standard practice. By answering a question solely by experience, you could unknowingly give an incorrect answer. Although experience is helpful, it is still to your benefit to look up each answer.

Sample
Question: The sky is _____.

    Blue

    Green

    Red

    Orange

If the reference book says that the sky is green, guess what the correct answer to the question the sky is green. If you mark blue, you are wrong for not following the directions of finding the correct answer in the book.

This is not a test of what you know, this is a text of problem-solving techniques. The State or County has research that has proven that all good business owners

MUST have problem-solving skills. If they do not possess these skills, they have 4 times more of a chance of going out of business.

For best performance, go through the examination several times.

On the first pass, answer all the easy questions and write what book(s) (and chapter) you think the answer will be in.

On the second pass, take one book at a time and go from the front to the back of each book, by chapter, and answer the questions in the most efficient manner.

On each successive pass of the test, you will find the harder questions:

DO NOT SPEND 5 MINUTES ON A QUESTION UNTIL THE END OF THE TEST.

ALL MATH QUESTIONS ARE ATTEMPTED LAST.

DO NOT LEAVE ANY ANSWERS UNANSWERED. TAKE OU BEST GUESS, YOU WILL HAVE A 25% CHANCE OF GUESSING CORRECTLY. Many of my students have passed the test on this method only.

4. Relax, take a 30 second- or 1-minute break every 30-45 mins.

5. You do not have to answer any of the very hard questions to pass the test. Learn to identify them early in the process, skip them and take 25% at the end.

Most people think that they have 2 minutes and 24 seconds per question (120 mins / 50 questions). Where if you do not attempt the very hard questions, you will have 3 mins and 10 seconds per question (120 minutes / questions).

Cross out the question on your test after you have found the correct answer.

This will ensure that you do not waste any time rereading a question that you have already answered, thus wasting your most valuable asset..... TIME!

Important Tip: If you are taking a paper and pencil exam, place a small check mark on the answer sheet next to any question you are going to skip.

This will do two things for you:

1. Reserve the answer line of the questions you are skipping

Instantly tell you which questions you need to look at again

Only one answer is right. If two answers mean the same thing, then they are both wrong. - Use scratch paper for math computations and work neatly. Place the number of the question next to the computation, and draw a line to separate it from the rest of your work. That way, if you decide to go back and check your answers, you can easily find your math for a question.

Do not use your scratch paper as an answer sheet. Some candidates number down the side of the scratch paper, record their answers there and then transcribe them onto the answer sheet later. This practice is time-consuming and increases the risk of error. Even worse, some candidates do not remember to transcribe their answers and turn in blank answer sheets!

Remember: only the answer sheet will be scored.

Your final score will be determined from the answers you record on the answer sheet. Allow time to record an answer for each question, but **DO NOT** mark more than one answer per question. After the time is called, no further marking of the answer sheet will be allowed. If you are unsure of an answer, it may be better to guess, since you will **NOT** receive credit for any question left blank. Select the closest or best answer for each question.

If you want to change an answer, make sure before you do so that you have clearly made an error and have seen the mistake. Then, erase carefully and completely.

When you have finished the examination, take a close look at your answer sheet. Check each line to make sure there is only one answer marked for each question and that you have completely erased any changes, check marks, or stray lines. Candidates taking computer-based tests may scroll back through the test to review and change answers if necessary.

After you finish the examination, raise your hand and wait for the examiner to check your papers for completeness before leaving your seat. You may then leave the room.

Filling Out Your Answer Sheet

For Paper and Pencil testing, you will be given a scan-able answer sheet and will be asked to bubble in your answers to each question. You may also be asked to bubble in some additional information such as your name, social security number, and the test number that is printed on your test booklet. You may be asked to sign a statement that you will comply with the test administration rules, procedures, and guidelines and that you will not divulge the test questions.

For computer-based testing, you will be using a keyboard and/or a mouse to enter your response to each question. You will be given time and a tutorial to familiarize yourself with using the keyboard or mouse to select your answers. If you complete your test and have time remaining, you will be able to review any or all questions and change your responses. You may also be asked to indicate agreement with a statement that you will comply with the test administration rules, procedures, and guidelines and that you will not divulge the test questions. (LOL)

STRATEGIES FOR TAKING A STATE OR COUNTY EXAM

The amount of time spent studying is not the only factor in being prepared. It is also very important to study efficiently. If you want to retain what you are studying, you must set up a system. You are better off if you study for one hour in a quiet, private and relaxed atmosphere than if you study for 15 minutes at a time, 6 or 8 times a day. So, start your exam preparation by setting up a schedule and picking an appropriate area.

Rules to help you study more effectively

Make sure that you know the meaning of words that are unfamiliar to you. Keep a list of the unknown words, look up their definitions and then keep going back to review the list.

Always try to follow your study schedule and plan.

Practice the rules for answering multiple choice questions while you are doing practice questions.

Find your weakest areas and then concentrate your study in those areas.

Write down problem questions and go back over them later. Bring them to the class and ask the instructor to review questions.

Be sure to tab the books and become familiar with the tabs, indexes, and table of contents so you can find things quickly.

Time yourself, so you know how long you are spending on each question.

The Test Day

Remind yourself how well you will do on the exam.

Get a good night's rest. Get up early and remind yourself how well you will do on the exam. Eat a good breakfast. Remind yourself how well you will do on the exam.

Be sure to wear comfortable clothes. Wear or bring a sweater that you can add or remove depending on the room temperature. Remind yourself how well you will do on the exam.

Get to the exam site early. If you have to rush to find the site or get to the room, you may not do as well on the exam. Remind yourself how well you will do on the exam.

Don't get nervous or excited. Remember, if all else fails, there is always another day.

General rules to answer multiple choice questions

Read the directions carefully and be sure that you understand them.

Look over the answer sheet and be sure you understand how to mark your answers.

Be carefully when transferring answers from the test to the answer sheet. Be sure to:

Mark answer completely,

Only mark one answer per question,

Make no extra marks on the answer sheet,

If you make an error, erase,

Be sure to mark the answer in the correct spot on the answer sheet. Repeat the answer to yourself as you transfer it to the answer sheet. And then check it again on the test sheet, repeating it.

Read the question carefully and be sure you understand what it is asking. Cross out any extraneous information. Read the question again.

Read all the answers before you make a choice. Quite often a "possible" answer is listed before the correct answer. **Don't be caught by this trap.**

Eliminate all choices that are wrong choices. After you read all the answers then cross out the wrong answers and chose from the remaining.

Never pick an answer because of a pattern to the answers on previous questions. There is no pattern. Just pick the answer you feel is correct.

Be aware of key words that may help select an answer. Absolute words, such as: always, never, only, all or none. These words usually indicate an incorrect answer. Limiting words such as: some, many, most, sometimes, usually, normally, occasionally, will often indicate the correct answer.

Skip over a question that gives you trouble or is taking too long to solve. Mark it in the question book so you can find it later. Continue through the exam and come back to the question after you are completed. Be sure to save five minutes at the end of the test period, so that if there are any unanswered questions, you can at least guess at the answer.

10. Never leave a question unanswered. There is no penalty for a wrong answer.

Watch for negative question, such as, "Which of the following would make the statement false?"

12. How to make an educated guess. If there are four choices, you have a 25% chance to pick the correct answer. But you may be able to improve those odds.

- Eliminate the incorrect answers.
- Look for answers with absolute or limiting words.
- Look for answers with obviously the wrong sign (+ or -).
- Look for two answers with the same meaning, they are probably both wrong.
- Look for two answers with the opposite meaning, one of them may be correct.
- If all else fails and you must guess, always guess the same choice.

13. Be careful changing answers. Remember that your first guess is normally the best. If you have time at the end of the exam you should go back through the test. But, only change answers if you are sure that your first choice is incorrect, *i.e.* you find a calculation error.

GOOD LUCK. Remember to keep reminding yourself that you will do fine and pass the exam!

If you have no confidence in yourself, you are twice defeated in the race of life. With confidence you have won before you've started-----MARCUS GARVEY

There are 24 hours in a day. If 8 of them are spent sleeping, that gives you 16 hours to get some efficient and productive study done, right?

It seems simple enough. There are plenty of hours in a day, so why is it so hard to use this time effectively, especially around exam time?

We've found that managing their time effectively is one of the things that students struggle the most with around exam time. However, time management is also one of the things that schools never teach – how frustrating?!

In the weeks leading up to study leave, every teacher you have for every class you go to seems to pile on the work: Mrs. Gibb from English class tells you that you have to prepare 3 practice essays for both your visual and written texts, your Geography teacher Miss Wood expects you to do every past exam paper for the last three years before the exam, Mr. West your Math teacher says that you have to finish all of the questions in that darned AME textbook if you want to do well on the exam.

But they expect you to do all of this without giving you any time management tips. Mrs. Gibb, Miss Wood and Mr. West all fail to tell you how it's humanly possible to complete all this work without
collapsing when you walk into the exam hall.

That's where we come in!

Read on for the time management tips that your teachers never gave you!

1. Focus on what you must study – not what you don't.

It seems obvious, but think of all the times you've sat down to study, and you've ended up spending 2 hours studying the concepts you already know like the back of your hand.

It's easier to study the subjects you like. Studying the concepts that you're already confident in is a lot less challenging than studying the concepts that you find the most difficult, as your brain will have to work less to learn this information.

Studying what you already know is a bad time management strategy because you'll leave all the important stuff to the last minute meaning you won't have the time to cover these concepts in depth.

The trouble with this tip is that it's often hard to decipher what you know and what you don't.

To figure out what concepts you already know, and what concepts you still need to learn, complete a subject audit. A subject audit involves breaking down a subject into several points or sections and then analyzing how well you know each of these points. You should spend most of your time studying those concepts that you have rated the most difficult.

The key for effective time management is to review the easier material, but allow enough time to cover the harder concepts in depth so you're not left to study all of the most difficult concepts the night before the exam.

2. Work in sprints.

You may think that to have good time management skills you have to spend all your time studying. However, this is a misconception that many students hold.

Think of studying for exams like training for a marathon.

On your first day of training, you wouldn't go out and run 42kms. You would burn-out quickly due to a lack of prior training, and you would probably be put off running for a long time. This would not be a good way to manage your time. The better route to success would be to slowly work up to running the 42kms by running a bit further every day.

This simple idea of training in short bursts has been proven effective in all areas of human performance. You don't have to be a marathon runner to use this strategy!

When studying, you should start out small by studying in short, focused 'sprints' followed by brief

breaks. Start by studying in 15-minute bursts followed by one 10 minute break. Over time, slowly increase the length of time you're studying (and breaking) for.

This strategy is effective because studying for short bursts promotes more intense focus and will give your brain the time to process and consolidate information as opposed to studying for long periods of time which is not effective and may increase your chances of burnout.

Don't think of effective time management as studying for three hours straight with no breaks, think of effective time management as using your time wisely and in ways that will best promote retention of information.

Follow these steps to practice effective time management and become an expert studier (or marathon runner!) in no time:

> **Set a timer for 15 minutes.**
>
> **Put in some solid study until the timer goes off, making sure you're spending every minute working with no distractions.**
>
> **Have a ten-minute break to check your phone, walk around, stretch, get outside etc.**
>
> **Rinse and repeat.**
>
> **Increase the amount of time you're studying for as you begin to feel more comfortable studying for extended lengths of time.**

Make a study system.
I'm sure you've been lectured by every teacher you've ever had to "make a study

plan!!!" Study plans are effective for your time management, however they're sometimes hard to stick to.

Here at Study Time, we find that the 'study system' is an effective strategy for really getting to the root of what you're studying. A study system is easier to stick to, and therefore fosters better time management
skills, because it breaks tasks down into small chunks.

A study system is basically a simple list of steps that you can make to outline the steps you're going to take when you study. The list should start simple (4-5 things), but over time it should become more complex as you add steps to it.

Just like a workout plan at the gym or for sport, it will give you a clear direction of what action to take, making study much more efficient.

Over time, you can experiment with new study methods, and add them in to optimize the system.

Below is an example study formula that you could use when studying:

- **Download the "Achievement Standard" from the NCEA website**
- **Turn this into a checklist for what you already know and what you need to know**
- **Break the checklist into main themes using a mind map**
- **For each theme, make a summary sheet**
- **After that, break down the key points of each summary and put these onto flash cards Read through your notes and ensure you understand them, and then hit the flash cards**
- **Test yourself on all of them first, then make two piles, one that's wrong and one that's right. Then redo the wrong pile again**
- **Get someone else to test you**
- **Practice exam papers – test yourself using exam papers from the past 2-3 years and time yourself**
- **Work through the answers**

Write a sheet of all tips/tricks i.e. things you got wrong in the practice exam papers Redo exam paper and make model answers

Adjust flashcards if necessary, i.e. make new ones based on the exam papers Re-test all your flashcards

Creating a study system will keep you on track and it will allow you to effectively plan out your time while studying.

4. Practice distributed learning.

Imagine your Math teacher gave you seven equations to do for homework. How would you answer these questions? Would you do one question per day for seven days, or would you do all seven questions in one day?

You may think that it would be a better time management strategy to do all seven questions at once and get them over and done with. However, this is an ineffective way to manage your time.

The brain works better when it has time to process information. Neuroscience has shown that your brain needs time to consolidate information that has been newly learned, in order to form strong links between neurons and thus strong memories.

If the learning is done in one big chunk, you'll just forget it after three days. However, if you review it a day after, then you'll retain it for seven days.

When making a study schedule, you should space out when you study for each subject.

For example, don't spend one day studying English, then the next day studying Math, then the next day studying Biology.

Instead, you should alternate studying for these subjects throughout the day. Do one hour of Math, then one hour of English study, then one hour of Biology, and so on.

This is a much better way to manage your time, because the more often you review a concept, the more solidified it will be in your mind. This is because there will be more time to consolidate this into your memory. Also, taking breaks between reviewing certain concepts will give your brain time to process the information.

Try it out!

APPLICATION FOR THE ROOFING CONTRACTORS QUALIFYING PARTY EXAMINATION

FOR OFFICIAL USE ONLY

After carefully reading the Instruction Sheet, complete the following application. Type or print legibly with black ink only.

PART I: Applicant Identifying Information - You must notify the Department of Financial and Professional Regulation and/or Continental Testing Service in writing, of any address changes after you file this application in order to receive any further information.

1. NAME LAST FIRST MIDDLE

2. UNITED STATES SOCIAL SECURITY NO.

3. PERMANENT MAILING ADDRESS STREET CITY STATE/COUNTRY ZIP CODE COUNTY

4. MAIDEN, GIVEN SURNAME, OR OTHER USED NAME(S)

5. MOTHER'S MAIDEN NAME

6. PLACE OF BIRTH CITY STATE/COUNTRY

7. DATE OF BIRTH Month / Day / Year

8. AGE ☐ Female ☐ Male

9. TELEPHONE NUMBER WHERE YOU MAY BE REACHED
   Work: (Area Code)
   FAX: (Area Code)
   Home: (Area Code)
   FAX: (Area Code)

10. E-MAIL ADDRESS(ES) [REQUIRED]

PART II: Examination - There are three separate types of examinations. Check the box of the type of examination for which you are applying and complete date and location. (See Reference Sheet for appropriate date and location.)

☑	TYPE OF EXAMINATION	DATE	LOCATION
	Illinois Residential		
	Illinois Residential, Commercial and Industrial		
	Illinois Commercial and Industrial (This category is for individuals who already possess a Limited Roofing license and want to upgrade to an Unlimited Roofing license.		

PART III: Identify the name and address of the individual and roofing company where you intend to practice (if applicable).

1. CONTRACTOR

   NAME OF CONTRACTOR BUSINESS

   LICENSE NUMBER OF CONTRACTOR BUSINESS
   104-_____

2. ADDRESS OF CONTRACTOR BUSINESS
   (Include Street, City, and ZIP Code)

IL486-1921 2/16 (RF-QP)

Additional application forms can be downloaded from the IDFPR Web site at www.idfpr.com.

PART IV: Personal History Information *(This part must be completed by all applicants)*	YES	NO
Have you been convicted of or pled guilty or nolo contendere to any criminal offense in any state or in federal court? Please do not give details on minor traffic charges, but do include information relating to Driving While Intoxicated (DWI) charges. *If yes, attach a certified copy of the court records regarding your conviction, the nature of the offense and date of discharge, if applicable, as well as a statement from the probation or parole office.*		
Have you been convicted of a felony?		
If yes, have you been issued a Certificate of Relief from Disabilities by the Prisoner Review Board? *If yes, attach a copy of the certificate.*		
Have you had or do you now have any disease or condition that interferes with your ability to perform the essential functions of your profession, including any disease or condition generally regarded as chronic by the medical community, i.e., (1) mental or emotional disease or condition; (2) alcohol or other substance abuse; (3) physical disease or condition, that presently interferes with your ability to practice your profession? *If yes, attach a detailed statement, including an explanation whether or not you are currently under treatment.*		
Have you been denied a professional license or permit, or privilege of taking an examination, or had a pro-fessional license or permit disciplined in any way by any licensing authority in Illinois or elsewhere? *If yes, attach a detailed explanation.*		
Have you ever been discharged other than honorably from the armed service or from a city, county, state or federal position? *If yes, attach a detailed explanation.*		

PART V: Child Support and/or Student Loan Information (Every applicant is required by law to respond to the following questions)

In accordance with 5 Illinois Compiled Statutes 100/10-65(c), applications for renewal of a license or a new license shall include the applicant's Social Security number, and the licensee shall certify, under penalty of perjury, that he or she is not more than 30 days delinquent in complying with a child support order. **Failure to certify shall result in disciplinary action, and making a false statement may subject the licensee to contempt of court.**

Are you more than 30 days delinquent in complying with a child support order?   Yes [ ]   No [ ]
(NOTE: If you are not subject to a child support order, answer "no.")

In accordance with 20 Illinois Compiled Statutes 2105/2105-(5), "The Department shall deny any license or renewal authorized by the Civil Administrative Code of Illinois to any person who has defaulted on an educational loan or scholarship provided by or guaranteed by the Illinois Student Assistance Commission or any governmental agency of this State; however, the Department may issue a license or renewal if the aforementioned persons have established a satisfactory repayment record as determined by the Illinois Student Assistance Commission or other appropriate governmental agency of this State." (Proof of a satisfactory repayment record must be submitted.)

Are you in default on an educational loan or scholarship provided/guaranteed by the Illinois Student Assistance Commission or other governmental agency of this State?   Yes [ ]   No [ ]

PART VI: Certifying Statement

Under penalties of perjury, I declare that I have examined the application and all supporting documents submitted by me in connection therewith, and to the best of my knowledge, they are true, correct, and complete.

_____   _____
Signature of Applicant   Date

~~INSTRUCTIONS~~

ROOFING CONTRACTORS QUALIFYING PARTY EXAMINATION APPLICATION

In order for your application to be processed, <u>ALL REQUIRED SUPPORTING DOCUMENTATION MUST BE SUBMITTED</u> with the application and required fee unless otherwise directed in the instructions.

Effective July 1, 2003, to apply for licensure as a roofing contractor under the provisions of the Illinois Roofing Industry Act, every roofing contractor applicant must designate a qualifying party who is required to take and pass a State examination.

"**Qualifying Party**" means: The individual filing as a sole proprietor, partner of a partnership, officer of a corporation, trustee of a business trust, or party of another legal entity, who is legally qualified to act for the business organization in all matters connected with its roofing contracting business, has the authority to supervise roofing installation operations, and is actively engaged in day to day activities of the business organization.

The Illinois Roofing Industry Act makes available two separate types of roofing contractor licenses-- limited roofing license and unlimited roofing license. "**Limited Roofing License**" means a license made available to contractors whose roofing business is limited to residential roofing, including residential properties consisting of 8 units or less. "Unlimited Roofing License" means a license made available to contractors whose roofing business is unlimited in nature and includes roofing on residential, commercial, and industrial properties.

To be scheduled for the qualifying party examination, you must complete and submit the attached Application for the Roofing Contractors Qualifying Party Examination (IL486-1921) along with the required examination fee, made payable to Continental Testing Services, Inc. The fee must be in the form of a certified check or money order. Forward this document and required fee to:

        Continental Testing Services, Inc.
        P.O. Box 100
        LaGrange, Illinois 60525-0100; *or*

Apply Directly On-Line. Register for the examination by referring to the Continental Testing Web site (www.continentaltesting.net) for information on how to apply for the examination on-line and pay the test fee by credit card.

If assistance is needed, direct your request to the following telephone number:

        Continental Testing Services, Inc.: 708-354-9911
        Telecommunication Device for the Deaf: 1-800-869-1313

When an operator answers, state the profession for which you are applying and that you need assistance with your application. Please allow 3 weeks from mailing your application before making an inquiry concerning its status.

DPR-RF-QP 04/06 (RF)

1 Exam Prep Tabs Roofing Construction & Estimating Tabs and Highlights

These 1 Exam Prep Tabs are based on *Roofing Construction and Estimating by Daniel Atcheson, 1995*.

Each 1 Exam Prep Tabs sheet has five rows of tabs. Start with the first tab at the first row at the top of the page; proceed down that row placing the tabs at the locations listed below. Place each tab in your book setting it down one notch until you get to the bottom of a page. Then start back at the top again.

After each 1 Exam Prep Tab, under "Reason" is a brief explanation of the purpose of the tab, and / or items to highlight in the section.

1 Exam Prep Tab	Page #	Reason
Measurement	6	Starts Chapter. Start by Measuring the Length of the eaves. On a roof, you only have to measure in one direction... Next, measure the width of the roof....Now measure the ips and valleys by hooking the tape to a building corner
	7	Note the example of how to measure and calculate roof areas.
	8	Note example of perimeter measure
	10	Note example of how to find slope and then how to find the rise when you know the slope and the run. Note the definition of pitch, as opposed to slope.
Definitions	13	Definition of common rafter, ridge rafter
	14	hip rafter, valley rafter, hip jack rafter, valley jack rafter
Conversion Table	15	This table is a conversion table that allows you to calculate the roof area given a roof slope, the lengths of hips and valleys. If you are a 1 Exam Prep student, see roofing manual for a more complete explanation.
	17	Notice example of perimeter of a sloped roof, then explanation of net vs. gross area
	18	Example to factor in an allowance Follow the example on calculating Total net Roof Area
	21	When you calculate the net area of a roof, be careful you don't omit the roof overhang
Sheathing	25	A sagging roof will also stretch asphalt shingles...You can use 1 x 4, 1 x 6 ... don't recommend you use anything wider than a 1 x 6...
	25	Figure 2-2 names support components

1 Exam Prep Tab	Page #	Reason
	27	Minimum plywood grade of C-D Interior and exterior glue. The index number is a rating that says the plywood can span a (should be maximum, not minimum) of 32 inches... The dead load on a roof is the weight of the roof deck, underlayment and shingles
Supports, Tables	28	Tables for spacing of supports, panel ratings live loads. Table 22 is for low slope roofs, also shows panel clips per span
	29	Figure 2-7 notice minimum spaces shown. Figure 2-8 Waferboard spans 30 Spaced sheathing is usually square-edged 1 x 4's and wider for wood shingles, or 1 x 4's, 1 x 6's and wider for shakes ....don't space the sheathing more than 21 inches in order to prevent underlayment from sagging into the attic
	31	The minimum roof sloop recommended for wood shingles is 4 in 12 lower slopes if you install 2 x 4 spacers
	32	Figure 2-13 Spaced sheathing over a solid sheathing notice dimensions
	33	Special care not to overload the roof at the mid span of rafters. Figure 2-17 Loading tiles on gable roof
	34	Allow a horizontal space of about 1 foot between stacks. Notice example on estimating roof sheathing in terms of labor cost.
Underlaying	35	Definitions capping in, drying in or prefelting, Purpose 1-6
	36	Figure 3-1, saturated felt underlayment must be water resistant, but not vapor resistant
	37	Organic felts can deteriorate due to oxidation and wicking. Fiberglass felts don't rot or absorb water....
	38-39	Recommended underlayment table
	40	When a long life roof fails, it's usually because the flashing or underlayment failed... drip edge under the felt...28guage min. ....over the roof deck approx. 3 inches
	41	Gravel Stop definition
	43	Never install felt over a wet deck. Figures 3-10 and 3-11 application of single and double underlayment
	44	Tin caps....32 gauge at least 1 5/8 inches diameter, 3/4 inch long on any roof with a valley....6 inches beyond the ridge. Install all felt....overhand drip edge at the eaves by at least 3/8 inch.

1 Exam Prep Tab	Page #	Reason
Felt Lap	45	Lap felt 6 inches...overlap...in the valley by 6 inches.... extend felt 3 to 4 inches up any vertical surface....Use a 2 inch top lap for single underlayment.
	46	Figure 3-19 End lap requirements definition, single 43 pound coasted base....sealed underlayment system see detail figures, next page.
	48	Definition 30/90 hot mop, 2 ply sealed system....walking in
	51	Covering capacity of underlayment lap allowance formula... add 1 sq. ft. to the roof area to be covered for each linear foot of ridge, hp, and valley.
	52	Over cut allowance formula
	53	Figures 3-32, 33 show the percentage you add to the net roof area for overlaps at the hips and ridge.
	54	Example 3-3 follow the solution.
	57	Definition Interlayment. Install the first 18 inch underlayment course so the bottom edge of the felt is twice the exposure distance above the butts of the starter course. See figure 3-36 for dimensions.
	58	Figure 3-37 Table for Interlayment Coverage Follow example 3-5 and 3-6 on the next page.
	63	Follow example 3-8 for length of flashing
Valleys	64	Definition of Closed and open valleys...Splash diverter and water guards
	65	Valley Flashing Materials....Galvanized steel & Aluminum are the least expensive so they're used the most... 26 or 29 gauge... 16 ounce copper, 12 once tin, 3 pound hard lead, 11 gauge zinc
	67	Non metal Valley flashing...36 inch wide...lap the upper strip over the lower by at least 12 inches and bond the lap with roofing cement
	68	Open valley...flash the valley with two layers of mineral surfaced roll roofing.
	69	Don't Fabricate heavy- gauge metal flashing pieces Longer than 10'. On wood shingle roofs, extend metal valley flashing at least 10 inches beyond each side of the centerline of the valley....6 in 12; 7 inches with 6 in 12 or steeper.
	70	On Shake roofs, extend the metal valley flashing at least 10'.

1 Exam Prep Tab	Page #	Reason
Asphalt Shingles	73	Starts chapter. Defines Saturant
	74	...materials most often used: naturally colored slate, Rock granules, ceramic coated rock granules
	75	Def: A (withstand severe fire exposure), B (moderate), C (light) UL classifications
	76	Store in warm location, stacks no more than 4' height
Slopes	77	Figure 4-4 minimum pitch and slope requirements for various asphalt products
	78	Figure 4-8, table, weight per square
	79	Table, typical asphalt shingles
	80	Installing Asphalt Strip Shingles
	82	6 inch method
	83	Diagonal method; 5 inch method (pattern)
	84	4 inch pattern low slope roofs, from 2 to 3 in 12; 5 inch pattern sometimes on hip roofs; 6 inch on Gable roofs; hip roofs...start shingling at the center of the roof and proceed in both directions
Valleys	89	Def: Open, Closed cut, woven
	96	Flashing; chimney width over 2', install saddle flashing
	97	Make this piece so the lower part goes at least 4 " over the shingles and the upper section goes at least 12" up the chimney Install the base flashing... Extend the flashing at least 6 inches onto the roof sheathing and 6 inches up the chimney
	98	Chisel and rake clean the mortar joints to a depth of 1 1/2 inches before you install the cap flashing
	99	Install each piece into mortar joints so each cap flashing unit overlaps the base by at least 3" 100 Install continuous flashing....where a sloping roof and a vertical side wall meet....
	105	For added leak protection on low sloped roofs, embed a strip of mineral surfaced roll roofing into roofing cement under the vent pipe
Nail Sizings	106	Recommended Nail Lengths table. 11 or 12 gaugehot dipped galvanized or aluminum roofing nails with 3/8" (min.) heads

1 Exam Prep Tab	Page #	Reason
	107	Stapling: ...use galvanized 16 gauge with minimum crown of 15/16 of an inch....go at least 3/4 " into the sheathing.
	108	Estimating number of shingles per square
	109	Estimating number of shingle courses
	111	Head lap, top lap and exposure
	113	Estimating Asphalt strip shingle quantities
	115	10% waste on small to average gable roofs, ; 15% on hip roofs. Add 2% on gable and 3% on hip laminated shingles with prefabricated ridge and hip units.
	121	Example 4-12, number of bundles problem factors in starter course, waste
	124	Def.: Ribbon Course
	128,129	Def: Dutch lap, American method
Mineral Surfaced Roll Roofing	131	Starts chapter
	132	Def: selvage, roll roofing or split sheet roofmg Single and double coverage, Pattern edge modified Bitumen Asphalt (MBA)
	133	Installing mineral surfaced roll roofing...rules apply:
	134	Figure 5-3 application methods. Exposed nail
	136	Concealed nail
	139	Hip, ridge units, cut roofing material into 12" x 36" strips
	140	Apply roofing cement at the rate of 1 1/2 gallons per
	100	square feet over the 19 inch selvage strip.
	142	Vent pipes
	144	Estimating Mineral Surfaced Roll Roofing
	147-9	Tables, total percentage to add for materials overrun
Wood Shingles & Shakes	159	Starts chapter...Unless you use pressure impregnated fire retardant shingles or shakes, a house with a wood roof costs more to insure...over 1/2" plywood a Class B
	160	Site applied surface treatments are only temporary.. ...are rigid, so they're extremely resistant to uplift...

1 Exam Prep Tab	Page #	Reason
	162	Number 2 grade cut for wood free of knots. One square of 16" shingles weights about 144 lbs...You don't need underlayment or interlayment with wood shingles, but you do with shakes.
	165	To allow for expansion when wet, space shakes 3/8 to 5/8" apart; offset adjacent shake or shingle courses by at least 1 1/2 inches
	167	Table, minimum nail length for shingles or shakes
	170	The minimum recommended roof slope for shakes is 4 in 12 and 3 in 12 for wood shingles
	172	Def. false deck
	173	If you install a vapor barrier, put it under the rigid insulation
	175	Cover, bundles of shakes per square, exposure tables
Estimating	176	Estimating Wood Shingle and shake quantities
	177	Shortcut method: 10% waste small jobs 15% on hip roofs with pre fabricated hp and ridge units; 5% on gable roofs with prefab hip and ridge units; 10% on hip roofs with prefabricated hip and ridge units
	185	Def. Staggered, Dutch weave patterns
	186	Installing sidewall shingles and shakes
	189	Double coursing
	190	Over existing walls
	192	All roof junctures must be weather tight. ...Use at least 26 gauge galvanized steel painted on both sides... If you have to bend the flashing ... over 15 degrees, paint the flashing after.
Tile Roofing	197	Starts chapter; concrete tiles weigh about 900 pounds per sq.
	198	Def. weather check; nose lug
	199	Three basic underlayment systems: one ply non sealed, one ply sealed; two ply sealed
	200	Installing roof tiles
	203	Type M mortar
	208	...nails go at least 3/4 inch into the framing...
Valleys	213	Valleys

1 Exam Prep Tab	Page #	Reason
	217	Flashing at Vertical Walls
	220	Flashing Soil Stacks and Vents
	225	Estimating Tile Quantities
	226	Filler mortar ...1 part type M or 1 1/2 parts type S and 4 parts sand
Slate Roofing	231	Starts chapter, lists advantages
	234	Standard slate on a residence can be installed over 15 lb saturated felt. For a textural roof, use 30 lb felt. For slates up to 3/4 inch thick on graduated roof use one layer. For thicker slates use 45, 55, or 65 roll roofing.
	235	Table, weights
	236	Determining the head lap
Strips, Spacing	239	Table spacing of nailing strips ridges, 3 basic types: saddle, strip saddle and comb
	242	Valleys Open and Closed
	245	Flashing
	249	When you use zinc flashing, install at least 11 zinc gauge rolled zinc. Don't drive nails through zinc. Use an acid flux solder to solder all joints. Estimating Slate Quantities
Metal Roofing & Siding	255	Starts Chapter; any metal sheet heavier than 30 gauge is called sheet metal.
	257	Installing Metal Roofing Panels
	260	Valley Flashing; Vent Flashing
	263	...simplest, strongest is riveted soldered seam
Seams	264	Flat and Flat locked Seams
	265	Standing Seams
	266	Batten seams
	268	Cross Seams. The most common type of solder used on sheet metal roofing is 50-50 lead-tin alloy.
	269	Estimating Metal Roofing and Siding
	272-76	Tables, waste factors, illustrations types panels

1 Exam Prep Tab	Page #	Reason
	277	Table of coefficient of thermal expansion
	278	Terne Metal
	279	Terne Coated Stainless Steel
	280-282	Tables, design factors terne coated steel
	285	Chrome Nickel; Monel metal
	286	Lead, zinc, copper roofing
	287	Copper Bearing Steal roofing
Built Up Roofing	291	Introduces chapter; 3 types of BUR: Aggregate surfaced, smooth surface, mineral surfaced
	292	Roof slope varies with type of interply and surface bitumen and roofing surface you use. Substrate design.
	293	Metal decks, 22 gauge min. with 1 1/2 inch ribs Lightweight insulating decks, types
	294	Fastener types, recommendations
Venting	295	Top venting, one per 900 to 1000 sf. 10 days to cure lightweight insulating concrete. Gypsum concrete decks min. 2" thick. Never install lightweight concrete decks on roofs with slopes greater than 1 in 12. Seal joints between precast gypsum panels with an 8" wide felt strip embedded in roofing cement
	297	Back nailing and nailing placement table
	298	Base Sheets
	300	Most manufactures recommend that you apply roll material with its long dimension perpendicular to the slope of the roof Rosin paper
	301	Roofing felts, formula to determine exposure: 34 inches (36 inches minus 2 inch end lap) / number of plies.
	302	3 ply BUR system
	303	4 ply. Hot Bitumens- asphalt and coal tar pitch are the most widely used bitumens in the roofing industry. Asphalt and coal tar pitch are generally incompatible except: You can install asphalt flashing material with coal tar pitch and you can use hot type II asphalt over coal tar saturated felts. EPDM insulation before you apply the membrane.
	304	4 types of asphalt (dead level, flat, steep, special steep)

1 Exam Prep Tab	Page #	Reason
	305	Cold Applied Bitumens
	306	Def: Resaturant. Surface aggregate
	308	Smooth Surface Roofing. Cap Sheets
	309	Aluminum Roof Coatings
	310	Phasing
	311	Cant strip... run the cant strip out over the roof at least 3 inches and up the vertical surface at least 5 inches.
	315	Water Retaining Roofs. Flashing on Flat roofs: locations
	316	Flashing at parapet walls... extend the flashing 8 to12 inches up the parapet wall and at least 5 inches out over the roofing surface.
	318-19	On nailable decks, you nail the flange edges on 3 inch centers. ... Don't install penetrations within 15 inches of the lower edge of a cant strip. Notice details of counter flashing.
	320	Table, equipment width = # of legs. Notice detail of roof drain 10-25
	321	Locations for expansion joints
Estimating BUR	323	Estimating BUR Systems... Don't deduct anything for openings less than 100 sq. feet ....deduct the entire opening area for openings 500 sq. ft. and larger
	327	Testing BUR Systems...Cut out an area at least 10 by 42 inches at right angles to the length of the felts..weight must be within 15%
	329	Built Up Roofing Repairs and re-roofing. Voids happen if...
	320	Fishmouths are caused by inadequate booming of felt edges or improper alignment of the felts ...make the patch 6 inches wider than the area you are repairing.
	331	Never solidly mop a new roof over an old roof.
Elastomeric Roofing	333	Starts chapter. Definition ....petroleum based materials such as bitumen or coal tar pitch adversely affect PVC membranes
	334	On re-roofs over BUR systems, you don't have to completely remove the old roof ...you only have to remove loose aggregate and install a layer of rigid
	335	You can get liquid applied elastomers in four consistencies: caulk, trowel, brush and spray. Normally, two layers of silicone rubber coatings are sprayed on over polyurethane insulation. This process

1 Exam Prep Tab	Page #	Reason
		provides a UL Class A fire rating. Apply a total minimum coating thickness of 15 dry mils 337 EPDM definition; ...not compatible with and should never be installed with either plastic cement or dead-level asphalt.
	338	You can install EPDM systems loosely laid and ballasted, fully adhered, or mechanically fastened.... install a butted insulation protection course over any substrate that has cracks or joints 1/4 inch wide or wider. Loosely laid system...compatible with lightweight concrete decks provided:
	339	Membrane thickness for a ballasted system is normally .045 inch. Installation tips for fully adhered EPDM systems
	340	Mechanically fastened EPDM System
	342	CPE Elastomeric Roofing
	343	PVC Elastomeric Roofing... incompatible with bituminous material
	344	Flashings
	345	Estimating Elasomeric Roofing
Insulation Vapor / Waterproofing	347	Starts chapter
	349	R values of fiberglass bat insulation
	350	R values for loose fill
	352	R values, material requirements for blown insulation
	353	R values of various types of rigid insulation
	354	Tapered Rigid Insulation; reflective; sprayed on 361 R = 1/U; U = 1/R;
	363	Vapor barriers come with a rating of .1 perm or less. Polyethylene film has the lowest perm ratings, ranging from .02 to .08.
	364	A sealant is a lower grade
	365-70	Butyl caulk; Acrylic latex caulk, polysulfide caulk, Polyurethane, solvent acrylic, silicone, vinyl acrylic, Epoxy sealant, backer rod, fireproof caulk and putty
	371	Water under pressure: hydrostatic head
	373	Installing Built up Membranes

1 Exam Prep Tab	Page #	Reason
	375	Estimating Built up Waterproofing and Damp proofing
	376	Table: plies of membrane required for head of water
	377	Use damp proofing materials where there's no hydrostatic head
	378	You can use emulsified asphalts for damp proofing, but don't apply these products in cold weather... Definition: parge coat
Roofing Repair & Maintenance	381	Starts chapter
	382	You can prevent water from entering mortar joints by tuck pointing the joints and applying a brush coating of clear silicone sealer.
	384	At vent flashings....Install shingles under the lower end of the flashing instead of on top
	386	Roof maintenance - list
	388	Def. Efflorescence
	390	A roof is considered beyond economical repair when the repair cost exceeds 80 % of the replacement cost
	392	Pointers for various reroofing situations
	394	Three layers of shingles is usually the most a roof can support
	395	Never install new shingles over tiles, slates or metal panels
	398	Use T lock shingles over a rough roof and you won't have to tear off the old roof
	400	Never install roll roofing over any type of asphalt shingle or over an aggregate surfaced built up roof
	402	A rule of thumb for adequate attic ventilation is to allow 1 sw. foot of net free vent opening for 150 sq. ft with no vapor barrier, 300 sq. feet with barrier or when half the vent openings are located at the ridge
	403	Run a ridge vent to within 18 inches of each end of the ridge.
	407-09	Gutters and downspouts; 28 gauge metal or 16 oz copper. Types, connections
Estimating Production Rates	411	Starts chapter. This chapter has examples of how to use published or historical data to determine worker efficiency

1 Exam Prep Tab	Page #	Reason
	415	The industrial and commercial wage rates do include a 30 % markup for supervision expense, contingency allowance, overhead and profit...there is a 15% markup on materials.
	425	Set the base of the ladder away from the roofs edge a distance equal to 1/4 the working height of the ladder
Appendix Slope Factors	427	Starts section
	428	A -Roof slope factors for determining rafter lengths
	429	B - Valley length factors
	430-35	Summary of all formulas used in book

1 Exam Prep
NRCA Roofing Manual:
Architectural Metal Flashing, Condensation and Air Leakage Control – 2018
Tabs and Highlights

These 1 Exam Prep Tabs are based on the National Roofing Contractors Association (NRCA) manual listed below:

Architectural Metal Flashing, Condensation Control and Air Leakage Control - 2018

Each 1 Exam Prep tabs sheet has five rows of tabs. Start with the first tab at the first row at the top of the page; proceed down that row placing the tabs at the locations listed below. Place each tab in your book setting it down one notch until you get to the last tab. Then start with the highlights.

1 Exam Prep Tab	Page #
Table of Contents	7
Contents - Architectural Metal Flashing	13
Materials	19
Low-Slope Roof Guidelines	47
Steep-Slope Roof Guidelines	85
Construction Details	105
Index of Construction Details	113
Appendixes – Arch Metal Flashings	177
Contents - Condensation & Air Leakage Control	183
Fundamentals of Condensation & Leakage Control	185
Low-Slope Condensation Control	195
Steep-Slope Condensation Control/Ventilation	215
Air Retarders for Roof Assemblies	237
Appendixes – Condensation/Air Leakage	259
Appendixes	283
Glossary	294

This concludes the tabs for this book. Please continue with the highlights below.

Page #	Highlight
17	NRCA defines these categories as follows: **Low-slope roofs:** a category of roof systems that generally includes weatherproof membrane types of roof systems installed on slopes at or less than 3:12. **Steep-slope roofs:** a category of roof systems that generally includes water-shedding types of roof systems installed on slopes exceeding 3:12.
19	Metals used in roofing can be divided into several categories: those that are naturally weathering ... which a corrosion-resistant metallic coating is applied; and those that require a protective coating. **Naturally Weathering Metals:** For a metal to be appropriately considered a naturally weathering metal, the base metal itself must be able to oxidize sufficiently to form its own protective layer to withstand environmental exposures common to roof systems. **Metallic-coated Metals:** Of the wide variety of metals used in manufacturing sheet-metal roof accessories, metal metallic-coated carbon steel is the most prevalent. This category of roofing material comprises of metal types that contain a base layer of carbon steel to which a corrosion-resistant metallic coating is applied.
20	**1.1 Metal Types** **Aluminum:** Aluminum provides a lightweight, easily formed metal that does not require a protective coating for most exposures.
21	**Figure 1-1:** Metal thickness and weight information for aluminum sheets **Aluminized Steel:** Aluminized steels rely almost solely on the aluminum's ability to act as a barrier for protecting the base steel.
22	**Figure 1-2:** Metal thickness and weight information for aluminized sheets **Copper:** Copper does not require a protective finish. Copper's appearance typically changes during its exposure to the elements; however, this change depends on geographic and atmospheric conditions, such as exposure to moisture and air pollutants.
23	**Copper-coated Stainless Steel:** Copper-coated stainless steel is Type 430 stainless steel in sheet or coil form coated with a thin copper layer on each side. **Figure 1-4:** Metal thickness and weight information for copper-coated sheets **Galvalume® (aluminum-zinc-coated steel):** "Galvalume is aluminum-zinc-coated steel and frequently used for roofing applications. This alloy coating is reported to be 55 percent aluminum and 45 zinc by weight."
24	**Figure 1-5:** Metal thickness and weight information for Galvalume sheets. **Galvanized Steel:** Galvanized steel is one of the oldest and most common metallic-coated metals.
25	**Figure 1-6:** Metal thickness and weight information for galvanized sheets. **Lead:** Lead is used as a roofing accessory metal because of its workability. Lead is extremely soft, can be formed by hand, and is useful for flashing irregular shapes and junctures.

Page #	Highlight
	Weather and Corrosive Environments: A weight range of 2 pounds per square foot to 4 pounds per square foot is typical for roofing applications, but heavier weights may be desirable when soldering is necessary.

Figure 1-7: Metal thickness and weight information for lead sheets.

Lead-coated Copper: Lead-coated copper was developed in the early 1900s to provide a roofing and flashing material with the appearance and corrosion-resistant characteristics of lead but with less cost and weight than lead alone. |
| 26 | **Figure 1-8:** Metal thickness and weight information for lead-coated copper sheets.

Stainless Steel: Stainless steel is a corrosion-resistant material. It is often used in harsh environments when other metals or metal paint finished may not be appropriate. |
| 27 | **Figure 1-9:** Metal thickness and weight information for stainless-steel sheets

Zinc: Zinc is a self-healing metal that weathers to a soft blue-gray patina. This soft architectural metal offers a combination of aesthetics, design flexibility, malleability, and durability. |
| 28 | **Figure 1-10:** Metal thickness and weight information for zinc sheets

Tin-zinc-coated Copper (FreedomGray): Tin-zinc-coated copper is composed of copper conforming to ASTM B370, "Standard Specification of Copper Sheet and Strip for Building Construction," coated on both sides with an alloy consisting of 50 percent tin and 50 percent zinc approximately 0.05 mils thick.

Zinc-tin-coated Stainless Steel (TCS): Zinc-tin-coated stainless steel is a Type 304 stainless-steel base metal coated on both sides with a thin layer of a zinc and tin alloy. The alloy is composed of 50 percent zinc and 50 percent tin.

Figure 1-11: Metal thickness and weight information for zinc-tin-coated copper sheets |
| 29 | **Figure 1-12:** Metal thickness and weight information for zinc-tin-coated stainless steel sheets

Terne-coated Stainless Steel: Terne-coated stainless steel is stainless steel coated on both sides with lead and tin. Today's version of terne-coated stainless steel is a Type 304 … with a thin layer of zinc and alloy most commonly referred to as TCS II. |
29-31	**1.2 Protective Coatings:** Note and highlight the definitions for each of the seven different types of coatings: Paint Systems; Fluoropolymers; Siliconized Acrylics and Polyesters; Pearlescent and Metallic Additives; Clear-coat Finishes; Anodizing.
35	**1.4 Oil Canning:** Oil canning refers to physical distortions in the flatness of metal; however, this condition is only aesthetic in nature and does not have any adverse effect on the structural integrity or the weather proofing capability of the metal.
36	**1.5 Cleats, Clips and Fasteners: Cleats:** NRCA defines a cleat as a continuous metal component installed behind the leading edge of a metal accessory, such as a coping cap or edge metal, used to engage and secure the metal accessory to the adjacent substrate or another metal component by means of a slip joint or by crimping the leading edge of the metal accessory to the cleat.

Page #	Highlight
37	**Clips:** NRCA defines a clip as an individual metal component installed at predetermined locations behind the leading edge of a flashing metal, used to engage and secure the sheet-metal flashings intermittently to the adjacent substrate or another metal component.
	Fasteners: Sheet-metal fasteners are mechanical anchors that provide anchorage of sheet metal. Fasteners are differentiated by the type of substrate or material being fastened.
38-39	**Figure 1-18: Fasteners commonly used with sheet metal.**
41	**1.7 Joinery:** Joinery is the method of joining two or more pieces of sheet metal. Joints can be made with mechanical fasteners, interlocking seaming methods, sheet metal cover plates, sealants, metals (e.g. solder, welding) or combinations of these methods.
	Mechanical Fasteners: Screws, bolts, and rivets are perhaps the simplest and most common method of joining two pieces of sheet metal.
	Crimping and Locking: Pre-painted metals and nonsolderable metals are commonly joined without the use of soldering or welding because the coating does not allow for soldering or welding. Crimping and locking is a typical method used to join laps in sheet-metal components.
	Soldering or Welding: Welded or soldered joints are those that form a chemical bond between two metal shapes.
44	**Figure 1-22:** Weldable and solderable metals
	Joinery Types: Following are examples with descriptions of joinery (seam) types commonly used in roofing applications.
44-46	Note and highlight each of the 14 different seam types: Overlap Standing Seam; Single-lock Standing Seam; Double-lock Standing Seam; Capped Standing Seam; Flat Lock Seam; Double Flat Lock Seam; Drive Cleat Seam; "S" Cleat Seam; Double "S" Cleat Seam; Cover Plate Seam; Backer Plate Seam: Cover Plate With Backer Plate Seam; Lap Seam; and Pittsburg Lock Seam.
50	**Figure 2-3:** Minimum metal thickness guidelines for flatness and weatherability - copings.
54	**A-type Profile Edge Metal:** A-type profile edge metal, commonly called "gravel stop," is often used in low-slope applications.
56	The roof flange should be a minimum of 3 inches, recessed a minimum 1/2 inch from the back of the wood nailer.
57	**Figure 2-10:** Minimum metal thickness guidelines for weather ability – perimeter edge metal
	L-type Profile Edge Metal: In low-slope applications, L-type profile is commonly used with roof systems without an aggregate surfacing or in draining edge locations with smooth-surfaced roof systems.
	Fascia Cap Edge Metal: Fascia cap edge metal is used in low-slope roof systems and is preferred because its design does not require the edge metal to be embedded or sandwiched into the roofing membrane.

Page #	Highlight
62	**Fascia Metal Accessories:** Depending on the design of the roof edge, fascia metal components may also be used with the perimeter edge metal.
66	**2.3 Counterflashing:** A counter-flashing is defined as a formed metal component secured on or into a wall or curb or to another component … to cover and protect the upper edge of the membrane base flashing and its associated fasteners from mechanical damage and exposure to weather.
67	Overlapping counterflashing joints should be about 3 inches and sealed.
71	**2.5 Area Dividers:** If roof area dividers are used, they should be flashed to a minimum height of 8 inches above the roof surface and should be located at high points in the roof with drainage away from or parallel to the divider.
77	**2.8 Gutters and Downspouts:** There are two types of gutters; built-in and externally attached (hanging). **Externally Attached (Hanging) Gutters:** Maintenance, durability, and longevity of the metal and securement type are important factors to consider when designing gutters and downspouts.
80	**Built-in Gutters:** Built-in gutters may be used with low-slope roof systems; however, they primarily are used on steep-slope roof systems.
81	**Downspouts:** Sheet-metal downspouts are shop-fabricated or pre-manufactured in a wide variety of shapes and sizes. Plain, corrugated, round, rectangular or square downspouts are typical.
85	**3.1 Drip Edge Metal:** Drip edge metal is a sheet-metal roof component designed to provide a continuous finished edge along the outer edges of a roof system.
86	**Figure 3-2:** Minimum metal thickness guidelines for weatherability based on steep-slope covering - drip edge metal.
87	**3.2 Gutters and Downspouts:** One way of controlling drainage of some steep-slope roof systems is by using gutters and downspouts. Special consideration must be taken when determining size, style, attachment, location, and construction to ensure adequate drainage and strength.
88	**Externally Attached (Hanging) Gutters:** Maintenance, durability, and longevity of the metal and securement type are important factors to consider when designing gutters and downspouts.
88	There are two common types of support systems typically used with externally attached gutters: - Support brackets - Straps
90	**Figure 3-5:** Minimum metal thickness guidelines for weatherability - gutters
94	**3.4 Valleys:** A valley is created at the downslope intersection of two sloping roof planes. Water runoff from the portions of the roof areas sloping into a valley flows toward and along the valley. **Fastener Placement:** Generally, fasteners should be kept back from the center of the valley a minimum of 8 inches.

Page #	Highlight
95	**Figure 3-12:** Minimum metal thickness guidelines for weatherability based on steep-slope covering - valley metal
96	**Clay and Concrete Tile Roof Systems:** NRCA recommends valley metal for use with tile be a minimum of 18 inches wide.
98	**Figure 3-13:** Minimum metal thickness guidelines for weatherability based on steep-slope coverings - flashings (apron, headwall, backer, cricket, sidewall, pipe penetration)
99	**Cricket Flashing:** NRCA recommends designers specify crickets at the upslope side of chimneys or curbed roof penetrations when the chimney of the curb is 24 inches wide or greater.
	3.7 Sidewall Flashing: Where a sloped roof area intersects a vertical side wall, either step flashing or channel flashing is installed.
100	**Figure 3-15:** Wood cricket built on upslope side of a chimney
	Figure 3-16: Metal cricket flashing for the upslope side of a masonry chimney
100	**Clay and Concrete Tile Roof Systems**
101	The step flashing width should be sufficient to obtain a 4-inch extension onto each underlying tile and about a 4-inch vertical height over the exposed face of each overlying tile.
	Metal Shingle Roof System
	Slate: The step flashing width should be a minimum of 8 inches to obtain a 4-inch extension onto each underlying shingle and about a 4-inch vertical height over the exposed face of each overlying shingle.
102	Counterflashing should extend over the top of the base flashings approximately 2 inches and have a ½ inch minimum drip edge at the bottom.
107	**Preservative-treated Wood:** Since Jan. 1, 2004, preservative-treated lumber for consumer use is no longer chromated copper arsenate (CCA) treated.
111	**Figure 4-2:** Guide for sheet-metal coping
144	**Expansion Joint with Cleats on Both Sides** (EJ-2)
155	**Gutter with Perimeter Edge Metal - Low-Slope Roof Systems** (G-2)
153	**Sidewall Flashing (Step Flashing)** (SW-1)
178	**Appendix 1** - Expansion Coefficients of Metals
189	**Water Vapor Movement in Buildings**
190	**Diffusion:** Diffusion occurs as the result of water vapor pressure differences across materials.
	Some materials allow diffusion to occur more rapidly than others. A material's ability to allow diffusion of vapor is measured by its permeability and permeance.

Page #	Highlight
190	**Permeability:** The time rate of vapor transmission through a flat material of a unit thickness induced by vapor pressure difference between two specific surfaces under specified temperature and humidity conditions.
	Permeance: The time rate of vapor transmission through a flat material or construction assembly induced by vapor pressure difference between two specific surfaces under specified temperature and humidity conditions.
191	**Figure 1-4:** Typical water vapor permeance or permeability values for common building materials
210	**Bituminous Vapor Retarders:** Modern bituminous vapor retarders generally membranes composed of self-adhering polymer-modified bitumen sheet products … installed in adhered applications.
	Nonbituminous Vapor Retarders: Included in the nonbituminous category of vapor retarders are: (2 bullets).
212	**Securement:** Over nailable roof decks, the base ply of the vapor retarder should be nailed to the roof deck, and then the first (and if necessary, the second) ply should be adhered to the base sheet.
	High-Humidity Interiors: NRCA suggests vapor retarders for such facilities or high-humidity sections of facilities be durable, effective, multilayer membranes with a perm rating as close to zero as possible.
215	Roofs can generally be divided into two categories: low-slope and steep-slope.
216	**3.1 Preventing Condensation Accumulation:** Depending on climate zone, preventing condensation accumulation in steep-slope roof assemblies requires some combination of the following measures: (5 bullets).
223	**3.2 Attic Ventilation:** Generally, ventilation of attic spaces can be accommodated by using one of two methods: (2 bullets).
	Static Ventilation: The most common means of providing attic ventilation for steep slope roof assemblies is by non-mechanical, static ventilation.
224	**R806.2 Minimum Area.** The minimum net free ventilating area shall be 1/150 of the area of the space vented space.
218	**R806.4 Installation and weather protection.**
219	When designing for attic ventilation, NRCA recommends designers provide for attic ventilation in the minimum amount of 1 square foot of net free ventilation area for every 150 square feet of attic space (1:150 ventilation ratio) measured at the attic floor level (e.g., ceiling).
	Mechanical Ventilation: A ventilation airflow rate in the amount of 1.0 cubic foot per minute per square foot of attic space measured at the attic floor is generally considered to be equivalent to a 1:150 ventilation ratio.
232	**3.5 Roof Vents**
	Intake Vents: Air intake vents are used to allow outside air to enter into attic spaces and ventilation cavities. Intake vents should be located along a roof assembly's lowest eave, at or near soffits or eaves.

Page #	Highlight
233	**Exhaust Vents:** Air exhaust vents are used to allow air in attic spaces and ventilation cavities to exit to the exterior.
	Exhaust vents should be placed at or near a roof assembly's ridge or high point.
233-234	Note and highlight the definition for each of the 5 most common types of exhaust vents: Ridge Vents; Static Vents; Gable-end Vents; Turbine Vents; and Mechanical Vents.
237-238	Note and highlight the definition for each of the following: air barrier, air leakage, air infiltration, air retarder, air retarder system, continuity, air retarder accessory, air leakage rates.
238	**Fundamental Concepts:** The primary function of an air retarder system is to reduce air leakage through a building thermal envelope.
249	**Figure 4-4:** U.S. climate zone map
260	**Appendix 1:** Psychrometric Chart
261	**Appendix 2:** Climate Zones (Note and highlight all charts of pages 239-250)
273	**Appendix 3:** Typical Thermal Properties of Building Materials

1 Exam Prep
NRCA Roofing Manual:
Architectural Metal Flashing, Condensation Control and Reroofing – 2014 Tabs and Highlights

These 1 Exam Prep Tabs are based on the National Roofing Contractors Association (NRCA) manual listed below:

Architectural Metal Flashing, Condensation Control and Reroofing - 2014

Each 1 Exam Prep tabs sheet has five rows of tabs. Start with the first tab at the first row at the top of the page; proceed down that row placing the tabs at the locations listed below. Place each tab in your book setting it down one notch until you get to the last tab. Then start with the highlights.

Special Note to our Students: If you are a 1 Exam Prep student, here is how to really get the most from the 1 Exam Prep Tabs. Follow the above instructions, but before placing the tab, find the tab's topic in the outline of your appropriate module. Now locate and highlight several items listed in the outline just before the topic, and just after. See how the topic fits in the outline and how it relates as a concept to the broader concept spelled out in the outline. If you take a few minutes to do this, when you take the test, key words in the test questions will remind you of where the information is in the manual!

1 Exam Prep Tab	Page #
Table of Contents	7
Chapter 1 - Materials	17
Chapter 2 - Low-Slope Roof Guidelines	47
Chapter 4 - Construction Details	107
Chapter 3 - Steep-Slope Roof Guidelines	85
Index of Construction Details	116-18
Chapter 1 - Condensation & Leakage Control	187
Chapter 2 - Condensation Low-Slope	197
Chapter 3 - Condensation Steep-Slope	213
Chapter 4 - Air Retarders For Roof Assemblies	227
Charts	238

1 Exam Prep Tab	Page #
Chapter 1 - Intro to Reroofing	264
Chapter 2 - Evaluation of Existing Roof	269
Chapter 3 - Building Code Requirements	281
Chapter 4 - Roof Decks for Reroofing	285
Chapter 5 - Roof Replacement Guidelines	309
Appendixes	315
Glossary	325

This concludes the tabs for this book. Please continue with the highlights below.

Page #	Highlight
15	**Introduction:** "The incline, or slope, or a roof is the primary factor in determining into which of these categories a particular roof falls. NRCA defines these categories as follows: **Low-slope roofs:** a category of roof systems that generally includes weatherproof membrane types of roof systems installed on slopes at or less than 3:12. **Steep-slope roofs:** a category of roof systems that generally includes water-shedding types of roof systems installed on slopes exceeding 3:12."
17	"Metals used in roofing can be divided into several categories: those that are naturally weathering … metallic-coated metals …"
	Naturally Weathering Metals: "For a metal to be appropriately considered a naturally weathering metal, the base metal itself must be able to oxidize sufficiently to form its own protective layer to withstand environmental exposures common to roof systems."
	Metallic-coated Metals: "… metallic-coated carbon steel is the most prevalent. This category of roofing material comprises of metal types that contain a base layer of carbon steel to which a corrosion-resistant metallic coating is applied."
18	**1.1 Metal Types:**
	Aluminum: "Aluminum provides a lightweight, easily formed metal that does not require a protective coating for most exposures."
19	**Figure 1-1:** Metal thickness and weight information for aluminum sheets
	Aluminized Steel: "Aluminized steels rely almost solely on the aluminum's ability to act as a barrier for protecting the base steel."

Page #	Highlight
20	**Figure 1-2:** Metal thickness and weight information for aluminized sheets
	Copper: "Copper does not require a protective finish. Copper's appearance typically changes during its exposure to the elements; however, this change depends on geographic and atmospheric conditions, such as exposure to moisture and air pollutants."
21	**Figure 1-3:** Metal thickness and weight information for copper sheets
	Copper-coated Stainless Steel: "Copper-coated stainless steel is Type 430 stainless steel in sheet or coil form coated with a thin copper layer on each side."
	Figure 1-4: Metal thickness and weight information for copper-coated sheets
	Galvalume® (aluminum-zinc-coated steel): "Galvalume is aluminum-zinc-coated steel and frequently used for roofing applications. This alloy coating is reported to be 55 percent aluminum and 45 zinc by weight."
22	**Figure 1-5:** Metal thickness and weight information for Galvalume sheets.
	Galvanized Steel: "Galvanized steel is one of the oldest and most common metallic coated metals." "For sheet-metal flashings, the most common thickness is 24 gauge. Galvanized steel is also available in 16, 18, 20, 22, 26, and 28-gauge thicknesses."
23	**Figure 1-6:** Metal thickness and weight information for galvanized sheets.
	Lead: "Lead is used as a roofing accessory metal because of its workability. Lead is extremely soft, can be formed by hand, and is useful for flashing irregular shapes and junctures."
	"A weight range of 2 pounds per square foot to 4 pounds per square foot is typical for roofing applications, but heavier weights may be desirable when soldering is necessary."
	Figure 1-7: Metal thickness and weight information for lead sheets.
	Lead-coated Copper: "Lead-coated copper was developed in the early 1900s to provided a roofing and flashing material with the appearance and corrosion-resistant characteristics of lead but with less cost and weight than lead alone."
24	**Figure 1-7:** Metal thickness and weight information for lead-coated sheets.
	Stainless Steel: "Stainless steel is a corrosion-resistant material. It is often used in harsh environments when other metals or metal paint finished may not be appropriate."
25	**Figure 1-9:** Metal thickness and weight information for stainless-steel sheets
	Zinc: "Zinc is a self-healing metal that weathers to a soft blue-gray patina. This soft architectural metal offers a combination of aesthetics, design flexibility, malleability, and durability."
	Figure 1-10: Metal thickness and weight information for zinc sheets

Page #	Highlight
26	**Tin-zinc-coated Copper:** "Tin-zinc-coated copper is composed of copper conforming to ASTM B370, "Standard Specification of Copper Sheet and Strip for Building Construction," coated on both sides with an alloy consisting of 50 percent tin and 50 percent zinc approximately 0.05 mils thick."
	Figure 1-11: Metal thickness and weight information for zinc-tin-coated copper sheets
	Zinc-tin-coated Stainless Steel (TCS): "Zinc-tin-coated stainless steel is a Type 304 stainless-steel base metal coated on both sides with a thin layer of a zinc and tin alloy. The alloy is composed of 50 percent zinc and 50 percent tin."
27	**Figure 1-12:** Metal thickness and weight information for zinc-tin-coated stainless steel sheets
	Terne-coated Stainless Steel: "Terne-coated stainless steel is stainless steel coated on both sides with lead and tin. Today's version of terne-coated stainless steel is a Type 304 … with a thin layer of zinc and alloy most commonly referred to as TCS II"
27-29	**1.2 Protective Coatings:** Note and highlight the definitions for each of the seven different types of coatings: Paint Systems; Fluoropolymers; Siliconized Acrylics and Polyesters; Laminates; Pearlescent and Metallic Additives; Clear-coat Finishes; Anodizing; and Powder Coatings.
34	**1.4 Oil Canning:** "Oil canning refers to physical distortions in the flatness of metal; however, this condition is only aesthetic in nature and does not have any adverse effect on the structural integrity or the weather proofing capability of the metal."
	1.5 Cleats, Clips and Fasteners: Cleats: - "NRCA defines a cleat as a continuous metal component installed behind the leading edge of a metal accessory, such as a coping cap or edge metal, used to engage and secure the metal accessory to the adjacent substrate or another metal component by means of a slip joint or by crimping the leading edge of the metal accessory to the cleat."
35	**Clips:** "NRCA defines a clip as an individual metal component installed at predetermined locations behind the leading edge of a flashing metal, used to engage and secure the sheet-metal flashings intermittently to the adjacent substrate or another metal component."
35	**Fasteners:** "Sheet-metal fasteners are mechanical anchors that provide anchorage of sheet metal. Fasteners are differentiated by the type of substrate or material being fastened."
37-38	**Figure 1-19: Fasteners commonly used with sheet metal.**
40	**1.7 Joinery:** "Joinery is the method of joining two or more pieces of sheet metal. Joints can be made with mechanical fasteners, interlocking seaming methods, sheet metal cover plates, sealants, metals (e.g. solder, welding) or combinations of these methods."
	Mechanical Fasteners: "Screws, bolts, and rivets are perhaps the simplest and most common method of joining two pieces of sheet metal."
41	**Crimping and Locking:** "Pre-painted metals and nonsolderable metals are commonly joined without the use of soldering or welding because the coating does not allow for soldering or welding. Crimping and locking is a typical method used to join laps in sheet-metal components"

Page #	Highlight
41	**Soldering or Welding:** "Welded or soldered joints are those that form a chemical bond between two metal shapes."
43	**Figure 23:** Weldable and solderable metals
43-45	**Joinery Types:** "Following are examples with descriptions of joinery (seam) types commonly used in roofing applications." Note and highlight each of the 14 different seam types: Overlap Standing Seam; Single-lock Standing Seam; Double-lock Standing Seam; Capped Standing Seam; Flat Lock Seam; Double Flat Lock Seam; Drive Cleat Seam; "S" Cleat Seam; Double "S" Cleat Seam; Cover Plate Seam; Backer Plate Seam: Cover Plate With Backer Plate Seam; Lap Seam; and Pittsburg Lock Seam.
42	**Figure 26:** Minimum metal thickness guidelines for weather ability - copings.
54	**A-type Profile Edge Metal:** "A-type profile edge metal, commonly called "gravel stop," is often used in low-slope applications."
56	"The roof flange should be a minimum of 3 inches, recessed a minimum 1/2 inch from the back of the wood nailer."
	L-type Profile Edge Metal: "In low-slope applications, L-type profile is commonly used with roof systems without an aggregate surfacing or in draining edge locations with smooth-surfaced roof systems."
	Figure 2-10: Minimum metal thickness guidelines for weather ability – perimeter edge metal
	Fascia Cap Edge Metal: "Fascia cap edge metal is used in low-slope roof systems and is preferred because its design does not require the edge metal to be embedded or sandwiched into the roofing membrane."
62	**Fascia Metal Accessories:** "Depending on the design of the roof edge, fascia metal components may also be used with the perimeter edge metal."
66	**2.3 Counterflashing:** "A counter-flashing is defined as a formed metal component secured on or into a wall or curb or to another component … to cover and protect the upper edge of the membrane base flashing and its associated fasteners from mechanical damage and exposure to weather."
67	"Counterflashing should extend over the top of the base flashings approximately 4 inches and have a ½ inch minimum drip edge at the bottom."
67	"Overlapping counterflashing joints should be about three inches and sealed."
71	**2.5 Area Dividers:** "If roof area dividers are used, they should be flashed to a minimum height of 8 inches above the roof surface and should be located at high points in the roof with drainage away from or parallel to the divider."
77	**2.8 Gutters and Downspouts:** "There are two types of gutters; built-in and externally attached (hanging)."
	Externally Attached (Hanging) Gutters: "Maintenance, durability, and longevity of the metal and securement type are important factors to consider when designing gutters and downspouts."

Page #	Highlight
80	**Built-in Gutters:** "Built-in gutters may be used with low-slope roof systems; however, they primarily are used on steep-slope roof systems."
81	**Downspouts:** "Sheet-metal downspouts are shop-fabricated or pre-manufactured in a wide variety of shapes and sizes. Plain, corrugated, round, rectangular or square downspouts are typical."
85	**3.1 Drip Edge Metal:** "Drip edge metal is a sheet-metal roof component designed to provide a continuous finished edge along the outer edges of a roof system."
86	**Figure 3-2:** Minimum metal thickness guidelines for weatherability based on steep-slope covering - drip edge metal.
87	**3.2 Gutters and Downspouts:** "One way of controlling drainage of some steep-slope roof systems is by using gutters and downspouts. Special consideration must be taken when determining size, style, attachment, location, and construction to ensure adequate drainage and strength."
88	**Externally Attached (Hanging) Gutters:** "Maintenance, durability, and longevity of the metal and securement type are important factors to consider when designing gutters and downspouts."
88	"There are two common types of support systems typically used with externally attached gutters:" - Support brackets - Straps
90	**Figure 3-5:** Minimum metal thickness guidelines for weatherability - gutters
94	**3.4 Valleys:** "A valley is created at the downslope intersection of two sloping roof planes. Water runoff from the portions of the roof areas sloping into a valley flows toward and along the valley." **Fastener Placement:** "Generally, fasteners should be kept back from the center of the valley a minimum of 8 inches."
95	**Figure 3-12:** Minimum metal thickness guidelines for weatherability based on steep-slope covering - valley metal
96	**Clay and Concrete Tile Roof Systems:** "NRCA recommends valley metal for use with tile be a minimum of 18 inches wide."
98	**Figure 3-13:** Minimum metal thickness guidelines for weatherability based on steep-slope coverings - flashings (apron, headwall, backer, cricket, sidewall, pipe penetration)
99	**Cricket Flashing:** "NRCA recommends designers specify crickets at the upslope side of chimneys or curbed roof penetrations when the chimney of the curb is 24 inches wide or greater." **3.7 Sidewall Flashing:** "Where a sloped roof area intersects a vertical side wall, either step flashing or channel flashing is installed."
100	**Figure 3-15:** Wood cricket built on upslope side of a chimney **Figure 3-16:** Metal cricket flashing for the upslope side of a masonry chimney

Page #	Highlight
100-1	**Clay and Concrete Tile Roof Systems:** "The step flashing width should be sufficient to obtain a 4-inch extension onto each underlying tile and about a 4-inch vertical height over the exposed face of each overlying tile."
101	**Slate:** "The step flashing width should be a minimum of 8 inches to obtain a 4-inch extension onto each underlying shingle and about a 4-inch vertical height over the exposed face of each overlying shingle."
109	**Preservative-treated Wood:** "Since Jan. 1, 2004, preservative-treated lumber for consumer use is no longer chromated copper arsenate (CCA) treated."
113	**Figure 4-2:** Guide for sheet-metal coping
147	**Expansion Joint with Cleats on Both Sides** (EJ-2)
155	**Gutter with Perimeter Edge Metal - Low-Slope Roof Systems** (G-2)
168	**Sidewall Flashing (Step Flashing)** (SW-1)
180	**Appendix 1** - Expansion Coefficients of Metals
192-93	**Water Vapor Movement in Buildings: Diffusion:** "Diffusion occurs as the result of water vapor pressure differences across material. Some materials allow diffusion to occur more rapidly than others. A material's ability to allow diffusion of vapor is measured by its permeability and permeance."
193	**Permeability:** "The time rate of vapor transmission through a flat material of a unit thickness induced by vapor pressure difference between two specific surfaces under specified temperature and humidity conditions." **Permeance:** "The time rate of vapor transmission through a flat material or construction assembly induced by vapor pressure difference between two specific surfaces under specified temperature and humidity conditions."
194	**Figure 1-4:** Typical water vapor permeance or permeability values for common building materials
208	**Bituminous Vapor Retarders:** "Modern bituminous vapor retarders generally membranes composed of self-adhering polymer-modified bitumen sheet products … installed in adhered applications."
208	**Nonbituminous Vapor Retarders:** "Included in the nonbituminous category of vapor retarders are: (2 bullets)."
209	**Securement:** "Over nailable roof decks, the base ply of the vapor retarder should be nailed to the roof deck, and then the first (and if necessary, the second) ply should be adhered to the base sheet."
209-10	**High-Humidity Interiors:** "NRCA suggests vapor retarders for such facilities or high-humidity sections of facilities be durable, effective, multilayer membranes with a perm rating as close to zero as possible."
213	"Roofs can generally be divided into two categories: low-slope and steep-slope."
214	**3.1 Preventing Condensation Accumulation:** "Depending on climate zone, preventing condensation accumulation in steep-slope roof assemblies requires some combination of the following measures: (5 bullets)."

Page #	Highlight
216	**3.2 Attic Ventilation:** "Generally, ventilation of attic spaces can be accommodated by using one of two methods: (2 bullets)."
216	**Static Ventilation:** "The most common means of providing attic ventilation for steep slope roof assemblies is by non-mechanical, static ventilation."
216-17	**1203.2 Attic Spaces.** "A minimum of 1 inch (25 mm) of airspace shall be provided between the insulation and the roof sheathing."
217	**R806.2 Minimum Area.** "The total net free ventilating area shall not be less than 1/150 of the area of the space ventilated."
218	**R806.4 Installation and weather protection.** "When designing for attic ventilation, NRCA recommends designers provide for attic ventilation in the minimum amount of 1 square foot of net free ventilation area for every 150 square feet of attic space (1:150 ventilation ratio) measured at the attic floor level (e.g., ceiling)."
218	**Mechanical Ventilation:** "A ventilation airflow rate in the amount of 1.0 cubic foot per minute per square foot of attic space measured at the attic floor is generally considered to be equivalent to a 1:150 ventilation ratio."
223	**3.5 Roof Vents: Intake Vents:** "Air intake vents are used to allow outside air to enter into attic spaces and ventilation cavities. Intake vents should be located along a roof assembly's lowest eave, at or near soffits or eaves."
	Exhaust Vents: "Air exhaust vents are used to allow air in attic spaces and ventilation cavities to exit to the exterior. Exhaust vents should be placed at or near a roof assembly's ridge or high point."
224-25	Note and highlight the definition for each of the 5 most common types of exhaust vents: Ridge Vents; Static Vents; Gable-end Vents; Turbine Vents; and Mechanical Vents.
227	Note and highlight the definition for each of the following: air barrier, air leakage, air infiltration, air retarder, air retarder system, continuity, air retarder accessory, air leakage rates.
228	**Fundamental Concepts:** "The primary function of an air retarder system is to reduce air leakage through a building thermal envelope."
233	**Figure 4-3:** U.S. climate zone map
238	**Appendix 1:** Psychrometric Chart
239-50	**Appendix 2:** Climate Zones (Note and highlight all charts of pages 239-250)
251	**Appendix 3:** Typical Thermal Properties of Building Materials
282	**1510.3 Recovering versus replacement.** "New roof coverings shall not be installed without first removing all existing layers of roof coverings down to the roof deck where any of the following conditions occur: (1-3)." "Exceptions: (1-3)."

Page #	Highlight
287	**Structural Concrete:** "Structural concrete is produced by mixing aggregate, usually stone or crushed gravel, with sand; portland cement; water; and, in some design mixes, various chemical additives. Steel reinforcing bars and/or steel wire mesh are used to reinforce the concrete."
287	**4.2 Concrete: Lightweight Structural Concrete:** "Structural lightweight weight concrete roof decks made with these type of aggregate and Portland cement have densities about 80 percent of the density of normal-weight structural concrete."
287	**Cast-in-place:** "Structural concrete that is poured and formed or cast at a job site is referred to as cast-in place concrete."
287	**Post-tensioned:** "Post-tensioned concrete contains high-strength steel strands or tendons that are embedded in the concrete."
287-88	**Precast and Prestressed:** "Precast concrete units are poured into forms. Typically off a job site, allowed to sufficiently cure, and then transported to the site for erection to make up a roof deck."
289-90	**4.3 Lightweight Insulating Concrete:** Note and highlight the definition for Lightweight-aggregate Insulating Concrete and Lightweight Cellular Concrete.
291	**4.4 Poured Gypsum:** "A poured gypsum roof deck consists of gypsum that is mixed with wood fibers or mineral aggregate."
292	**Precast Gypsum Panels:** "Precast gypsum panel roof decks are constructed of metal-bound gypsum, internally reinforced with a steel wire mesh or panels composed of two factory-laminated paper-faced gypsum sheets. Metal-edged precasts panels feature tongue-and-groove side section. "
294	**4.5 Steel:** "Steel roof decks are constructed of cold-rolled steel sheets or panels with ribs formed in each panel to provide strength and rigidity."
	Narrow-rib Steel Deck (Type A): "A steel deck panel with a rib-width opening of 1 inch maximum."
	Figure 4-7: Narrow-rib steel deck (Type A)
	Intermediate-rib Steel Deck (Type F): "A steel deck panel with a rib-width opening of 1 inch to 1-3/4 inches."
	Figure 4-8: Intermediate-rib steel deck (Type F)
	Wide-rib Steel Deck (Type B): "A steel deck panel with a rib-width opening of 1 ¾ inches to 2-5/8 inches."
	Figure 4-9: Wide-rib steel deck (Type B)
	Deep-rib Steel Deck (Type 3DR): "A steel deck panel with rib-width opening of 1-1/2 inches to 2-3/4 inches and a rib depth of 3 inches minimum."
	Figure 4-10: Deep-rib steel deck (Type 3DR)

Page #	Highlight
311	**Existing Metal Flashings**: "Reroofing projects typically incorporate new metal flashings, metal counterflashings and copings."
313	**Figure 5-2:** NRCA guidelines for clearance for equipment support strands
313	**Roof Curbs and Equipment Supports:** "NRCA suggest roof curb heights be sufficient to maintain 8-inch minimum base flashing heights for roof-mounted curbs."
313	**Roof Slope:** "For roof penetrations that are 24 inches wide or wider, NRCA recommends installing a cricket on the upslope side of penetrations."

1 Exam Prep
NRCA Roofing Manual:
NRCA Roofing Manual: Membrane Roof Systems – 2019
Tabs and Highlights

These 1 Exam Prep Tabs are based on the National Roofing Contractors Association (NRCA) manual listed below:

Membrane Roof Systems – 2019

Each 1 Exam Prep tabs sheet has five rows of tabs. Start with the first tab at the first row at the top of the page; proceed down that row placing the tabs at the locations listed below. Place each tab in your book setting it down one notch until you get to the last tab. Then start with the highlights.

1 Exam Prep Tab	Page #
Table of Contents	8
Introduction	12
Ch. 1 – Roof Assembly Configs	15
Ch. 2 - Roof Decks	78
Ch. 3 - Air & Vapor Retarders	110
Ch. 4 - Rigid Board Insulation	122
Ch. 5 - Roof Membranes	172
Polymer-modified Bitumen	186
Single-Ply Roof Membranes	200
Ch. 6 – Fasteners	220
Ch. 7 - Surfacings	234
Ch. 8 -Roof Accessories	252
Ch. 9 – Reroofing	258
Ch. 10 – Construction Details	288
Index of Construction Details	332
Appendix 1 – Wind Uplift	546
Appendix 2 – Chemical Comp of Roof Membranes	558

1 Exam Prep Tab	Page #
Appendix 3 – Temp Roof Systems	560
Appendix 4 – Flood Testing	562
Appendix 5 – Bldg Code Comp	564
Appendix 6 – History of Updates	578

This concludes the tabs for this book. Please continue with the highlights on the following page.

Page #	Highlight

Roof assembly: An assembly of interacting roof components including the roof deck, air or vapor retarder4 (if present), insulation and membrane or primary roof covering designed to weather proof a structure

Roof Systems: A system of interacting roof components generally consisting of membrane or primary roof covering and roof insulation (not including the roof deck) designed to weatherproof the sometimes to improve the building's thermal resistance

Low-slope roof systems: A category of roof systems that generally includes weatherproof membrane types of roof systems installed on slopes at or less than 3:12

Steep-slope roof systems: A category of roof systems that generally includes water-shedding types of roof coverings installed on slopes greater than 3:12

CHAPTER 1 – ROOF ASSEMBLY CONFIGURATIONS: Roof assembly configurations are designated in the following order: project type, roof covering type, number of plies or layers (if applicable) attachment method (if applicable) and substrate type. Following is a description of these categories and the options listed under each category. Highlight all of the following and become familiar with each one

Project Type: There are three project types: new construction or roof replacement, roof re-cover and temporary roof, new construction or roof replacement and roof re-cover are included for every roof covering type.

16 **Roof Covering Type**

Number of Plies or Layers

Attachment Method

Substrate Type
- **Nonnailable deck**
- **Insulated deck**
- **Nailable deck**
- **Steel deck**

77 **CHAPTER 2 – ROOF DECKS:** The following types of roof decks are addressed in this manual: Highlight the six (6) bullet points and become familiar with **Cementitious wood fiber panels, Lightweight insulating concrete, Steel, Structural concrete (cast-in-place, post-tensioned and precast-prestressed), Wood panels (plywood, oriented strand board) and Wood planks and wood boards**

78 **2.1 – Guidelines Applicable to All Roof Deck Types - Structural Support:** A roof deck transfers live and dead loads to supporting framing members (e.g. joists, purlins, subpurlins). Live loads include environmental loads, such as wind, snow, rain and ice, and other nonstationary loads such as workers and mobile installation equipment.

Dead loads include stationary loads, such as topside and underside mechanical equipment, weight of the deck, any sheathing overlayment, roof membrane, insulation and ballast.

Page #	Highlight
	Roof Expansion Joints: Roof expansion joints are used to minimize the elects of stresses and movements of a building's components and to limit the effects of and potential for theses stresses to cause splitting, buckling/ridging or damage to a roof system. Highlight the four (4) bullet points and become familiar with **The building's thermal movement characteristic, The structural supports and roof deck, The roof system selected and The climatic conditions**
	Slope and Drainage: For new construction projects, *The International Building Code, 2018 Edition* indicates a design minimum slope of ¼:12 is required for membrane roof systems, except for coal tar built-up roof systems where a design minimum slope of 1/8:12 is permitted.
80	The criterion for judging proper slope for drainage is that there be no ponding water on the roof 48 hours after a rain during conditions conducive to drying.
	Slope generally is provided by: Highlight the four (4) bullet points and become familiar with **Sloping the structural framing or roof deck, Designing a tapered insulation system, Proper location of roof drains, scuppers and gutters and A combination of the above**
	Drains should be located at low points in a roof (points of maximum deck deflection), not a column or bearing walls (points of minimum deflection).
	Electrical Conduits and Other Piping: If metallic conduit or wiring needs to be placed near the roof assembly, NRCA recommends it be positioned and supported at least 1 ½ inches from the bottom side of the roof deck or substrate to which the roof system is applied.
	Additional Insulation and Consideration for a Vapor Retarder: Based on the dew-point calculation and to limit possible condensation and premature degradation of materials, a designer should consider provisions for a vapor retarder.
	2.2 - Cementitious Wood Fiber Panels: Cementitious wood fiber panels intended as roof decks provide for structural support of the roof system and can provide for a finished interior ceiling surface that has acoustical properties.
83	**Vertical Alignment:** Elevation differences in excess of 1/8 of an inch between panels are considered unacceptable. Uneven joints of 1/8 of an inch or more should be grouted with the grout feathered to a slope of 1/8 of an inch per foot.
84	**Attachment of Roof System Components:** NRCA does not recommend the use of seam-fastened, mechanically attached single-ply membranes over cementitious wood fiber panel roof decks because of the potential for fastener holes to reduce a cementitious wood fiber panel roof deck's structural integrity and alignment of fastener penetrations likely resulting in significant loss of the roof deck's structural integrity.
	2.3 - Lightweight Insulating Concrete: Lightweight-aggregate insulating concrete and lightweight-cellular insulating concrete are used as a fill material, usually to add slope to drain or as a topping over another substrate, such as a corrugated metal form deck, structural concrete deck, wood deck or other structural components.
85	**Design:** NRCA recommends lightweight insulating concrete roof decks be a minimum of 2 inches thick, not including the thickness of any form board or other underlying substrate.

Page #	Highlight
87	**Attachment of Roof System Components:** NRCA does not recommend directly adhering base sheets, rigid board insulation or roof membrane to lightweight insulating concrete roof decks without installing a mechanically fastened venting base sheet or other coated base sheet separator.
88	**2.4 - Steel:** Steel roof decks are constructed of cold-rolled steel sheets or panels with ribs formed in each panel to provide strength and rigidity. The panels are available in several gauges, rib depths, flute spacings and yield strengths.
	Narrow-rib Steel Deck (Type A): A steel deck panel with a rib-width opening of 1inch maximum. See Figure 2-2.
	Intermediate-rib Steel Deck (Type F): A steel deck panel with a rib-width opening of 1 inch to 1 ¾ inch. See Figure 2-3.
	Wide-rib Steel Deck (Type B): A steel deck panel with a rib-width opening of 1 ¾ inches to 2 5/8 inches. See Figure 2-4.
	Deep-rib Steel Deck (Type 3DR): A steel deck panel with rib-width opening of 1 ½ inch to 2 ¾ inches and a rib depth of 3 inches minimum. See Figure 2-5.
89	**Design:** Most conventional steel deck panels are fabricated from steel with a minimum yield strength of 33 ksi or Grade 33 steel.
	NRCA recommends steel roof decks be 22-gauge or heavier and have a minimum G-90 galvanized coating complying with ASTM A653.
	End Laps and Side Laps: Deck panel end laps should not be less than 2 inches and should be centered over structural supports. All side laps should be mechanically fastened. Side-lap fastener spacing should not exceed 3 feet.
90	**Deck Attachment:** SDI permits powder-actuated fasteners, pneumatically driven fasteners or screws instead of welding to fasten steel decks to supporting framing if fasteners meet project strength and service requirements.
94	Also, ANSI/SDI RD-2010 specifies the following dimensional tolerances for steel roof deck panels: Highlight all five (5) bullet points and become familiar with each one
95	**Attachment of Roof System Components:** Rigid board insulation should be applied in a minimum of two layers to minimize gaps and thermal breaks at board joints.
95-96	NRCA does not recommend the use of low-rise foam or liquid-applied adhesive as the primary means of attaching rigid board insulation to steel roof decks.
96	**2.5 Structural Concrete:** There are two general types of structural concrete used in roof decks: normal-weight structural concrete and light-weight structural concrete.
	Normal-weight Structural Concrete: Steel reinforcing bars and / or steel wire mesh are used to reinforce the concrete. The density of reinforced, normal-weight structural concrete generally is about 150 pounds per cubic foot (pcf).
	Lightweight Structural Concrete: Lightweight structural concretes have densities ranging from 95 to 120 pounds per square foot, about 80 percent of the density of normal-weight structural concrete.

Page #	Highlight
96	The most commonly used lightweight aggregate is expanded shale.
97	The three general installation types for structural concrete roof decks are cast-in-place, post-tensioned and precast-prestressed. Highlight headings and become familiar with **Cast-in-place Concrete, Post-tensioned Concrete and Precast-prestressed Concrete**
98	**Precast-prestressed concrete:** called "camber", which precast Figure 2-9. The prestressing process generally results in upward deflection, also member at center of the span above the elevation of the supports. See
99	**Design:** Also, designers need to consider additional factors when using structural concrete roof decks, including drainage, curing and drying, high-humidity areas, roof openings, and weather and temperature. **Curing and Drying:** Normal-weight and lightweight structural concrete contain significant amounts of water when mixed, formed and poured, and finished. As concrete cures and hardens, it consumes large amount of this water through hydration and evaporation. For example, a 4-inch-thick concrete slab of normal weight concrete will release about 1 quart of water for each square foot of surface area.
101	Until recognized pass-fail criteria applicable for determining concrete's internal humidity is developed, NRCA suggests a maximum 75 percent relative humidity value be used; lower values may be necessary when using organic-based materials, such as wood fiberboard, perlite board and some insulation facer sheets, as roof system components. **Attachment of Roof System Components:** Structural concrete roof decks are considered to be "nonnailable"; that is, mechanical fasteners such as screws and plates and nails are not used to attach rigid board insulation, base sheets or membrane components. NRCA recommends designers specify a separator layer or rigid board insulation over a structural concrete roof deck before installing a single-ply membrane over the deck.
102	**2.6 Wood Panels:** There are two general types of wood panels used for roof decks: Plywood and oriented strand board (OSB). Panels consists of a number of cross-laminated layers that vary in number according to the panel's thicknesses. OSB panels are composed of layers of compressed, glued wood strands. **Design:** When plywood is used as a roof deck material, NRCA recommends the use of a minimum of four ply, 15/32-of-an-inch-thick or four-ply, nominal ½-of-an-inch-thick plywood for 16-inch joist or rafter spacings, and four-ply, nominal 5/8-of-an-inch-thick plywood for 24-inch joist or rafter spacings.
103	When OSB is used as a roof deck material, a minimum of 15/32-of-an-inch-thick OSB is recommended for 16-inch rafter spacings and nominal 5/8-of-an-inch-thicknesse OSB for 24-inch rafter spacings. Generally, unless a panel manufacturer recommends otherwise, spacing between panel edges is recommended to be about 1/8 of an inch.

Page #	Highlight
104	**Fire-retardant-treated Panels:** NRCA does not recommend using FRT wood as a roof deck material.
	Attachment of Roof System Components: Built-up and polymer-modified bitumen membranes should not be adhered directly to wood panel roof decks.
	NRCA does not recommend the torch application of polymer-modified bitumen membrane sheets directly to combustible substrates, such as wood panel roof decks.
105	Liquid-applied membrane roof systems should not be adhered directly to wood panel roof decks.
	2.7 – Wood Planks and Wood Boards: Wood plank and wood board roof decks are composed of solid-sawn dimensional lumber. They are typically supported by wood beams, glue-laminated timber (glulams), and/or solid lumber joists or purlins.
	Use of nominal 6-inch-wide wood boards is suggested for roof decks to prevent excessive movement and splitting. Boards thinner than nominal 1 inch are not considered strong enough to support roof loads.
109	**CHAPTER 3 – AIR AND VAPOR RETARDERS:** NRCA defines the terms "air retarder" and "vapor retarder" as follows:
	Air retarder: Layer(s) of material used to minimize the amount of air intrusion and air leakage into and out of a roof assembly.
	Vapor retarder: Layer(s) of material or a laminate used to reduce the flow of water vapor into a roof system.
110	**3.1 – Air Retarders – Terminology:** In this manual, NRCA has adopted and will use the term "air retarder" for what some will refer to as an "air barrier." Following is additional terminology applicable to air retarders: Highlight all seven (7) bullet points and become familiar with **Air leakage, Air infiltration, Air retarder, Air retarder system, Continuity, Air retarder accessary and Air leakage rate**.
111	**Fundamental concepts:** To be considered can effective air retarder material, the air permeance for that material has been established by some building and energy codes as no greater than 0.004 cubic foot per minute per square foot (cfm/ft^2) at a pressure difference of 0.3 inches of water.
112	**Roof Membrane Air Retarders:** For example, IECC and ASHRA 90.1 recognize the following types of roof systems as deemed-to-comply air retarder materials: Highlight all four (4) bullet points and become familiar with **Built-up membranes, Polymer-modified bitumen membranes, Adhered single-ply membranes and 1.5 pcf density closed-cell spray foam, minimum 1 ½ inches thick**
	The deemed-to-comply option's criteria for closed-cell spray foam, minimum 1.5 pcf density, minimum 1 ½ inches thick, can be interpreted to include spray polyurethane foam (SPF) roof systems.
	NRCA Recommendations: NRCA considers a continuous, air-impermeable roof membrane to function as an air retarder. Examples of continuous, air-impermeable roof membranes include built-up, polymer-modified bitumen and single-ply membrane roofing systems.
117	**3.2 – Vapor Retarders:** The materials used to construct vapor retarders in roof assemblies using membrane roof systems may be classified into two broad categories: Highlight the two (2) bullet

Page #	Highlight
118	points and become familiar with **Bituminous vapor retarders and Plastic sheet or film vapor retarders**
	Bituminous Membrane Vapor Retarders: Bituminous membrane vapor retarders are the most commonly used type of vapor retarders.
	Such a vapor retarder provides a perm rating that approaches 0 perms.
	Plastic Sheet or Film Vapor Retarders: Depending on material type and thickness, permeance of these plastic sheets or film retarders ranges from approximately 0.04 to 0.50 perms.
	Selecting Vapor Retarder Materials: The term "vapor retarder" refers to a broad range of materials used to control the flow of moisture vapor from the interior of building into the roof system. The following are important considerations when selecting a vapor retarder: Highlight the four (4) bullet points and become familiar with **Roof deck type and possible puncture damage, Sandwich-type vapor retarder construction, Insulation type, Securement and Compliance with fire-and wind-resistance classifications**
121	**CHAPTER 4 – RIGID BOARD INSULATION:** The purpose of roof insulation is to provide a substrate for the application of a roof membrane and thermal resistance.
	4.1 – Guidelines Applicable to All Insulation Types: Roof insulation that is properly manufactured, designed and installed serves several vital purposes: Highlight all six (6) bullet points and become familiar with
122	While reducing the potential for interior moisture condensation, rigid roof insulation sandwiched between a roof deck and roof membrane can increase the probability of condensation occurring within the roof system.
	Desirable Properties of Roof Insulation: An ideal roof insulation would have the following properties. Highlight the ten (10) bullet points and become familiar with **Compatibility with bitumen and other adhesives, Component compatibility, Impact resistance, Fire resistance, Moisture resistance, Thermal resistance, Stable R-value, Attachment capability, Dimensional stability and Compressive strength**
123	**Usage Guidelines:** In low-slope membrane roof system construction, use of two or more layers of rigid board insulation is preferred.
125	**Principles of Thermal Insulation:** The primary function of insulation is to provide thermal resistance. Heat is a form of energy, and energy can be measured using a British thermal unit (Btu). A Btu is defined as the energy required to raise the temperature of 1 pound of water 1-degree Fahrenheit.
	Terminology: Highlight all four (4) bullet points and become familiar with **Thermal conductivity (k), Thermal conductance (C), Thermal resistance ® and Thermal transmittance (U or U-factor).**
126	The following table provides a range of U-factor values and corresponding total assembly R-values.
127	**Table with U-factor values and corresponding total assembly R-values**
130	**4.2 – Cellular Glass:** The following properties of cellular-glass roof insulation make it an effective insulating material: Highlight all nine (9) bullet points and become familiar with these properties

Page #	Highlight
130	**R-value:** Cellular-glass roof insulation has an R-value of 3.44 per inch thickness tested at a 75 F mean temperature. Cellular-glass roof insulation is recognized for having a stable R-value.
131	**Combustibility:** Cellular-glass roof insulation is noncombustible. It can be exposed directly to hot bitumen, torch flame or high temperatures, such as those produced by hot-air welders. **4.3 – Expanded Polystyrene (EPS):** The following recognized properties of expanded polystyrene insulation make it an effective insulating material: Highlight all seven (7) bullet points and become familiar with these properties
132	Typically, expanded polystyrene insulation is used in walls and roofs of commercial, industrial and residential buildings. **Product Standard:** When expanded polystyrene insulation is used, NRCA recommends designers specify expanded polystyrene insulation with a compressive strength appropriate for specific project conditions.
133	**Compatibility:** Expanded polystyrene insulation is affected by exposure to the sun, organic solvents and some adhesives.
134	**Application and Securement:** NRCA recommends designer specify a maximum 4-by-4-foot board size for expanded polystyrene insulation adhered to a substrate. The 4-by 8-foot board size is appropriate for loosely laid and mechanicaly attached membrane application.
135	**4.4 – Extruded Polystyrene (XPS):** The following recognized properties of polystyrene board roof insulation make it an effective insulating material: Highlight all seven (7) bullet points and become familiar with these properties Typically, extruded polystyrene insulation is used in buildings with low-temperature interior spaces, such as refrigeration rooms, and in walls and roofs of other commercial, industrial and residential buildings.
138	NRCA recommends designers specify a maximum 2-by 4-foot board size for extruded polystyrene insulation adhered to a substrate. The 2-by 8-foot board size is appropriate for loosely laid and mechanically attached membrane applications.
139	**4.5 – Glass-faced Gypsum:** Although glass-faced gypsum is not typically classified as an insulating product, information about glass-faced gypsum is included here because glass-faced gypsum is used in roof assemblies as a thermal barrier to provide fire resistance, substrates for air and vapor retarders, and cover boards beneath roof membranes. **R-value:** Glass-faced gypsum has R-values based upon thicknesses as follows. **Table: Glass-faced Gypsum**
140	**Combustibility:** Glass-faced gypsum boards are noncombustible. Gypsum boards are inherently fire-resistant because of gypsum calcination.
141	**4.6 – Fiber-reinforced Gypsum:** **R-value:** Fiber-reinforced gypsum has R-values based upon thicknesses as follows. Highlight Table Fiber-reinforced Gypsum
143	**4.7 – Stone Wool:** Stone wool insulation intended for roofing purposes is manufactured as a rigid insulating material. It is manufactured using rock and slag as base ingredients.

Page #	Highlight
143	Natural mineral materials are combined, heated until molten and then spun into a fibrous material that is often referred to as stone wool. The stone wool fibers are bound together with a binding agent to form a rigid insulation board.
144	**4.8 – Perlite:** Perlite board insulation intended for roofing purposes is a rigid insulating material manufactured from expanded volcanic minerals combined with organic fivers and binders. The top surface of perlite board roof insulation is generally treated with an asphalt emulsion to minimize bitumen absorption. The common R-value used to calculate the total thermal resistance of a perlite board roof insulation system is 2.78 per inch of thickness.
148	**4.9 – Polyisocyanurate – R-value:** NRCA recommends designers specifying polyisocyanurate insulation determine roof system thermal resistance using an in-service R-value of 5.0 per inch.
152-153	**4.11 - Wood Fiberboard:** The common R-value used to calculate the total thermal resistance of a wood or cane fiberboard insulation system is about 2.78 per inch of thickness.
153	Wood-fiber "sheathing" boards generally do not possess sufficient physical properties to be suitable for use as roof insulation. **R-value:** The common R-value used to calculate the total thermal resistance of a wood or cane fiberboard insulation system is about 2.78 per inch of thickness.
155	**4.12 – Cement Board - R-value:** Cement board does not contribute significant thermal resistance when used a part of roof assemblies.
158	**4.14 - Tapered Insulation:** Tapered insulation can be used to meet the requirements for slope in new construction and reroofing projects, as well as in cases where a roof deck will not provide adequate slope to drain water off a roof surface.
159	Although the primary reason for using tapered roof insulation is to improve slope and promote drainage, there are other advantages: Highlight two (2) bullet points and become familiar with
161	**Thermal Insulation Value:** The minimum R-Value approach establishes R-value for a tapered roof insulation system by determining the R-value of the tapered material at the thinnest point in the tapered system layout. The average R-Value approach establishes the R-value for a tapered roof insulation system by determining the R-value of the tapered material at the representative average thickness in the tapered system layout. Arithmetic Average Thickness Method: Arithmetic average thickness is the thickness of tapered and flat stock insulation at the midpoint between the minimum thickness (i.e., low point) and the maximum thickness (i.e., high point) in a tapered insulation system. See Figure 4-5.
164	**Design:** Tapered insulation layouts should be designed to form a sump that measures the size of the drain bowl's diameter plus approximately 24 inches at roof drains, and crickets should be installed on the high sides of all roof curbs.
165	**Slope Pattern:** A general rule of thumb for designing sufficiently sloping saddles and crickets is that they be twice the slope of the adjacent field of the roof. See Figure 4-12 (on page 166).
166	**Hips and Valleys:** When using performed tapered insulation boards of one consistent slope, all valley centerlines should be 45 degrees from the direction of slope, that is, the valley centerlines are 90 degrees apart.

Page #	Highlight
171	**CHAPTER 5 – ROOF MEMBRANES:** Most low-slope roof membranes have two principal components: weatherproofing layer or layers and reinforcement.
	The weatherproofing component is the most important element within a roof membrane because it keeps water from entering a roof assembly.
	The reinforcement adds strength, puncture resistance and dimensional stability to a membrane.
	This chapter describes four types of common roof membranes: built-up membranes, polymer-modified bitumen sheet membranes, single-ply membranes, and liquid-applied membranes.
172	**5.1 – Guidelines Applicable to All Membrane Types:**
	Slope and Drainage: For new construction projects, *The International Building Code, 2018 Edition* indicates a design minimum slope of ¼:12 is required for membrane roof systems, except for coal tar built-up roof systems where a design minimum slope of 1/8:12 is permitted.
	Slope generally is provided by: Highlight the four (4) bullet points and become familiar with
173	**Weather Conditions During Application:** When membrane roofing materials are applied, entrapment of moisture should be prevented. Moisture in or on materials may cause membrane blistering. If precipitation occurs before completely installing the roof membrane, the membrane surface in the immediate work area and the substrate should be dried or allowed to dry before work resumes.
	5.2 - Built-up Roof Membranes: A built-up roof membrane, sometimes referred to as BUR, consists of multiple layers of saturated felts, coated felts, fabrics or mates assembled in place shingle fashion with alternate layers of bitumen and surfaced with mineral aggregate, bituminous materials, a liquid-applied coating or a granule-surfaced cap sheet.
174	The principal components used in constructing built-up roof membranes are: Highlight four (4) bullet points and become familiar with **Bitumens, Reinforcement layers, such as felts and ply sheets, Membrane flashings and Accessories.**
174	**Bitumens:** Asphalts have excellent resistance to moisture, good resistance to weathering and excellent cohesive and adhesive characteristics. These properties also make asphalts useful as adhesives for adhering rigid board insulation and applying surfacings.
	Many coal tar built-up membranes remain in service, but coal tar is no longer widely used for built-up roof membrane construction.
	Cold-applied Asphalt Adhesives: These liquid versions of asphalt are referred to as "cutbacks". Cutting the asphalt back with solvents makes it possible to apply the weatherproofing asphalt material with heating it in a kettle or tanker.
176	**Hot-applied Asphalt:** For most roof system applications, including the construction of built-up membrane roof systems, oxidized asphalt bitumens are used.
	…classifies asphalt into four different types based on the asphalt's softening point, penetration (hardness) and ductility. The following table lists the ranges of softening point values for the four types of asphalt defined by ASTM D312.

Page #	Highlight
176	**Table: Asphalt Softening**
	An asphalt's penetration value is used as a measure of consistency (relative hardness).
	Table: Asphalt Penetration
	An asphalt's ductility value provides one measure of an asphalt's tensile properties and can be used as a measure of ductility for specification requirements.
	Table: Asphalt Ductility
177	Currently, asphalts complying with ASTM D312's, Type I or Type II are seldom used.
	As a result, ASTM D312 now indicates a maximum heating temperature for asphalt as 550°F. For mop application of asphalt, EVT is the temperature at which asphalt has a viscosity of 125 centipoise (cP). For mechanical spreader application of asphalt, EVT is the temperature at which the asphalt has a viscosity of 75 cP.
	Table: Asphalt EVT Values
	NRCA recommends at the point of application asphalt be within a ± 25 F range from an asphalt's initial EVT.
178	Asphalt complying with ASTM D312, Type III is generally appropriate for interplay moppings in built-up membrane application where the slope of the completed membrane is 1:12 or less. Use of asphalt complying with ASTM D312, Type V is suggested for slopes greater than 1:12.
	Hot-Applied Polymer-modified Asphalt: This polymer-modified asphalt is made from standard roofing asphalt modified by the addition of styrene ethylene butadiene styrene (SEBS).
	ASTM D6152 specifies a 500F minimum FP temperature; however, actual FP temperatures in excess of this value are desirable and common.
	NRCA recommends kettle and tanker temperatures be maintained lower than 25 F below the asphalt's actual FP temperature and never heated to or above the actual FP temperature.
178-179	**Reinforcement Felts and Sheets:** Roll-roofing materials used as reinforcement inbuilt-up roof membrane construction fall into three categories as follows: Highlight the three (3) bullet points and become familiar with **Base sheets, Ply sheets, and Mineral-surfaced cap sheet**
179	**Base Sheets:** Base sheets work well to separate roof systems from substrates. When mechanically attached, a base sheet can serve as a separation layer or adhesive bond break between a roof deck and roof system so the roof system may move thermally, independently from the roof deck.
	Ply Sheets: Ply sheets are installed directly over base sheets or over rigid board insulation as interplay sheets in built-up roof membranes. Historically, ply sheets have been either fiberglass-mat or organic-mat reinforced.
180	**Asphalt-coated Polyester and Fiberglass-mat Sheets:** Asphalt-coated polyester and fiberglass-mat sheets may be used as ply sheets, including flashing applications.

Page #	Highlight
180	Ply sheets are produced in a standard width of 36 inches
	Membrane Flashings: Membrane flashings are used to terminate a built-up roof membrane at a roof's perimeter and at roof penetrations. Membrane flashings typically consist of a base or backer layer or layers and a cap sheet.
182	**SBS Polymer-modified Bitumen Base Sheets:** Several types of bituminous roofing sheets are becoming more commonly used as multiple-ply membrane flashings in built-up roof systems and base plies in polymer-modified bitumen roof systems. Among the most common are several styrene butadiene styrene (SBS) polymer-modified asphalt base sheets.
	Liquid-applied flashings: Liquid-applied flashings commonly are used in situations where penetrations or surfaces are irregularly shaped and difficult to flash using a membrane flashing.
183	**Rosin-sized Sheathing Paper:** One purpose of the rosin-sized sheathing paper is to prevent the first ply of felt from adhering to wood decking. Another purpose is to prevent bitumen from dripping through some roof decks.
	Application of Built-up Membrane Materials: A complete built-up membrane roof system may include a slip sheet; air retarder or vapor retarder; rigid board roof insulation; cover board; interplay bitumen or adhesive; and layers of base sheet, ply sheet, cap sheet or other roof surfacing option.
184	**Fasteners for Built-up Roof Membranes:** Large-head, annular-threaded nails; barbed; ring-shank nails; or specifically approved mechanical fasteners should be used to fasten base sheets for built-up roof membranes to nailable decks, for back-nailing and to fasten base flashings in built-up roof membranes.
	Bitumen Heating: The following guidelines apply to the heating of bitumen: Highlight all seven (7) bullet points and become familiar with each
185	**Membrane Application:** On low-slope roofs, roof membrane plies should be applied so the slow of water runoff will not be against the laps. When possible, all plies should be installed in shingle fashion. When slopes are greater than 2:12, consideration should be given to laying the felts parallel to the slope. This application method, consisting of plies laid parallel to the slope, is referred to as "strapping the plies" and also may be used on slopes less than 2:12.
186	**5.3 - Polymer-modified Bitumen Roof Membranes:** Polymer-modified roof membranes are composed of reinforcing fabrics, usually polyester, fiberglass or both, that serve as the carriers for the polymer- modified bitumen as it is manufactured into a roll material. The purposes for reinforcements in polymer-modified bitumen sheets essentially are the same as felts in built-up roof membranes. The reinforcements help keep the bitumen in place within the sheet, provide tensile strength and allow for varying degrees of sheet elongation.
	Generally, APP polymers modify the asphalt to give the resultant material a "plasticized" nature. SBS polymers modify the asphalt to give the resultant material a "rubberized" nature.
	The principal components used in constructing polymer-modified bitumen roof membranes are: Highlight all five (5) bullet points and become familiar with **Adhesives, Base layer, such as a base sheet or interplay sheets, Polymer-modified bitumen cap sheet, Membrane flashings and Accessories**
191-192	**Interply Sheets:** In place of single-layer base sheets, the following sheets, sometimes referred to as "interply sheets", are often used in multiple layers beneath APP or SBS polymer-modified bitumen sheets. Highlight the four (4) bullet points and become familiar with **Asphalt, Fiberglass Ply Sheet, APP Polymer-modified Interply Sheets, SBS Polymer-modified Bitumen Interply Sheets, and Self- adhering (SA) Polymer-modified Bitumen Interply Sheets**

Page #	Highlight
192	**Polymer-modified Bitumen Membrane Cap Sheet:** All polymer-modified bitumen-coated sheets are factor-coated on one or both sides with polymer-modified bitumen. Some sheets are surfaced on one or both sides with fine materials, such as sand, mica or talc, that serve as parting agents and prevent adhesion of the material while in roll form. Some manufacturers use liquid parting agents, and others use plastic films either removed by hand or intended to be burned off during the installation.
194	**Accessories:** Accessory products commonly used when constructing polymer-modified bitumen roof membranes include roof cements, adhesives and asphalt core board.
195	**Asphalt Core Board:** Asphalt core boards may be installed over structural substrates, rigid board insulation and existing roof membranes to provide substrates for torch-applied, hot mopped, cold adhesive applied and self-adhering asphalt-based membranes. Once the adhesive cures or cools to ambient temperature, the asphalt core boards become fused with the membrane.
196	Asphalt core board for roof system applications typically is available as 4-by 4-foot, 4-by 5-foot and 4- by 8-foot panels that are 1/8-of-an-inch, 3/16-of-an-inch, ¼-of-an-inch or ½-of-an-inch in thickness.
197-198	**Torch-applied application:** Beginning with this edition of the NRCA Roofing Manual, NRCA no longer recommends designers specify torch-applied polymer-modified bitumen membranes over combustible substrate roof decks, even where a thermal barrier insulation layer has been laid over the combustible roof deck. NRCA considers the potential fire risk associated with torch-applied application over combustible roof decks to outweigh any advantages torch application provides.
199	**Membrane Application:** Blisters have been reported in some SBS polymer-modified bitumen membrane systems. Most have involved installation with hot asphalt and occurred between the cap sheet and base sheet or ply sheets. Application factors that can contribute to blistering include insufficient asphalt temperature at the point of application, long mop lead and lack of cap sheet embedment into the asphalt mopping.
200	**5.4 - Single-ply Roof Membranes:** There are two principal types of materials used in the construction of single-ply roof membranes: thermoset polymer sheets and thermoplastic polymer sheets. The terms describe the materials' different behaviors on heating that arise from their different molecular arrangements and chemical properties.
	Currently, EPDM sheets are the only thermoset materials commonly used in construction of single-ply roof membranes in the North American market.
	There are four common subcategories of thermoplastic membranes: Highlight all three (3) bullet points and become familiar with **Polyvinyl (PVC), PVC alloys, including copolymer alloy (CPA), ethylene interpolymer (EIP) and nitrile alloy (NBP), Ketone ethylene ester (KEE) and Thermoplastic Polyolefin (TPO)**
201	**Ethylene Propylene Diene Monomer (EPDM):** EPDM is a synthetic rubber material that can be formulated with extensive flexibility for use as membrane sheet roofing.
	EPDM membranes exhibit good resistance to ozone, ultraviolet (UV) rays, weathering and abrasion. EPDM also has good low-temperature flexibility. EPDM is resistant to same acids; alkalis; and oxygenated solvents, such as ketones, esters and alcohols. On the other hand, exposure to aromatic, halogenated and aliphatic solvents, as well as animal and vegetable oils and petroleum-based products, should be avoided to prevent membrane swelling and distortion.
	The most common thicknesses of EPDM single-ply roofing sheet materials are 45 mils and 60 mils.
202	**Polyvinyl Chloride (PVC):** PVC Sheets are resistant to bacterial growth, many industrial chemical atmospheres and plant-root penetration. Properly formulated, PVC sheets are fire-resistant and have hot-air welding seaming characteristics. PVC sheets are chemically incompatible with bituminous materials

Page #	Highlight
202	and as such, should be separated from asphalt products.
	NRCA recommends designers specify PVC sheets with a minimum thickness of 45 mils for use in conventional single-ply roof systems.
203	**PVC Alloys:** PVC alloys compound various polymers with PVC. Sheets produced with PVC alloys are somewhat akin to PVC sheets in that they, too, are thermoplastic in nature; however, each has its own unique properties. PVC alloy materials manufactured for use as roof membranes typically are produced as reinforced sheets.
204	**Ketone Ethylene Ester (KEE):** KEE Sheets are reported to be resistant to certain chemicals, air-conditioning coolants, jet fuels and restaurant grease, as well as UV radiation, airborne bacteria, acid rain and industrial pollutants.
	KEE sheets are compatible with asphalt.
	Thermoplastic Polyolefin (TPO): TPO sheets are compounded from a blend of polypropylene (PP) and ethylene-propylene rubber (EPR) polymers. Flame retardants, pigments, UV absorbers and other proprietary ingredients may be included in TPO sheet formulations.
205	**Application of Single-ply Membranes:** Single-ply membrane roof systems are typically designed and installed in three configuration types: loose-laid ballasted, mechanically attached and adhered.
	Single-ply sheets should be unrolled and allowed time to relax and lie flat before application. Manufacturers commonly indicate a minimum period of 30 minutes for this.
206	**Loose-laid, Ballasted:** Loose-laid, ballasted systems seldom require field-membrane securement other than perimeter and base flashing attachment. As the system's name implies, the weight of the ballast and the force of gravity serve to secure the entire roof system.
	The most common application rate for aggregate or stone ballast is 1,000 pounds to 1,200 pounds per 100 square feet for 1 ½ -inch to ¾-of-an-inch round, river-washed gravel designated a Size Number 4
	Mechanically Attached: Mechanically attached systems use a variety of fasteners and fastening patterns to secure a membrane to a substrate. Among these methods are metal disks placed within a seam and attached through a membrane to a roof deck; metal or plastic bars placed within a seam and attached through a membrane to a roof deck; metal and plastic disks and/or bars placed over a membrane and covered with membrane stripping; polymer-coated metal disks used with fasteners to attach rigid board insulation to roof decks and heat welded to the underside of thermoplastic membranes using electromagnetic induction welding equipment; and other specialized proprietary securement systems.
207	**Heat Induction Welding:** An alternative method of attachment of single-ply roof membranes is heat welding a thermoplastic single-ply roof membrane to specially coated fastening plates using an electromagnetic heat-induction-welding tool.
211	**Air Intrusion:** Air intrusion has significance for roof assembly performance for two primary reasons. It contributes to mechanical fatigue of roof assembly components, including field membrane, flashings, mechanical attachment components and roof deck. It also provides a mechanism for depositing excess moisture inside a roof assembly.
	Adhered: Adhered membrane systems are generally applied using a liquid-applied contact adhesive. Some membranes are made with a factory-laminated fleece backing that allows adhesion with alternative types of adhesives, such as hot asphalt and low-rise polyurethane foam.

Page #	Highlight
212	Depending on the liquid carrier(s) used, cold-applied single-ply roof membrane adhesives currently available can be placed into one of three categories: Highlight all three (3) bullet points and become familiar with **Volatile organic compound (VOC) solvent-based adhesives, Low-VOC (also known as VOC-exempt solvent-based) adhesives and Water-based adhesives**
214	**5.5 – Liquid-applied Membranes:** Liquid-applied roof membranes are constructed in place from a liquid resin and reinforcing material. The liquid resin is available as a one- or two-component product and is typically applied in two coats. Depending on the resin chemistry, a catalyst or hardener may be added to induce the curing process. In most instances, a primer is required.
217	**Application:** Liquid-applied roof membranes should be installed as continuously as possible. To do this, it is important wood nailers, curbs, drains and other penetrations be in place before roofing.
219	**CHAPTER 6 – FASTENERS: Design Considerations:** These characteristics are a function of the substrate type and strength and the fastener's size, shank, point or tip type, and thread design. The corrosion resistance of a fastener should also be considered, along with its desired service life, which should be equivalent to that of the roof system. A fastener should be compatible with the material being secured and the substrate into which it is embedded. The shear strength and tensile strength of a fastener also are important considerations.
220	**Fasteners and Preservative-treated Wood:** NRCA is of the opinion the corrosion-related concerns regarding the use of currently available preservative-treated wood possible outweigh the benefits that preservative-treated wood provides as a component in roof assemblies. In many instances, nontreated, construction-grade wood is suitable for use in roof assemblies as blocking or nailers provided reasonable measures are taken to ensure the nontreated wood remains reasonable dry when in service.
221	**6.1 – Base Sheet Fasteners - Material Types:** A majority of fasteners are fabricated from hardened carbon steel or stainless steel. Often, such designations as 1022 for carbon steel and 304 for stainless steel are included and refer to properties such as alloys, strength and corrosion resistance. Fasteners are often surfaced (or coated) with various corrosion-resistant coatings, such as zinc, epoxy, fluorocarbons or other proprietary materials. In some cases, fasteners are fabricated plastics, such as glass-reinforced nylon and other polymer materials. Fasteners made of metal are thermal bridges.
223-224	**6.2 – Insulation Fasteners – Fastener Spacing:** Because center-to-center metal rood deck rib spacing typically is 6 inches, the spacing for insulation fasteners typically is some multiple of 6 inches.
229	**6.3 - Membrane Fasteners – Fastener Spacing:** Spacing between the rows of fasteners and fastener spacing within the rows are two parameters that determine uplift resistance. Common fastener spacing with a row is 6 inches and 12 inches. See Figure 6-9 (on page 230). Some common field-sheet row spacings are 6 ½ feet, 7 feet, 8 feet and 10 feet.
233	**CHAPTER 7 – SURFACINGS:** Membrane surfacing is the component that protects the weatherproofing component of some roof systems from the effects of direct sunlight, ultraviolet rays and weather exposure. Some surfacings provide other benefits, such as increased fire resistance, improved traffic and hail resistance, and aesthetic properties.
234	**7.1 – Guidelines Applicable to All Surfacing Types:** Solar reflectance: The fraction of solar flux reflected by a surface expressed as a percent or within the range of 0.00 and 1.00 Thermal emittance: The ratio of the radiant heat flux emitted by a sample to that emitted by a black-body radiator at the same temperature (total thermal emittance)

Page #	Highlight
234	**ENERGY STAR:** ...for low-slope roof system products:

        Initial solar reflectance must be greater than or equal to 0.65

        Solar reflectance three years after installation under normal conditions must be greater than or equal to 0.50 without cleaning prior to testing

    For steep-slope roof systems:

        Initial solar reflectance must be greater than or equal to 0.25

        Solar reflectance three years after installation under normal conditions must be greater than or equal to 0.15

235	**7.2 - Aggregate:** When aggregate is used to surface a built-up roof system, it generally is for the following reasons: Highlight all seven (7) bullet points and become familiar with

Table: Aggregate Gradation Amounts Finer than Sieve Specified, Mass Percent

238	**7.3 - Ballast:** When single-ply membrane sheets are used in loose-laid, ballasted configurations, the surfacing commonly used are rounded aggregate or concrete roof pavers. Generally, ballasted roof systems are limited to roods with slopes of 2:12 or less.
239	**7.4 – Coatings:** A roof coating is a fluid material applied in the field as a film to the roof surface to provide weather protection to the original roof membrane. A coating protects the roof substrate from weather (solar radiation, heat and moisture) and determines its radiative properties.
241	When properly designed and installed, roof coatings can: Highlight all eight (8) bullet points and become familiar with

    Roof Coating Types: Most roof coatings consist of two general components:

- Primer
- Coating

    Primer: Primers are intended to prepare a roof surface for accepting a coating and improve the overall adhesion of the coating to the substrate.

242	**Coatings:** The coating material itself is the topmost surface of the coating system application and the layer that provides the primary characteristic of the coating.
247	**Coating Application:** The three common application methods for roof coatings are:

- Airless Spray
- Roller
- Brush or broom

248	**Figure 7-6: General guideline for primer and coating selection**
249	**Brush or Broom:** Most coatings should not be broom-applied.

Page #	Highlight
249	**Weather Conditions:** Wind preferably should be less than 6 mph. Ambient temperatures should be moderate, with most coating applications specified to be conducted between 40 F and 100 F depending on manufacturers' recommendations.
251	**CHAPTER 8 – ROOF ACCESSORIES:** Examples of premanufactured accessories that may be encountered on a membrane roof system include.

- Equipment curbs
- Expansion joint covers
- Skylights and roof/smoke hatches
- Prefabricated pipe flashings
- Pipe support systems.

Page #	Highlight
252	**8.1 – Equipment Curbs:** NRCA recommends a minimum of 24 inches of clearance between walls and curbs and minimum 12 inches of clearance between pipes and curbs.
	For most membrane roof systems, equipment curbs should be detailed and constructed to a height of 8 inches above the finished roof membrane.
	8.2 – Expansion Joint Covers: NRCA considers raised curb type expansion joints to be preferred, though for ballasted single-ply membrane roof systems, low-profile expansion joints in the same plane as the roof membrane are considered acceptable.
252-253	For most membrane roof systems, expansion joints should be detailed and constructed to a height of 8 inches above the finished roof membrane.
253	**8.3 – Skylights and Roof/Smoke Hatches:** Skylights and hatches should be installed with curbs tall enough to allow for an 8-inch vertical flashing height.
253-254	**8.4 – Prefabricated Pipe Flashings:** Pre-molded pipe flashings – commonly referred to as flashing boots or collars – are often used in single-ply membrane roof systems for sealing pipes or irregularly shaped penetrations.
254	NRCA recommends a minimum of 12 inches of clearance between pipes and a minimum 12 inches of clearance between pipes and curbs or walls.
	For most membrane roof systems, pipe flashings should be detailed and constructed to a height of 8 inches above the finished roof membrane.
	8.5 – Pipe Support Systems: It is common for the roofing contractor to be responsible for installation of pipe support systems in reroofing scenarios.
257	**CHAPTER 9 – REROOFING:**
258	**9.1 – Definitions:** Highlight all five (5) bullet points and become familiar with **Reroofing, Re-covering, Replacement, Roof assembly and Roof system**
259	

- **Low-slope roof systems:** A category of roof systems that generally includes weatherproof membranes types of roof systems installed on slopes of 3:12 or less
- **Steep-slope roof systems:** A category of roof systems that generally includes water-shedding types of roof coverings installed on slopes greater than 3:12

Page #	Highlight
259	**9.2 – Evaluation of Existing Roof Systems – Interior Inspection:** An evaluation of an existing roof system for the purpose of determining whether to re-cover or replace it should include a visual inspection of the interior of the building in the area underneath the roof area being considered.
262	**Hidden Conditions:** NRCA does not recommend metallic conduit or wiring be embedded within roof assemblies or placed directly below roof decks. If metallic conduit or siring needs to be placed near the roof assembly, NRCA recommends it be positioned and supported at least 1 ½ inches from the bottom side of the roof deck or substrate to which the roof system is applied.
263	**Roof System Inspection:** Inspection of the roof system should include evaluation of installed materials, as well as design, and should take account of: Highlight all seven (7) bullet points and become familiar with **Perimeter edge-metal flashings, Penetrations, Roof surface condition, Drainage and slope, Roof system composition, Moisture with the existing roof assembly, and Rooftop mechanical equipment**
265	**Moisture with the Existing Roof Assembly:** When evaluating moisture content of roof assemblies, nondestructive moisture evaluation techniques should be considered. Nondestructive moisture evaluation techniques include infrared thermography, neutron (nuclear) thermalization and electrical capacitance. **Other Leak Sources:** There are many building components that may be sources for leakage, including: Highlight all eleven (11) bullet points and become familiar with
268	**1511.3.1.1 Exceptions.** A *roof recover* shall not be permitted where any of the following conditions occur: Where the existing roof or roof covering is water soaked or has deteriorated to the point that the existing roof or roof covering is not adequate as a base for additional roofing Where the existing roof covering is slate, clay, cement or asbestos-cement tile Where the existing roof has two or more applications of any type of roof covering
269	Reuse of existing metal flashing materials only is permitted when the materials' remaining service life of the new roof system.
270	**Cementitious Wood Fiber Panels - Roof Replacement Considerations:** When existing toggle bolts and auger-type fasteners are removed, NRCA recommends installation of a new structural roof deck because the structural capacity of the cementitious wood fiber roof deck can be reduced by the voids left by the removed fasteners.
271	**Vertical Alignment:** Elevation differences in excess of 1/8 of an inch between panels are considered unacceptable. Uneven joints of 1/8 inch or more should be grouted with the grout feathered to a slope of 1/8 of an inch per foot. **Lightweight Insulating Concrete – Roof Replacement Considerations:** Securing a replacement roof system over an aged lightweight insulating concrete deck with new lightweight insulating concrete fasteners can be considered if the replacement roof system-specific pullout resistance can be achieved. NRCA suggests a minimum of four tests per continuous pour area be conducted when determining fastener withdrawal resistance for lightweight insulating concrete decks.
272	**Steel – Roof Replacement Considerations:** NRCA is concerned with the structural capacity and potential fastener-holding power of steel roof decks lighter than 22 gauge (0.028 inches thick).

Page #	Highlight
272	Installing new steel deck without removing the existing metal deck is called nesting. Nesting can be accomplished by using the same type and grade of steel or a steel roof deck with narrower flutes so the new deck fits into the existing deck.
274	**Structural Concrete – Roof Replacement Considerations:** For prestressed or post-tensioned concrete decks, drilling into the deck can be detrimental to the load-bearing capacity of the deck because to the possibility of severing a tension cable. NRCA does not recommend attaching the roof insulation or membrane to prestressed or pos-tensioned concrete decks with mechanical fasteners.
275	**Curing and Drying:** Sealing the concrete's moisture into the deck by using a high-bond strength vapor retarder adhered directly to the deck followed by an adhered roof system is another option. A high-quality, 12- to 15- mil thick two-part epoxy has successfully been used as a vapor retarder in the flooring industry.
276	**Wood Panels – Roof Replacement Considerations:** NRCA does not recommend installing roof systems over structural wood panel roof decks, such as plywood and OSB, that re less than 15/32 of an inch thick. **Wood Planks and Wood Boards – Roof Replacement Considerations:** NRCA does not recommend installing roof systems over wood board roof decks with less than ¾ of an inch minimum thickness.
277	**Gypsum- Poured Gypsum:** Three general requirements are: Highlight all three (3) bullet points and become familiar with
278	**Roof Replacement Considerations:** If the existing roof system was sprinkle- or strip-mopped to the deck, the removal process may only cause minor damage to the deck. If the exiting roof was solid-mopped, the removal process may cause major damage to the deck. If major damage occurs, consideration should be given to replacing the roof deck or using a re-cover system.
280	**Thermal-setting Insulating Fill – Roof Replacement Considerations:** In a roof replacement situation, reusing thermal-setting insulating fill is generally not practical because a new roof system cannot be mechanically attached to it, and adequate adhesion typically cannot be achieved to provide for adequate uplift resistance of the new roof system.
281	**9.6 – Re-cover Guidelines for Membrane Roof Systems:** The following is a list of general recommendations for re-covering over an existing roof system with a new built-up, polymer-modified bitumen, single-ply or liquid-applied membrane roof system: Highlight all five (5) bullet points and become familiar with
282	**9.7 – Design Guidelines for Roof Replacement with New Membrane Roof Systems – Fire Resistance:** An in-depth review of the code's criteria for classifying construction types is beyond the scope of this manual. The following brief descriptions provide a general idea of the classifications: Highlight the four (4) bullet points and become familiar with **Type IA, IB, IIA, IIB, Types IIIA and IIIB, Type IV and Types VA and VB**
283	**Condensation Control:** When designing a replacement roof system, one or more of the following considerations may need to be addressed with regard to its water vapor transport performance: Highlight all four (4) bullet points and become familiar with
284	**Perimeter Edge-metal Flashings:** Because of unknow attachment methods, NRCA suggests existing perimeter edge-metal flashings not be reused.

Page #	Highlight
285	**Roof Curbs and Equipment Supports:** Figure 9-5 provides NRCA's guidelines for clearance for equipment support stands. **Figure 9-5: NRCA guidelines for clearance for equipment support stands**
285	**Pipe Penetrations:** Different types of pipe penetrations require different methods of flashing during reroofing projects. Highlight all three (3) bullet points and become familiar with
287	**CHAPER 10 – CONSTRUCTION DETAILS:** In this chapter, construction details are provided for the following membrane roof system types: Highlight and become familiar with **Built-up membrane, Polymer-modified bitumen membrane, EPDM membrane, Thermoplastic membrane and Liquid-applied membrane**
289	**Wood Nailers and Blocking:** Among other advantages, the nailers provide protection for the edges of rigid board insulation and provide a substrate for anchoring flashing materials. Wood nailers should be a minimum of 2 x 6 nominal-dimension lumber.
291	**Penetrations and Clearance:** The maximum amount of space should be provided between pipes, walls and curbs to facilitate proper installation of membranes and flashings. NRCA recommend a minimum of 12 inches of clearance between pipes, a minimum of 12 inches of clearance between pipes and curbs or walls, and a minimum of 24 inches of clearance between walls and curbs.
295	**Combustible Substrates:** Lumber and wood fiberboard cant strips are generally not considered to be noncombustible. NRCA suggest the use of noncombustible perlite, stone wool or other similar noncombustible material for cant strips.
297	**Independent Securement of Mechanically Attached Single-ply Roof Membrane:** For mechanically attached single-ply membrane roof systems, NRCA suggest the designer consider the inclusion of a mechanically fastened batten bar or plates approximately 6 inches to 12 inches away from the outside edge of the roof system, drain sumps, curbs and penetrations as independent membrane securement. This is commonly referred to as a peel-stop.
306	**Drains and Drain Sumps:** Drain sumps should be square or rectangular and typically are 4 feet or 8 feet per side where premanufactured sump insulation is used. NRCA suggest drain sump dimensions not be less than the drain bowl diameter plus 24 inches to allow for correct drain flashing installation. **Crickets and Saddles:** To help reduce the amount of residual surface water between drains, behind curbs and along roof edges between scuppers, NRCA recommend installing crickets and saddles. Figures 10-13 (on page 309) and 10-14 (on page 310) provide additional information regarding cricket and saddle slope and length-to-width (L:W) ratios.
308	**EPDM Membrane Corner Flashings:** For flashing inside corners, it is suggested field membranes be used to bridge the roof-to-wall transition to provide a continuous wall flashing. Figure 10-17 (on pages 319-321) illustrates the sequencing of steps for this technique.

1 Exam Prep
NRCA Roofing Manual: Metal Panel and SPF Roof Systems – 2016
Tabs and Highlights

These 1 Exam Prep Tabs are based on the National Roofing Contractors Association (NRCA) manual listed below:

Metal Panel and SPF Roof System - 2016

Each 1 Exam Prep tabs sheet has five rows of tabs. Start with the first tab at the first row at the top of the page; proceed down that row placing the tabs at the locations listed below. Place each tab in your book setting it down one notch until you get to the last tab. Then start with the highlights.

1 Exam Prep Tab	Page #
Metal Panel - Table of Contents	7
Roof System Configurations	21
Structural Substrates	47
Metal Guidelines	67
Metal Panel Roof Guidelines	87
Architectural Metal Panel	105
Metal Panel Assemblies	129
Fasteners	145
Roof Accessories	151
Re-Roofing	155
Construction Details	191
Index of Drawings	201
SPF Roof Systems - Table of Contents	289
SPF Roof Decks	321
Other Substrates	347
SPF	353
Protective Surfacings	365
Roof Accessories	377

1 Exam Prep Tab	Page #
Re-roofing	383
Construction Details	411
Unit Conversions	499

This concludes the tabs for this book. Please continue with the highlights below.

Page #	Highlight
47	"The following types of structural substrates are addressed in this manual: (6 bullets)"
48	**Deflection:** "Structural substrate deflection should be limited to 1/240 of the structural substrate's total span to accommodate the stresses of concentrated or uniform loading."
49	**Slope and Drainage:** "The criterion for judging proper slope for drainage is that there be no ponding water on the roof 48 hours after a rainfall during conditions conducive to drying."
50	**Electrical Conduits and Other Piping**
51	"NRCA does not recommend metallic conduit or wiring be embedded within roof assemblies or be placed directly on the roof surface or directly below the roof deck."
	2.2 Steel
52	"Furthermore, NRCA recommends steel decks be 22-gauge or heavier and have a minimum G-90 galvanized coating complying with ASTM A653.
67	**Naturally Weathering Metals**
	Metallic-coated Metals: "Corrosion results from the steel reacting with oxygen ... undesirable for two reasons: performance and appearance."
68	"The primary purpose of metallic coatings is to protect ... reduce change of rapid oxidation."
	Aluminum: "Aluminum provides a lightweight, easily formed metal that does not require a protective coating for most exposures." "It is not recommended aluminum be used as an in-wall flashing embedded in concrete or masonry."
69	**Aluminized Steel:** "Aluminized steels rely almost solely on the aluminum's ability to act as a barrier for protecting the base steel."
70	**Copper:** "Over time copper develops a bronze, brown, or blue-green color resulting from the formation of a protective layer of copper sulfate, referred to as patina."
	Copper-coated Stainless Steel (Copper Plus)

Page #	Highlight
71	"Copper-coated stainless steel was developed to provide a roofing or flashing material with the appearance, malleability and corrosion-resistance characteristics of copper but the strength of stainless steel."

Figure 3-4: Metal thickness and weight information for copper-coated stainless steel sheets.

Galvalume® (aluminum-zinc-coated steel): "This alloy coating is reported to be 55 percent aluminum and 45 percent zinc by weight." |
| 72 | **Galvanized Steel:** "Galvanized steel is one of the oldest and most common metalliccoated metals. Although the zinc coating extends the weatherability of the base steel, it is generally not considered adequate by itself for providing long-term service life in exposed applications."

Lead: "Lead is used as a roofing accessory metal because of its workability." |
| 73 | "Sheet lead has little structural strength and puncture resistance and therefore must be installed over solid substrates."

Weather and Corrosive Environments: "A weight range of 2 pounds per square foot to 4 pounds per square foot is typical for roofing application, but heavier weights may be desirable for soldering purposes."

Lead-coated Copper: "Lead coated copper has limited availability; however there still may be small regional manufacturer's that provide it."

"The weight of lead coating should be at least 12 pounds and should not exceed 15 pounds." |
| 74 | **Figure 3-8:** Metal thickness and weight information for lead-coated copper sheets.

Stainless Steel: "Stainless steel is a corrosion-resistant material." "Types 302 and 304 are the most common." |
| 75 | "For sheet metal flashings, 300-series stainless-steel material is preferred."

"Stainless-steel sheets greater than 24-guage in thickness may be more difficult to work with."

Zinc: "Zinc is a self-healing metal that weathers to a soft blue-gray patina."

"The rate of patina varies with the environment and application." |
| 76 | Figure 3-10: Metal gauge, thickness and weight information for zinc sheets. |
| 77 | **Terne Metal:** "Terne metal is a carbon-steel-based metal coated on both sides with a thin layer of zinc and tin."

"The coating is not applied solely to protect the steel but also to serve as a paintable surface and allow for ease of soldering." |
| 83 | **3.4 Oil-Canning:** "Oil-canning refers to physical distortions in the flatness of metal; however, this condition is only aesthetic in nature and does not have any adverse effect on the structural integrity or the weatherproofing capability of the metal." |

Page #	Highlight
87	**4.1 System Types: Architectural Metal Panel Roof Systems:** "Architectural metal panel roof systems require continuous or closely spaced decking. Architectural metal panel roof systems are typically water-shedding roof systems."
88	"Architectural metal panel roof systems perform well on slopes of 3:12 or greater."
	"A minimum underlayment of an ASTM D4869 Type III or Type IV (No. 30) asphalt-saturated felt underlayment and separate slip sheet, such as rosin-sized sheathing paper or underlayment with slip-sheet capabilities is recommended beneath architectural metal roof panels."
	Structural Metal Panel Roof Assemblies: "Metal panel used in structural metal panel have the strength and capability of spanning structural members, such as joists or purlins, without being supported by a continuous or closely spaced roof deck. Structural metal panel roof assemblies are typically weatherproof. They are designed to resist the passage of water oat joints, laps and junctures under minimal hydrostatic pressure."
	"NRCA recommends 1/2 inch per foot as the minimum slope for structural metal panel roof assemblies even though numerous manufacturers will allow structural metal panel roof systems to be installed on slopes as low as 1/4 inch per foot."
90	**4.3 Seam Types/Configurations**
	Flat Seam: "Flat-seam metal panel roof systems are adaptable to many types of surfaces."
	Flat Seam, Nonsoldered: "A flat seam is created with individual flat-pan panels applied in an overlapped. interlocking shingle fashion. See Figure 4-2."
92	**Flat Seam, Soldered:** "When the joints of flat-seam panels are joined together on low-slope roofs, the joints are soldered to make the system weatherproof. See Figure 4-3."
	"For those metals that require pre-tinning (e.g. copper), sheet edges should be pre-tinned to a minimum width of 1 1/2 inches before folding the edges."
	Standing Seam: "The term "standing seam" refers to almost any kind of metal roof panel with a raised vertical seam."
93	**4.4 Seaming Methods:** "There are four basic panel-to-panel seaming techniques: (4 bullets)."
	Mechanical Seam: "A mechanical seam is completed by hand seamers, tongs, or electrical seaming devices."
	Snap-lock Seam: "In a snap-lock seam, male and female legs are adjoined to secure the seam in place … See figure 4-4 for an example of a snap-lock seam."
	Snap-on Seams: "A snap-on seam is usually simple to install. A separate cap or batten snaps onto a panel's rib and clip to complete the seam."
	Hooked Seam: "A hooked seam is a flat-lock, flat seam used in some types of architectural metal systems, such as Bermuda horizontal panels or metal shingles."

Page #	Highlight
99	**4.12 Thermal Movement Considerations:** "The term "thermal movement" refers to a material's dimensional changes resulting from changes in temperature …The net change in any one dimension is proportional to the net temperature change and is a material-specific property called the coefficient of See Figure 4-11."
105	"Architectural metal panel roof systems are typically water-shedding roof systems."
	"Architectural metal roof panel systems perform well on slopes of 3:12 or greater."
	"A minimum underlayment of an ASTM D4869, Type III and IV (No. 30) asphalt-saturated felt underlayment …recommended beneath architectural metal roof panels."
106	"Although metal panels classified as "structural panels" also can be used as architectural metal roof panels... See Chapter 6."
	Slip Sheets: "A slip sheet is a layer of rosin-sized or unsaturated building paper."
	"Before metal panel application, a rosin-sized slip sheet may be necessary to protect the underlayment from damage as panels can adhere to and tear the underlayment."
	Single Layer of Underlayment: "For single-layer underlayment, a minimum of one layer of No.30 asphalt-saturated, non-perforated felt or laminated or reinforced polyethylene or polypropylene-based synthetic underlayment should be applied horizontally, perpendicular to the slope of the roof."
108-109	"All sheets should have a minimum side lap of 2 inches over the preceding sheet, and end laps should be a minimum of 4 inches."
109	**Ice-dam Protection Membranes:** "water and ice-dam protection membranes generally consist of a single layer of self-adhering polymer-modified bitumen underlayment."
110	**5.3 Insulation:** "The primary purposed of roof insulation is to provide thermal resistance."
	Rigid Board Insulation: "Rigid roof insulation can be installed over continuous or a closely spaced roof decking under an architectural metal panel roof system."
112	**5.5 Panel Profiles:** "Panel profiles vary depending on the different methods used for forming panels."
	Figure 5-6: Examples of seam types for common architectural metal roof panels
114	**5.7 Panel Attachment**
115	"NRCA recommends a minimum of two fasteners per clip be installed."
116	**5.8 Drainage:** "An architectural metal panel roof system must provide localized positive drainage….NRCA does not recommend drains with internal drainage systems, including built-in gutters with drains."
	5.9 Sheet-metal Flashing
	"Designers should consider the following factors for proper detailing of an architectural metal panel roof system and related sheet-metal flashings (9 bullets)."

Page #	Highlight
123	**Support Penetrations**
129	"Structural metal panel roof assemblies have the strength and capability of spanning structural members, such as joists or purlins, without being supported by a continuous or closely spaced roof deck. Structural metal panel roof assemblies are typically weatherproof roof systems. They are designed to resist the passage of water at joints, laps, and junctures under minimal hydrostatic pressure." "NRCA recommends ½ inch per foot as the minimum slope for structural panel roof assemblies." "Structural metal roof panels can also be used in architectural applications closely spaced substrates"...
131	**6.4 Panel Profiles**
132	"There are three general panel profiles common to structural metal panels:(3 bullets)."
134	**Figure 6-3**: Example of structural metal roof panel profiles
136	**6.7 Drainage:** "A structural metal panel roof system must provide localized positive drainage. …NRCA does not recommend internal drainage systems, including built-in gutters with drains."
137	**6.8 Sheet Metal Flashing**: "Designers should consider the following factors for proper detailing of a metal roof system and related sheet-metal flashings (9 bullets)."
141	**Support Penetrations:** Note and highlight the chart which lists Width of Equipment and Clearance.
145	**Design Considerations**
146	"NRCA recommends a minimum of two fasteners per clip be installed."
147	**Figure 7-1**: Fasteners commonly used with sheet metal
149	**Figure 7-2**: Guidelines for the selection of fasteners based on galvanic action
153	**8.2 Skylights**: "Skylight frames should overlap the curb a minimum of 3 inches to act as counterflashing, or a separate counterflashing could be installed."
155	"When roofing system maintenance and repair can no longer prevent recurrent leakage or extend a roof system's useful service life, consideration needs to be given to reroofing." "Reroofing should also be considered in other situations, including the following (10 bullets)."
156	**9.1 Definitions**<ul><li>**Reroofing**</li><li>**Re-covering**</li><li>**Replacement**</li><li>**Roof assembly**</li><li>**Roof system**</li></ul>
177	**9.6 Re-cover Guidelines for Metal Panel Roof Systems:** "The following design considerations apply to roof re-covers with new metal panel roof systems: (9 bullets).

Page #	Highlight
179	**Insulation**: "Additional insulation may be added by installing rigid or blanket insulation over the existing roof system."
180	**Existing Flashings**: "Re-covering an existing roof system with new metal panel roof system typically requires new metal flashings and counterflashings."
	"Because of unknown attachment methods it is not recommended to use existing edge-metal flashings as cleats or forms of anchorage for new metal flashings."
181	**Drainage and Slope**: "NRCA suggest that design of metal framing systems provide for a minimum of ½:12 slope for structural metal panel roof systems in re-cover applications."
182	**Penetrations**: "When re-cover structural metal panel systems are used, all existing penetrations need to be extended or raised through the new roof system and flashed in a watertight manner; additional framing may be required."
321	"The following types of roof decks are addressed in this manual: (6 bullets)."
	2.1 Guidelines Applicable to All Roof Deck Types
323	**Slope and Drainage**: "The International Building Code 2012 Edition, minimum slope of ¼:12 is required for SPF roof systems."
325	**2.2 Cementitous Wood Fiber Panels:** "Cementitous wood fiber panels intended as roof decks provide for structural support of the roof system and can provide for a finished interior surface that has acoustical properties."
	Design: "It is recommended that the specifications require the joints between adjacent panels greater than ¼ of an inch be grouted with material recommended by the deck manufacturer."
326	**2.3 Lightweight Insulating Concrete**
327	**Design**: "NRCA recommends lightweight insulating concrete roof decks be a minimum of 2 inches thick…other underlying substrate"
328	**Structural support**: "Lightweight insulating concrete roof decks are designed for application over: - Galvanized metal from decks - Bulb-tee and form-board systems - Structural or precast concrete substrates"
329	**2.4 Steel**: "The most common steel roof deck panels are constructed in one of the following for configurations: narrow-rib steel deck (Type A); intermediate-rib steel deck (Type F); wide-rib steel deck (Type B) and deep-rib steel deck (type 3DR)."
	Design: "NRCA recommends steel decks be 22-gauge or heavier and have a minimum G-90 galvanized coating complying with ASTM A653."
	Structural Support: Spacing of attachment point is recommended to be no more than 12 inches on center… under concentrated, moving loads."
337	**2.5 Structural Concrete**: "There are two general types of structural concrete used in roof decks: normal-weight structural concrete and light weight structural concrete."

Page #	Highlight
342	**2.6 Wood Panels**: "There are two general types of wood panels used for roof decks: plywood and oriented strand board (OSB)."
	Design: "When plywood is used as a roof deck material, NRCA recommends the use of a minimum of four-ply, 15/32-inch-thick plywood or four-ply, nominal 5/8-inch-thick plywood for 24-inch rafter spacings."
344	**2.7 Wood Planks and Wood Boards**
347-348	**3.1 Base Sheets:** "Following are common varieties of base sheets that are used in SPF roof systems (4 bullets)."
348	**3.2 Rigid Board Insulation**: "Following are the common types of rigid roof board insulation used in conjunction with SPF roof systems (7 bullets)."
353	"SPF roof systems are constructed by mixing and spraying a two-component liquid that forms the base of an adhered roof system. Isocyanate, referred to as component A, reacts chemically with the polyol resin, referred to as component B, immediately when mixed. This mixture expands 20 to 30 times its original liquid volume to form a closed-cell foam."
354	**Applicability and Restrictions:** "The following are general applicability and restriction guidelines for the use of SPF roof systems. (7 bullets)."
355	**Weather Conditions During Application**
	Temperature: "The substrate temperature range for SPF application is between 50 F and 180 F. For temperatures below 50 F, low temperature, factory formulated materials and low temperature application techniques should be used." "This condition may develop when a roof deck temperature drops below 50 degrees Fahrenheit, depending on the SPF formulization ..."
	Wind: "Practical experience has shown that SPF should not be sprayed when wind speeds exceed 12 mph ... at roof height unless some form of wind screen is used."
	Equipment: "Application of SPF required equipment designed to meter and spray the Isocyanate (Component A) and the resin (Component B) components at a 1-to-1 ratio."
356	**Types of Primers:** "Commonly used primers are categorized as follows: (6 bullets)."
357	**Figure 4-1:** Primer application chart
359	**Thickness:** "Optimum lift thickness should be from 1/2 inch to 1 1/2 inches."
359-360	**Surface Texture:** "The following terms are used to describe SPF surface texture: (6 bullets)."
361	**SPF Application Guidelines**
362	**Lack of Isocyanate (Component A):** "SPF that lacks isocyanate will exhibit one or more of the following characteristics: (6 bullets)."
	Lack of Polyol (Resin) (Component B): "SPF that lacks polyol is more difficult to discover unless the condition is extreme."

Page #	Highlight
	"The more extreme condition of lack of polyol will exhibit one or more of the following characteristics: (6 bullets)."
362-363	**Aged or Improper Components:** An applicator cannot make equipment adjustments to improve the quality of the SPF. The obvious effects are one or more of the following: (11 bullets)."
363	**Ultraviolet Exposure/Degradation**: "The best way to prevent UV is to apply the first or base coat of the protective costing the same day the SPF is applied." "Where there are larger areas of UV degradation … at least an additional 1 inch of new SPF must be applied."
365	**5.1 Protective Surfacing Requirements**: "Protective surfacing are part of SPF roof systems to provide weatherproofing, UV protection, mechanical damage protection and fire resistance."
366	**5.2 Protective Coatings**: "Protective coatings for use over SPF must: (5 bullets)."
367	**Protective Coating Types**
368	"The following types of protective coatings: (6 bullets)."
373	**Figure 5-4:** Recommended minimum coating dry film thickness
377	"Examples of pre-manufactured accessories that may be encountered on an SPF roof system include: (6 bullets)."
383	**7.1 Definitions** - **Reroofing** - **Re-covering** - **Replacement** - **Roof assembly** - **Roof system**
383	**Roof Re-cover Using An SPF Roof Systems:** "When roofing system maintenance and repair can no longer prevent recurrent leakage or extend a roof system's useful service life, consideration needs to be given to reroofing." "Reroofing should also be considered in other situations, including the following (11 bullets)."
398	**Roof Replacement Considerations**
403-404	**7.5 – Preparation of Existing Roof Surfaces:** "The following are brief guidelines for applying SPF over each of the common types of roof membranes." - **SPF Application over Existing Built-up Roof System** - **SPF Application over Existing Polymer-modified Bitumen Roof Systems** - **SPF Application over Existing Single-ply Roof Systems** - **SPF Application over Existing SPF Roof Systems**
404-405	**7.2 Roof Re-cover Design Considerations:** "The following is a list of general recommendations for re-covering an existing roof system with a new SPF roof system." (8 bullets).

1 Exam Prep
NRCA Roofing Manual:
Steep-Slope Roof Systems – 2017
Tabs and Highlights

These 1 Exam Prep Tabs are based on the National Roofing Contractors Association (NRCA) manual listed below:

Steep-Slope Roof Systems - 2017

Each 1 Exam Prep tabs sheet has five rows of tabs. Start with the first tab at the first row at the top of the page; proceed down that row placing the tabs at the locations listed below. Place each tab in your book setting it down one notch until you get to the last tab. Then start with the highlights.

1 Exam Prep Tab	Page #
Table of Contents	7
Asphalt Shingle Roof Systems	13
Roof Decks	43
Underlayments	49
Asphalt Shingles	57
Reroofing	81
Construction Details	103
Index of Drawings (Asphalt Shingles)	109
Clay & Concrete Tile Roof Systems	135
Roof Decks	183
Underlayments	189
Clay & Concrete Tile	199
Reroofing	221
Construction Details	239
Index of Drawings (Tile)	245
Metal Shingle Roof Systems	323
Roof Decks	349
Underlayments	355

1 Exam Prep Tab	Page #
Metal Shingles	361
Reroofing	383
Construction Details	403
Index of Drawings (Metal Shingles)	409
Slate Roof Systems	431
Roof Decks	455
Underlayments	461
Slate	469
Reroofing	487
Construction Details	505
Index of Drawings (Slate)	511
Wood Shake & Shingle Roof Systems	535
Roof Decks	557
Underlayments & Interlayments	563
Wood Shake & Shingle	571
Construction Details	609
Index of Drawings (Wood Shake/Shingles)	615
Unit Conversions	691

This concludes the tabs for this book. Please continue with the highlights on the following page.

Page #	Highlight
44	Asphalt shingle roof systems may be applied directly to the following roof deck substrates: (2 bullets).
	2.1 Wood Panels. Wood-panel roof decks can be subdivided into two general types: plywood roof decks and oriented strand board (OSB) roof decks.
45	When plywood is used as a roof deck material, NRCA recommends the use of a minimum of four-ply, 15/32-inch-thick plywood for 16-inch rafter spacings, and four-ply, 5/8-inch-thick plywood for 24-inch rafter spacings.
	When OSB is used as a roof deck material, a minimum of nominal thickness of ½ inch-thick (15/32-inch-thick) OSB is recommended for 16-inch rafter spacings and 5/8-inch-thickness OSB for 24-inch rafter spacings.
	Plywood and OSB sheathing panels should be installed with about 1/8-inch minimum gaps at panel edges to allow for expansion of the panels.
45-46	**2.2 Wood Planks and Wood Boards.** Wood planks are long, relatively thick pieces of lumber. Specifications sometimes vary in thickness from 2 inches up to 5 inches with the width dimension in the plane of the roof deck.
46	Wood boards are pieces of lumber that are less than 2 inches thick with square edges.
49	An underlayment performs several functions, it provides: (3 bullets).
49-50	There are different underlayment configurations that can be used for asphalt roof systems. These configurations can be categorized as follows: (3 bullets).
52	**Roof Slope:** For roof substrates having slopes of 4:12 or more. NRCA recommends a minimum single-layer ... underlayment be specified and applied horizontally in shingle fashion.
	When specifying asphalt shingle roof systems over roof substrates having slopes less than 4:12 ... consider the following: (5 bullets).
53	**Underlayment Configurations**
	Single Layer of Mechanically Attached Underlayment: For single-layer applications, the underlayment should be applied horizontally in shingle fashion and lapped ... a minimum of 2 inches and the end laps of a minimum of 4 inches are recommended.
	Figure 3-2: Single-layer underlayment
	Single-layer of Self-adhering Underlayment: This configuration consists of one layer of self-adhering polymer-modified bitumen sheet applied over and entire roof deck.
	Typically manufacturer's recommend side laps of a minimum of 3 ½ inches and end laps a minimum of 6 inches for self-adhering polymer-modified sheets installed as rood underlayments.
57	Asphalt shingles are designed for use as multilayered, water-shedding roof components that rely on the slope of a roof substrate to effectively shed water.

Page #	Highlight
	Common dimensions for standard three-tab shingles are 12 inches by 36.
58	*Figure 4-1: Shapes and styles of asphalt shingles.*
59	**Self-sealing Strip:** Commonly, asphalt strip shingles and laminated shingles contain adhesive, self-sealing strips.
	Asphalt Shingle Classifications
60	Asphalt shingles classified according to ASTM D7158 as Class D are said to pass at a basic wind speed up to and including 90 mph; those classified as Class G are said to pass at a basic wind speed up to and including 120 mph; and those classified as Class H are said to pass at a basic wind speed up to and including 150 mph.
61	*Figure 4-3: Asphalt shingles' wind-resistance classifications.*
	Fasteners
65	Nails should be long enough to penetrate through all layers of roofing materials and achieve secure anchorage into a roof deck. Nails should extend a minimum of 1/8 inch through the underside of plywood or other acceptable wood panel decks less than 3/4 of an inch thick.
	Asphalt Roof Cement: There are two common types of asphalt roof dement: flashing cement and lap cement.
66	**Offset Patterns:** There are several offset or side-lap gauge patterns used with three-tab shingles, and the pattern used generally is selected based on manufacturer or installer preference, regional or climatic experience, or common practice.
68	**Shingle Attachment:** When attaching asphalt shingles, the intended location of fasteners depends on the particular shingle type.
	Attachment of three-tab strip shingles: Fastening of full-length three-tab shingles requires a minimum of four roofing nails per strip shingle … positioned about 5/8 of an inch above the top of the shingle cutouts.
	For areas considered to be high-wind regions, six-nail attachment of asphalt strip shingles may be required by the applicable building code.
	Figure 4-11: Four-nail attachment locations for three-tab strip shingles.
	Figure 4-13: Six-nail attachment locations for three-tab strip shingles.
69	**Attachment of laminated strip shingles:** Fastening of full-length laminated strip shingles requires a minimum of four roofing nails per strip shingle.
	For areas considered to be high-wind regions, size-nail attachment of laminated shingles may be required by some building codes.
	Figure 4-14: Four-nail attachment locations for laminated strip shingles

Page #	Highlight
	Figure 4-15: Six-nail attachment locations for laminated strip shingles.
71	**Hips and Ridges:** Asphalt shingles may be butted and nailed as work progresses up either side of a hip or a ridge.
	Drip Edge Metal: Drip edge metal is most common for asphalt shingle roof systems. Drip edge metal is typically fabricated in two configurations, L-type or T-type.
	NRCA suggests fastening drip edge metal at about 12 inches on center, slightly staggered. Spacing may need to be closer in highwind regions.
72	NRCA recommends drip edge metal should be fabricated from one of the following metal types and minimum thicknesses: (9 bullets).
	Valleys: A valley is created at the downslope intersection of two sloping roof.
	With asphalt shingle roof systems, there are four basic types of valleys: (4 bullets)
	Generally, fasteners should be kept back from the center of the valley a minimum of 8 inches.
	Open Valleys: "An open valley is constructed by installing typically 8-foot or 10-foot lengths of corrosion-resistant metal from the low point to the high point in the valley.
	Figure 4-20: Underlayment centered in valley to channel water runoff down the valley
73	*Figure 4-21: Open valley using metal valley flashing.*
	A minimum 36-inch-wide layer of heavy weight felt, polymer-modified bitumen membrane or self-adhering underlayment is centered in the valley under the field underlayment.
	NRCA suggests valley metal for asphalt shingle roof systems be fabricated from one of the following metal types and minimum thicknesses: (9 bullets)
	NRCA recommends valley metal for use with asphalt shingles be a minimum of 24 inches wide.
74	**Closed-cut Valleys:** "In closed-cut valleys, shingles on one side of the valley are installed across the valley and shingles from the other side are cut about 2 inches short of the centerline of the valley."
	Woven Valleys: NRCA does not recommend the use of woven valleys.
	Flashings: Because roof systems are frequently interrupted by the intersection of adjoining roof sections, adjacent walls or penetrations such a s chimneys and vent pipes - all of which create opportunities for leakage - special provisions for weather protection must be made at these locations.
75	**Vertical Surface Flashings**
76	Four types of metal flashings commonly used at locations where an asphalt shingle roof system intersects a vertical surface: apron flashing, step flashing, cricket or backer flashing, and counterflashing.
	Figure 4-25: Sheet-metal Flashing components used at chimney

Page #	Highlight
	Apron Flashings: Apron flashings provide a weatherproofing transition material where a roof area intersects a head wall.
	Step Flashings: Where a roof area intersects a vertical side wall, individual pieces of metal flashing are installed at the end of each shingle course.
	NRCA recommends using metal step flashing that is 7 inches long by 8 inches wide for standard-size shingles ... onto each underlying shingle and 4 inches up the vertical surface.
77	**Cricket or Backer Flashing:** When a roof area intersects the upslope side of a chimney or curbed roof penetration. a cricket or backer flashing is installed.
	Backer flashing is generally limited to penetrations that are 24 inches wide or less.
	Counterflashing: Apron, step, cricket and backer flashings require some form of counterflashing to cover and protect their top edges from water intrusion.
78	**Skylight flashings:** Skylights, in terms of roof flashing, are much the same as other vertical surface flashings, particularly chimney flashings.
82	**5.1 Definitions** - Reroofing - Re-covering - Replacement - Roof assembly - Roof system Roof systems generally can be dived into two categories: - Low-slope roof systems - Steep-slope roof systems
91	**5.4 Roof Decks for Reroofing** **Wood Panels:** Plywood and OSB sheathing panels should be installed with about 1/8-inch minimum gaps at panel edges to allow for panel expansion.
92	*Figure 5-1: APA recommendations for wood structural panel attachment in the steep-slope applications* **Roof Replacement Considerations:** NRCA does not recommend installing roof systems over structural wood panel roof decks that are less than nominal thickness of ½ of an inch.
96	**Drainage and Slope:** NRCA recommends installing a cricket on the upslope side of roof penetrations that are 24 inches wide or wider.
97	**Preparation of Existing Roof Surfaces**: Two items that should be verified when nesting new shingles over existing shingles are as follows: (2 bullets).
110	Note and highlight the figure titled: **Eave**
111	Note and highlight the figure titled: **Eave with Gutter**

Page #	Highlight
115	Note and highlight the information contained in the figure titled: **Rake**
118	Note and highlight the figure titled: **Ridge with Continuous Ridge Vent**
119	Note and highlight the figure titled: **Hip**
120	Note and highlight the figure titled: **Open Valley**
122	Note and highlight the figure titled: **Closed-Cut Valley**
128	Note and highlight the figure titled: **Chimney with Cricket Flashing**
129	Note and highlight the figure titled: **Chimney with Backer Flashing (24 inches or less)**
131	Note and highlight the figure titled: **Steep- to Low-Slope Roof System Transition**
184	Tile may be fastened directly to the following substrates: (3 bullets)
	2.1 Wood Panels Wood panel roof decks can be subdivided into two general types: plywood roof decks and oriented strand board (OS B) roof decks.
	2.2 Wood Planks and Wood Boards Wood plank and wood board roof decks are composed of solid-sawn dimensional lumber.
187	**2.3 Batten Systems** For some types of tile roofs, batten and counter-batten systems are used to hang tile that has head lugs.
	If battens are not raised or kerfed to allow drainage, they should not be longer than 4 feet. Battens may be installed with aligned or staggered joints and about 1/2-inch separation between ends to help drain moisture that may migrate into a roof system.
190	**3.1 Underlayment Materials**
	Asphalt Felts: Asphalt-saturated and asphalt impregnated felt underlayments traditionally have been the mostare the most commonly used steep slope roof underlayments.
191	**Polymer-modified Bitumen Sheets:** Polymer-modified bitumen sheet membrane products are sometimes used an underlayments in tile roof systems.
	3.2 Underlayment Design and Installation: Clay and concrete tiles are designed for use as multilayered, water-shedding roof components that rely on the slope of the roof substrate to effectively shed water.
	Roof Slope: NRCA recommends designers specify the substrates for clay or concrete tile roof systems have slopes of 4:12 or more.
	Underlayment Configurations: "There are different underlayment configurations that can be used for tile roof systems. There following configurations are addressed in this manual: (4 bullets)." Note and highlight each section which describes the 4 categories.

Page #	Highlight
199	Tile shapes commonly are categorized as follows: (4 bullets).
200	*Figure 4-1: Roof tile classification by profile.*
201	*Figure 4-2: Common clay profiles*
203	*Figure 4-6: S-tile dimensions*
203	**4.1 Clay and Concrete Tile Materials**
	Clay Roof Tile
204	Clay tiles are fired in kilns at temperatures ranging from 1800 F to 2000 F.
	Roof Tile Physical Characteristics: Concrete tile absorption values range from 3 percent to 20 percent.
	Freeze-thaw Resistance: Some types of tile are graded for their resistance to frost action. ASTM Standard C1167, "Standard Specification for Clay Roof Tiles," provides grades of clay tile, and each has a different resistance to freeze-thaw cycles.
206	**Securement Methods:** Roof tile commonly is secured using the following means and methods: (6 bullets).
208	**Asphalt Roof Cement:** There are two common types of asphalt roof cement: flashing cement and lap cement.
209	**4.2 Clay and Concrete Tile Design and Installation**
	Exposure and Appearance: Generally, a minimum 3-inch course-to-course overlap is recommended … requires a minimum of 2 inches for clay and concrete tile applied on very steep slopes.
210	**Hips and Ridges:** To weatherproof a roof at hips and ridges, special hip and ridge trim tiles are used as hip and ridge coverings.
	Rakes: To weatherproof a tile roof system along rake edges, specific details used depend on the tile type and profile, climate, and regional or area practices.
211	**Valleys:** A valley is created at the downslope intersection of two sloping roof planes.
	With tile roof systems, there are two basic types of valleys: Open valleys: Closed valleys.
	Open Valleys
212	NRCA suggests valley metal for tile roof systems be fabricated from one of the following metal types and minimum thicknesses: (7 bullets.)
	NRCA recommends valley metal for use with tile be a minimum of 24 inches wide.
213	**Closed Valleys:** In closed valley, tiles on both sides are cut at an angle parallel to the centerline of the valley and butted together to form a mitered joint.

Page #	Highlight
	Flashings: Flashings are divided into the following categories: (4 bullets).
	NRCA suggests metal flashings used in clay tile or concrete tile roof systems be fabricated from one of the following metal types and minimum thicknesses: (7 bullets).
215	*Figure 4-17: Sheet-metal flashing components used at a chimney*
	Figure 4-18: Apron flashing at masonry chimney for pan and cover tile
	Figure 4-19: Apron flashing at masonry chimney for interlocking or plain tile
216	*Figure 4-20: Step flashing at a masonry chimney for plain tile*
	Figure 4-21: Channel flashing at a masonry chimney with pan and cover tile
	Figure 4-22: Channel flashing at a vertical wall.
	NRCA suggests using metal step flashing pieces sized such that they match the tile in length so a minimum step flashing head lap is achieved. The step flashing width should be sufficient to obtain a 4-inch extension onto each underlying tile and about a 4-inch vertical height over the exposed face of each overlying tile.
217	*Figure 4-24: Sheet-metal backer flashing at chimney*
	Figure 4-25: Wood cricket built on upslope side of chimney
	Figure 4-26: Cricket flashing for upslope side of masonry chimney.
218	**Skylight Flashings:** Skylights, in terms of roof flashing, are much the same as other vertical surface flashings, particularly chimney flashings.
221	Reroofing also should be considered in other situations, including the following: (10 bullets).
222	**5.1 Definitions** - Reroofing - Re-covering - Replacement - Roof assembly - Roof system **5.2 Evaluation of Existing Roof Systems**
223	NRCA does not consider clay and concrete tile roof systems acceptable substrates for new re-cover applications.
226	**Base and Counterflashings:** When removing the existing roof system and installing new clay or concrete roof system, NRCA recommends the existing base flashings be removed and new base flashings be installed.

Page #	Highlight
231	**5.4 Roof Decks for Reroofing**
	Wood Panels: NRCA does not recommend OSB panels to be used as a substrate for clay and concrete tile roof systems.
	Wood sheathing panels should be installed with about 1/8 minimum gaps at panels edges to allow for panel expansion.
232	*Figure 5-1: APA recommendations for wood structural panel attachment in steep-slope applications*
	Roof Replacement Considerations
233	Roof decks should be continuous and without gaps. Gaps greater than ¼ of an inch should be covered or filled.
	NRCA does not recommend installation of clay or concrete tile roof systems …. That are less than nominal thickness of 5/8 inches.
237	**Roof Slope:** For roof penetrations that are 24 inches or wider, NRCA recommends installing a cricket on the upslope side of the penetrations.
239	Construction details are provided for the following tile shapes: (4 bullets.)
242	*Figure 6-2: Sheet-metal counterflashing options.* A. Through-wall Reglet and Counterflashing" and B. Insert Reglet and Counterflashing
248	Note and highlight the figure titled: **Eave**
249	Note and highlight the figure titled: **Eave With Gutter**
253	Note and highlight the figure titled: **Rake**
254	Note and highlight the figure titled: **Ridge**
255	Note and highlight the figure titled: **HIP**
256	Note and highlight the figure titled: **Open Valley**
257	Note and highlight the figure titled: **Headwall Flashing**
258	Note and highlight the figure titled: **Sidewall Flashing with Two-Piece Counterflashing**
259	Note and highlight the figure titled: **Sidewall Flashing With One-Piece Counterflashing**
262	Note and highlight the figure titled: **Chimney With Cricket Flashing**
263	Note and highlight the figure titled: **Chimney With Backer Flashing (24 Inches Wide or Less)**
264	Note and highlight the figure titled: **Curb-mounted Skylight**

Page #	Highlight
265	Note and highlight the figure titled: **Steep- to Low-slop Roof System Transition**
266	Note and highlight the figure titled: **Eave**
267	Note and highlight the figure titled: **Eave With Gutter**
271	Note and highlight the figure titled: **Rake**
272	Note and highlight the figure titled: **Ridge**
273	Note and highlight the figure titled: **Hip**
274	Note and highlight the figure titled: **Open Valley**
275	Note and highlight the figure titled: **Headwall Flashing**
276	Note and highlight the figure titled: **Sidewall Flashing With Two-Piece Counterflashing**
277	Note and highlight the figure titled: **Sidewall Flashing With One-piece Counterflashing**
280	Note and highlight the figure titled: **Chimney With Cricket Flashing**
281	Note and highlight the figure titled: **Chimney with Backer Flashing**
282	Note and highlight the figure titled: **Curb-mounted Skylight**
283	Note and highlight the figure titled: **Steep- to Low-slope Roof System Transition**
303	Note and highlight the figure titled: **Eave**
304	Note and highlight the figure titled: **Eave With Gutter**
308	Note and highlight the figure titled: **Rake**
309	Note and highlight the figure titled: **Ridge**
310	Note and highlight the figure titled: **Hip**
311	Note and highlight the figure titled: **Open Valley**
312	Note and highlight the figure titled: **Headwall Flashing**
313	Note and highlight the figure titled: **Sidewall Flashing With Two-Piece Counterflashing**
315	Note and highlight the figure titled: **Sidewall Flashing With One-piece Counterflashing**
317	Note and highlight the figure titled: **Chimney With Cricket Flashing**
318	Note and highlight the figure titled: **Chimney with Backer Flashing**

Page #	Highlight
319	Note and highlight the figure titled: **Curb-mounted Skylight**
320	Note and highlight the figure titled: **Steep- to Low-slope Roof System Transition**
353	**2.3 Batten Systems:** If battens are not raised or kerfed to allow drainage, they should not be longer than 4 feet. Battens may be installed with aligned or staggered joints and about 1/2-inch separation between ends to help drain moisture that may migrate into a roof system.
356	**2.1 Underlayment Materials:** Materials used as underlayment for metal shingle and synthetic component roof systems generally consist of asphalt felts, synthetic felts, polymer-modified bitumen sheets and water and ice-dam protection membrane.
358	**Roof Slope:** "NRCA recommends designers specify the substrate for metal shingle and synthetic component roof systems have slopes of 4:12 or more.
358	**Underlayment Configurations**
362	**Naturally Weathering Metals:** For a metal to be appropriately considered a naturally weathering metal, the base metal itself must be able to oxidize sufficiently to form its own protective layer to withstand environmental exposures common to roof system. The most common types of naturally weathering metals are: (4 bullets).
366	**Paint Systems**
367	A wide variety of available factory-applied paint systems, and some manufacturers have their own formulations for each. Two common types of factory baked-on, paint-based systems are fluoropolymer and siliconized acrylic, or siliconized polyester.
372	**Securement Methods** **Nail Applications:** Nails should be long enough to penetrate through all layers of roofing materials … acceptable wood panel decks less than ¾ of an inch thick.
375	**Valleys**
376	NRCA recommends valley metal for use with metal shingles be a minimum of 18-inches wide.
383	Reroofing should be considered in other situations, including the following: (10 bullets).
384	**5.1 Definitions** - Reroofing - Re-covering - Replacement - Roof assembly - Roof system
388	**Roof Covering Condition:** The following conditions may adversely affect steep-slope roof coverings' water shedding function: (17 bullets).

Page #	Highlight
393	**5.4 Roof Decks for Reroofing** **Wood Panels:** Plywood and OSB sheathing panels should be installed with about 1/8 minimum gaps at panels edges to allow for panel expansion.
395	*Figure 5-1: APA recommendations for wood structural panel attachment in steep-slope applications*
396	**Roof Replacement Considerations**
397	NRCA does not recommend installing roof systems over structural wood panel roof decks that are less than nominal thickness of 3/4 of an inch.
401	For roof penetrations that are 24 inches or wider, NRCA recommends installing a cricket on the upslope side of the penetrations.
406	*Figure 6-2: Sheet-metal counterflashing options.* A. Through-wall Reglet and Counterflashing" and B. Insert Reglet and Counterflashing."
410	Note and highlight the figure titled: **Eave**
411	Note and highlight the figure titled: **Eave With Gutter**
415	Note and highlight the figure titled: **Rake**
416	Note and highlight the figure titled: **Ridge**
418	Note and highlight the figure titled: **Hip**
419	Note and highlight the figure titled: **Valley**
420	Note and highlight the figure titled: **Headwall Flashing**
421	Note and highlight the figure titled: **Sidewall Flashing with Two-Piece Counterflashing**
422	Note and highlight the figure titled: **Sidewall Flashing With One-Piece Counterflashing**
425	Note and highlight the figure titled: **Chimney With Cricket Flashing**
426	Note and highlight the figure titled: **Chimney With Backer Flashing (24 Inches Wide or Less)**
427	Note and highlight the figure titled: **Curb-mounted Skylight**
428	Note and highlight the figure titled: **Steep- to Low-slope Roof System Transition**
456	NRCA recommends designers specify roof deck slopes intended for the application of slate roof systems at 4:12 or greater.
464	**Roof Slope**: NRCA recommends designers specify substrates for slate roof systems have roof slopes of 4:12 or more.

Page #	Highlight
470	**Colors:** The color of slate is determined by its chemical and mineral composition.
	Weight: A square of slate on a roof system set at the standard 3-inch head lap will vary in weight from 700 pounds to 8,000 pounds depending on the thickness of each slate.
	Figure 4-1: Approximate weight of roofing slate at various thicknesses
471	Figure 4-2: Common Slate sizes, slates per square and exposures
472	Figure 4-3: Physical Requirements for Roofing Slate
474	**4.2 Slate Roof System Design and Installation**
	Exposure and Appearance: Figure 4-5 shows the proper exposures for various length of slate if all are to be set with a 3-inch head lap.
	Figure 4-5: Slate exposures
487	Reroofing should be considered in other situations, including the following: (10 bullets).
488	**5.1 Definitions** - Reroofing - Re-covering - Replacement - Roof assembly - Roof system
497	**5.4 Roof Decks for Reroofing:**
	Wood Panels: NRCA does not recommend OSB panels be used as a substrate for slate roof systems.
498	*Figure 5-1: APA recommendations for wood structural panel attachment in steep-slope applications*
503	**Roof Slope**: For roof penetrations that are 24 inches wide or wider, NRCA recommends installing a cricket on the upslope side of penetrations.
508	*Figure 6-2: Sheet-metal counterflashing options.* A. Through-wall Reglet and Counterflashing" and B. Insert Reglet and Counterflashing
512	Note and highlight the figure titled: **Eave**
513	Note and highlight the figure titled: **Eave with Gutter**
517	Note and highlight the figure titled: **Rake**
518	Note and highlight the figure titled: **Ridge with Slate**
521	Note and highlight the figure titled: **Hip**
522	Note and highlight the figure titled: **Open Valley**

Page #	Highlight
524	Note and highlight the figure titled: **Headwall Flashing**
525	Note and highlight the figure titled: **Sidewall Flashing with Two-Piece Counterflashing**
529	Note and highlight the figure titled: **Chimney With Cricket Flashing**
530	Note and highlight the figure titled: **Chimney With Backer Flashing (24 Inches Wide or Less)**
532	Note and highlight the figure titled: **Steep- to Low-slop Roof System Transition**
559	**2.2 Wood Planks and Wood Boards**
560	When spaced sheathing is used, a roof deck may be composed of 1-inch nominal, 4-inch-wide boards for attaching wood shingles and 1-inch nominal, 6-inch-wide boards for attaching wood shakes.
567	**Roof Slope:** NRCA recommends designers specify the substrates for wood shake and wood shingle roof systems have slopes of 4:12 or more.
	NRCA recommends a minimum single layer of ASTM D4869, Type III, or Type IV asphalt felt underlayment be specified and applied horizontally in shingle fashion.
	Note and highlight the figure titled: *Figure 3-2: Single layer Underlayment*
572	*Figure 4-1: Wood shakes.*
573	*Figure 4-2: Wood shingles.*
576	*Figure 4-3: Nails used with wood roofing*
578	**Field Application:** Joints in the first exposed course of wood shakes or wood shingles should be offset a minimum of 1 ½ inches from the joints in the underlying starter course.
579	*Figure 4-4: Wood shake coverage and exposure table*
580	*Figure 4-5: Shingle coverage and exposure table.*
584	**Open Valleys**: NRCA recommends valley metal for use with wood shakes or shingles be a minimum of 24-inches wide sheet metal.
591	**Reroofing**
592	**5.1 Definitions** - Reroofing - Re-covering - Replacement - Roof assembly - Roof system
601	**5.4 Roof Decks for Reroofing**

Page #	Highlight
	Wood Panels: Plywood and OSB sheathing panels should be installed with about 1/8-inch minimum gaps at panel edges to allow for panel expansion.
602	**Roof Replacement Considerations:** NRCA does not recommend installing roof systems over structural wood panel roof decks that are less than nominal thickness of ½ of an inch.
	Figure 5-1: APA recommendations for wood structural panel attachment in the steep-slope applications
612	*Figure 6-2: Sheet-metal counterflashing options* A. Through-wall Reglet and Counterflashing" and B. Insert Reglet and Counterflashing.
618	Note and highlight the figure titled: **Eave**
619	Note and highlight the figure titled: **Eave with Gutter**
623	Note and highlight the figure titled: **Rake**
625	Note and highlight the figure titled: **Hip**
626	Note and highlight the figure titled: **Open Valley**
627	Note and highlight the figure titled: **Headwall Flashing**
628	Note and highlight the figure titled: **Sidewall Flashing with Two-Piece Counterflashing**
632	Note and highlight the figure titled: **Chimney With Cricket Flashing**
633	Note and highlight the figure titled: **Chimney With Backer Flashing (24 Inches Wide or Less)**
634	Note and highlight the figure titled: **Curb-Mounted Skylight**
636	Note and highlight the figure titled: **Eave**
637	Note and highlight the figure titled: **Eave with Gutter**
641	Note and highlight the figure titled: **Rake**
643	Note and highlight the figure titled: **Hip**
644	Note and highlight the figure titled: **Open Valley**
645	Note and highlight the figure titled: **Headwall Flashing**
646	Note and highlight the figure titled: **Sidewall Flashing with Two-Piece Counterflashing**
650	Note and highlight the figure titled: **Chimney With Cricket Flashing**
651	Note and highlight the figure titled: **Chimney With Backer Flashing (24 Inches Wide or Less)**
652	Note and highlight the figure titled: **Curb-Mounted Skylight**

Page #	Highlight
653	Note and highlight the figure titled: **Steep- to Low-slop Roof System Transition**
654	Note and highlight the figure titled: **Eave**
655	Note and highlight the figure titled: **Eave with Gutter**
659	Note and highlight the figure titled: **Rake**
661	Note and highlight the figure titled: **Hip**
662	Note and highlight the figure titled: **Open Valley**
663	Note and highlight the figure titled: **Headwall Flashing**
664	Note and highlight the figure titled: **Sidewall Flashing with Two-Piece Counterflashing**
665	Note and highlight the figure titled: **Sidewall Flashing with One-Piece Counterflashing**
668	Note and highlight the figure titled: **Chimney With Cricket Flashing**
669	Note and highlight the figure titled: **Chimney With Backer Flashing (24 Inches Wide or Less)**
670	Note and highlight the figure titled: **Curb-Mounted Skylight**
671	Note and highlight the figure titled: **Steep- to Low-slop Roof System Transition**
672	Note and highlight the figure titled: **Eave**
673	Note and highlight the figure titled: **Eave with Gutter**
677	Note and highlight the figure titled: **Rake**
679	Note and highlight the figure titled: **Hip**
680	Note and highlight the figure titled: **Open Valley**
681	Note and highlight the figure titled: **Headwall Flashing**
682	Note and highlight the figure titled: **Sidewall Flashing with Two-Piece Counterflashing**
683	Note and highlight the figure titled: **Sidewall Flashing with One-Piece Counterflashing**
686	Note and highlight the figure titled: **Chimney With Cricket Flashing**
687	Note and highlight the figure titled: **Chimney With Backer Flashing (24 Inches Wide or Less)**
688	Note and highlight the figure titled: **Curb-Mounted Skylight**
689	Note and highlight the figure titled: **Steep- to Low-slop Roof System Transition**

1 Exam Prep

NRCA Membrane Roof Systems Questions

1. The preferred method of installing rigid insulation board to cementitious wood-fiber roof decks is?

    Spot mopping
    Blind nailing
    Loose laid
    Adhesion to the base sheet

The recommended steel panel roof deck gauge is _____ or heavier.

    22
    20
    26
    18

Roofing materials normally should not be applied below what temperature?

    40 degrees
    50 degrees
    32 degrees
    90 degrees

Moisture in or on materials can cause?

    Slippage
    Fishmouths
    Blistering
    Skipping

The maximum mop application of Type IV asphalt is?

    450 degrees
    475 degrees
    500 degrees
    525 degrees

The minimum temperature for the application of Type I coal tar pitch is?

    360 degrees
    335 degrees
    330 degrees
    385 degrees

7. NRCA recommends steel decks be _____ gauge or heavier?

- 22
- 24
- 26
- 20

8. When installing cellular-glass, multiple-layer insulation is required when the total thickness of the insulation is greater than?

- 3"
- 2"
- 1 1/2"
- 1"

When using perlite insulation as the primary insulation NRCA recommends _____ layers.

- 2
- 2 1/2
- 1
- 3

Multiple-layer insulation of wood fiberboard is recommended when the total required thickness of the insulation is greater than how many inches?

- 1 1/2
- 1 1/3
- 1 3/4
- 2

The equiviscous temperature is?

- Proper melting point
- Minimum melting temperature
- Proper viscosity for application
- Flash point

Bitumen can be heated and held at the high temperatures for _____

- Long periods
- 1 hour
- 4 hours
- Short periods

The EVT range must be within _____ degrees of viscosity at 125 centistokes.

- 10° F
- 15° F
- 20° F
- 25° F

14. Coal-tar Type I Bitumen has an application temperature of_____. (2011 Only)

    375°F
    360°F
    350°F
    450°F

When using EPDM Membrane materials,_____ should be avoided to prevent swelling.

    Glues
    Sand
    Hypalon Coatings
    Aliphatic Solvents

EPDM single-ply requires the use of_____ to prevent wicking at exposed cut edges.

    Contact Solvents
    Silica Sand
    Sealant
    Cut sheets

Rosin sheets work well to_____

    Prevent drippage
    Divorce roof membranes
    Provide adhesion
    Provide vapor migration

Correctly designed penetration pockets should have compatible_____

    Projections
    Sealant
    Dripholes
    Sealing

NRCA recommends for slope and drainage that there be no ponding on the roof_____

    8 hours after raining
    24 hours after raining
    12 hours after raining
    48 hours after raining

When installing BUR roof drains, copper must be_____ inches square.

    28
    30
    6
    48

21. Overheating bitumens can cause _____

    Poor Adhesion
    Flash hazards
    Slippage
    Yellow smoke

Base flashing height for Atatic smooth surface roofing should not be lower than _____

    8 inches
    6 inches
    10 inches
    5 inches

Raised curbs using BUR roofing should be flashed a minimum of _____

    8"
    10"
    12"
    14"

There should be no evidence of standing water on the deck _____ hours after it stops raining.

    24
    48
    72
    86

When determining the thermal resistance of a tapered insulation system a common industry approach is _____

    Average thickness
    C value
    Minimum R value
    Maximum R value

Cold rolled ribs lighter than _____ gauge have little strength.

    18
    20
    22
    24

27. Intermediate rib decking has a maximum rib opening of how many inches?

    1
    1 3/4
    2
    2 ½

Spacing between side lap fasteners should not exceed how many feet?

    3
    4
    6
    21

The weld spacing along the perimeter should be _____ inches.

    18
    12
    6
    3

Cellular glass board is approved at _____ inches minimum thickness.

    1
    1 1/2
    1 3/4
    6

There should be no evidence of water on the roof _____ hours after it stops raining.

    24
    48
    36
    12

According to the NRCA manual, the Equiviscous Temperature range is defined as _____

    125 centistokes
    125 centistokes plus 25 degrees Fahrenheit
    125 centistokes plus or minus 25 degrees Fahrenheit
    125 centistokes minus 25 degrees Fahrenheit

According to the NRCA manual, the roofing contractor should take special precautions when the temperature is below how many degrees?

   60
   50
   40
   55

Loose-laid **EPDM** single-ply systems require the use of_____ to provide resistance against wind-uplift forces.

   Screw fasteners
   Special adhesives
   Heat applied seams
   Ballast

One of the more common types of insulation layers is_____

   15 pound asphalt felt
   30 pound fiberglass
   Fiberglass insulation
   Board insulation

According to the NRCA manual, asphalt shall be applied at a temperature within _____ degrees of the equiviscous temperature.

   10
   15
   20
   25

There are how many subcategories of common Thermoplastic membranes?

   4
   6
   7
   2

Field lap seams when installing EPDM are typically constructed with_____

   Durable locks
   Snap caps
   Seam tape
   Heat seams

39. A four-way slope, high point of 12 and low point of 3 can provide uniform perimeter_____

    Depth
    Width
    Temperature
    Thickness

When installing cementitious wood fiber decks,_____ type fasteners should be used.

    Auger
    One Piece Tube nails
    Three Piece Tube nails
    Nylon expansion fasteners

For added benefit NRCA recommends insulation be applied a minimum of _____ layers?

    1
    2
    3
    9

Mop Temperature for Type IV asphalt is_____

    350°F
    425°F
    450°F
    475°F

Type II ASTM D312 is _____ asphalt?

    Deadlevel
    Flat
    Steep
    Special

The Equiviscous Temperature range must be plus or minus_____

    10°F
    15°F
    20°F
    25°F

Substituting adhesives in thermoset single-ply roofing is_____

    Good
    Bad
    Ugly
    Recommended

46. When using EPDM Membrane materials, which of the following will prevent wicking?

>Seam sealant
>Corn oil
>Lard
>Solvents

Fishmouths in thermoset roofing should be_____

>Cut
>Spliced
>Bonded
>Hot mopped

The minimum square inches for the lead sheet when installing roof drains is_____

>18
>22
>24
>30

Base flashing height should not be lower than _____ inches.

>8
>6
>10
>5

The building is located in a 90 mph basic wind speed region in Exposure "B". The maximum allowable height of the building if using gravel is_____

>100 feet
>110 feet
>120 feet
>90 feet

Number 4 aggregate ballast is typically applied at a coverage rate of about _____ pounds per 100 square feet for loose-laid ballasted membrane roof systems.

>2,000
>1,300
>1,500
>2,500

52. When using nails with cementitious wood-fiber, NRCA suggests using _____

    Barbed clip fasteners
    Two-piece tube nails
    Three-piece tube nails
    Toggle bolts

Intermediate rib decking has a maximum nominal rib opening of _____ inches.

    1
    1 3/4
    2
    2 ½

A metal roof deck should be welded no more than how many inches on center?

    6
    8
    12
    16

Ballast systems should be designed using _____

    Patterns
    Thickness
    Porosity
    Weight calculations

Mineral surfaced cap sheets should be unrolled and allowed to relax for how long?

    Eight hours
    Until soft and pliable
    Four hours
    Until flat

The two general categories of metal roofing systems are _____ and _____

    Water shedding and water repellant
    Architectural and field engineered
    Waterproof and water-resistant
    Cold-rolled and panel

The tanker temperature should always be less than how many degrees below the actual flash point of coal tar bitumen?

- 25
- 50
- 75
- 10

When installing insulation board for cement-wood fiber decks, the maximum elevation difference allowed is _____

- 2"
- 1"
- 1/2"
- 1/8"

Type "F" decking has flute spacing of _____

- 1 inch maximum
- 1 to 1 3/4 inches
- 1 3/4 to 2 5/8 inches
- 1 1/2 to 2 3/4 inches

Vapor retarders should be used to _____

- Control the flow of moisture vapor from the interior of the building into the roof system
- Control the flow of moisture vapor from the exterior of the building into the roof system
- Remove the moisture vapor from the interior of the building
- Remove the moisture vapor from the exterior of the building

Which of the following is not a type of rigid roof insulation?

- Perlite
- Vermiculite
- Polystyrene
- Mineral fiber

Asphalt with a maximum softening point of 225 degrees is _____

- Type I
- Type II
- Type III
- Type IV

64. Moisture in or on materials can cause membrane_____

    Deterioration
    Softening
    Blistering
    Buckling

Type III asphalt is for slopes up to_____

    1/4:12
    1/2:12
    1:12
    3:12

Type IV asphalt is suggested for slopes greater than_____

    1/4:12
    1/2:12
    1:12
    3:12

The **NRCA** states lightweight structural concrete has a density of not less than _____ pcf?

    60
    85
    90
    120

Which of the following is not a type of rigid roof insulation?

    Cellular glass
    Spun glass modules
    Wood fiberboard
    Gypsum board

Type I asphalt requires a minimum mop application temperature of how many degrees?

    350
    325
    375
    400

According to the NRCA, 24 inch by 24 inch roof mounted equipment requires support height of _____ inches.

    14
    30
    36
    48

71. NRCA recommends the height of a base flashing be no lower than how many inches?

    8
    10
    12
    16

A typical Type F deck panel should have a minimum rib width of _____ inches?

    1
    1 1/2
    1 3/4
    ½

A rigid board made from crushing glass and mixing it with hydrosulfide gas is _____

    Roof covering
    Decking
    Cellular-glass
    A vapor barrier

The maximum slope required for low slope roofing is _____

    1:12
    2:12
    4:12
    3:12

The temperature of the hot asphalt should be measured _____

    At the kettle
    On the roof
    At the pipe
    After installation

TPO is available in all except _____ mils?

    40
    72
    45
    90

Based on dew-point calculation and to limit possible condensation and premature degradation of materials, a designer should consider _____

    Installing more than normal insulation
    Provisions for a vapor retarder
    An extra layer of hot mop or cold process depending upon the roof style
    The use of a deck sealer

78. Type 1 low-softening point asphalt cement is governed by _____

        ASTM D 312
        ASTM D 4586
        DBPR D 6977
        ASTM D 3019

Which is not an advantage of Ethylene Propylene Diene Monomer roofing?

        Resistance to ozone
        Weathering
        Abrasion
        Resistance to vegetable oils

According to the NRCA, the softening point for Type I asphalt is how many degrees Fahrenheit?

        210 to 235
        210 to 225
        185 to 176
        135 to 151

Which is not property of a rigid board roof insulation system?

        Moisture resistance
        R-value
        Compressive strength
        Tactile compatibility

Which of the following is not a common subcategory of thermoplastic membranes?

        PVC
        CPA
        EIP
        DIP

The ASTM standard governing polyisocyanurate foam board roof insulation is _____

        D1289
        D6163
        C578
        C1289

The minimum R-value approach establishes the thermal resistance for a tapered roof insulation system by determining the R-value of the tapered material at the _____

        Thickest point in the tapered system layout
        Thinnest point in the tapered system layout
        Average point in the tapered system layout
        Any point in the tapered system layout

85. Which is not a common subcategory of thermoplastic membranes?

> EPDM
> KEE
> TPO
> PVC

The tapered systems is 6 inches at the thickest point and 2 inches at the thinnest point. Using the Average R-Value approach, the R-value of the tapered system is Valued at how many inches of thickness?

> 8
> 6
> 4
> 2

Caution should be used when applying roofing materials below what temperature?

> 40 degrees Centigrade
> 50 degrees Fahrenheit
> 50 degrees Centigrade
> 40 degrees Fahrenheit

EVT is defined as the temperature at which the viscosity of roofing asphalt is _____

> Explosive
> At flash point
> Emits yellow smoke
> 125 Cs

Type III asphalt may be used on roof slopes _____ or less?

> 1/4 inch per foot
> 1/2 inch per foot
> 3/4 inch per foot
> 1 inch per foot

When applying polymer-modified asphalt roofing, the contractor should use _____

> Low kettle temperatures
> Detailed torch kits
> Coal tar roof cements
> Asphalt roof cements

Kettle temperature should be maintained at less than how many degrees below flash point?

> 100
> 75
> 50
> 25

When applying modified bitumen membrane sheets directly to combustible substrates such as wood decks, NRCA recommends _____

    Not using a torch
    Using a torch
    Nailing the rosin paper
    Not using rosin paper

The maximum temperature for the application of Type 2 asphalt for mop applications Is _____

    350 degrees F
    375 degrees F
    400 degrees F
    425 degrees F

The two types of vapor retarders are?

    Hydrostatic and hydrokinetic
    Bitumen and plastic sheet or film vapor retarders (non-bitumen)
    Semi-permeable and permeable
    Type 1 and Type 2

ANSWER KEY

		2011	2015
1.	D	17	124
2.	A	22	129
3.	A	78	198
4.	C	79	199
5.	B	81	202
6.	B	82	203
7.	A	22	129
8.	A	49	161
9.	A	61	174
10.	A	66	181
11.	C	80	202
12.	D	87	209
13.	D	80	202
14.	B	82	N/A
15.	D	98	224
16.	C	98	224
17.	A	86	208
18.	B	344	410
19.	D	15	122
20.	B	300	363
21.	B	87	209
22.	A	305	369
23.	A	282	342
24.	B	15	122
25.	C	69	187
26.	C	22	129
27.	B	21	128
28.	A	22	129
29.	B	22	129
30.	B	49	161

31.	B	15	122
32.	C	80	202
33.	C	78	200
34.	D	122	255
35.	D	42	155
36.	D	80	202
37.	A	97/98	223
38.	C	98	224
39.	D	68	187-188
40.	A	110	242
41.	B	43	155
42.	C	81	203
43.	B	81	203
44.	D	80	202
45.	B	97	223
46.	A	121	254
47.	C	97	223
48.	D	300/349	363/418
49.	A	400	440
50.	B	121	254
51.	B	122	255
52.	D	109	241
53.	B	21	128
54.	C	22	129
55.	D	122	255
56.	D	88	210
57.	D	21	128
58.	A	81	203
59.	D	17	124
60.	B	21	128
61.	A	39	151
62.	B	42	155
63.	D	80	202

64.	C	79	201
65.	C	81	203
66.	C	81	203
67.	B	18	125
68.	B	42	155
69.	B	81	203
70.	A	276/279	384/388
71.	A	392/400	469/477
72.	D	21	128
73.	C	48	161
74.	D	11	12
75.	B	81	203
76.	A	101	226
77.	B	38	150
78.	A	80	202
79.	D	98	224
80.	D	80	202
81.	D	42	154
82.	D	97/98	223
83.	D	72	192
84.	B	69	187
85.	A	97	223
86.	C	69	187
87.	D	78	200
88.	D	80	202
89.	D	81	203
90.	D	94	208
91.	D	81	203
92.	A	33	124
93.	D	98	224
94.	B	38	150

1 Exam Prep

NRCA Metal Panel and SPF Roof Systems, 2016

Questions and Answers

One of the advantages of heavier gauge galvanized steel is that if thick enough, a panel will not exhibit an objectionable amount of _____

- Oil canning
- Surface defects
- Glare
- Rusting

According to NRCA, architectural metal panel roof systems perform well on slopes of _____ in 12 or greater.

- 14
- 3
- 1/2
- 1/8

The height of a mechanical equipment stand supporting 12 inch wide equipment is _____

- 14"
- 18"
- 24"
- 30"

The nominal thickness of 16-ounce copper is how many inches?

- .0270
- .0216
- .0418
- .0340

Sixteen ounce copper weighs how much per square foot?

- 16 pounds
- 16 ounces
- 3/4 pounds
- 14 ounces

6. During a reroof pipe penetrations require?

   - Same type of flashing regardless of use
   - Different type of flashing
   - Stacks to have an unlimited height
   - None of the above

If unsatisfactory or questionable roof deck conditions are observed, the roofing contractor should _____?

   - Install new roofing system over existing deck
   - Replace and repair damaged area of roof deck
   - Promptly inform the building owner or other responsible parties
   - Place tarp over the area and continue working in order to avoid wasting time

Who is responsible for installing pipe support systems in reroofing?

   - Plumbing contractor
   - Mechanical contractor
   - Roofing contractor
   - At the discretion of the owner/property manager

Where should expansion joints be located in a roof assembly?

   - Expansion joints are never needed in a roof assembly
   - At the center of a commercial building
   - Every 12 ft
   - In the same location as the buildings structural expansion joint

Why would a recoat be needed for an SPF system?

   - Thin coat becoming slightly translucent
   - Extensive physical damage
   - Damage caused by hail, wind, or hurricane
   - All of the above

All stored materials should be stored according to _____?

   - International Building Code
   - Per NRCA guidelines
   - Within temperature range and guidelines required by the system manufacturer
   - All of the above

What is the standard time for testing and evaluating concrete's compressive strength and its dryness or suitability to be covered by a roofing system?

- 7 days
- 15 days
- 30 days
- 28 days

Where are metal panel roof systems fabricated?

- contractor's facility or jobsite
- manufacturing facilities
- Both A and B
- None of the above

How many different commonly used sheet metal fasteners are there?

- 8
- 12
- 13
- 18

What kind of material can be used as underlayment?

- asphalt felt
- synthetic sheets
- self-adhering polymer-modified bitumen sheets
- All of the above

1 Exam Prep
NRCA Metal Panel and SPF Roof Systems
2016 Answer Key

1. A   Page 83
2. B   Page 88
3. A   Page 141
4. B   Page 501
5. B   Page 71
6. B   Page 409
7. C   Page 394
8. C   Page 379
9. D   Page 378
10. D   Page 375
11. C   Page 354
12. D   Page 340
13. C   Page 95
14. C   Page 147
15. D   Page 106

1 Exam Prep
NRCA Steep-slope Roof Systems, 2017
Questions and Answers

For single-layer of mechanically attached underlayment applications, the underlayment should be applied in a single fashion and side laps are typically _____ inches.

    1
    2
    3
    4

Fastening of full-length three-tab strip shingles requires a minimum of _____ roofing nails per shingle.

    4
    6
    8
    32

With asphalt shingle roof systems, three basic types of valleys are _____ valleys.

    Open, shut and woven
    Open, California cut and closed
    Woven, closed and open
    Closed-cut, no-cut and woven

In closed-cut valleys, shingles on one side of the valley are installed across the valley and shingles from the other side are cut about _____ inches short of the centerline of the valley.

    2
    4
    6
    12

Drip edge metal is most common for asphalt shingle roof systems and mechanically attached underlayment should be installed _____ drip edge metal at eaves.

    Over
    Under
    With bull membrane
    Using fasteners every 6 inches

With tile roof systems, the two basic valleys are _____ valleys.

- Open and woven
- Closed and woven
- No-cut and closed
- Open and closed

Cricket or backer flashing generally is limited to penetrations that are _____ inches wide.

12
16
18
24

Asphalt shingle fasteners should be kept back a minimum of _____ inches from the center of the valley.

6
8
10
12

Metal flashings used in wood shake or shingle systems may be fabricated from any of the following EXCEPT _____.

26-gauge prefinished galvanized steel
3-pound lead
26-gauge stainless steel
16-ounce copper

A minimum _____ inch-wide layer of polymer-modified bitumen underlayment, base sheet or self-adhering underlayment is centered in the valley under the field underlayment

19
36
18
6

Fasteners should extend a minimum of _____ of an inch through the underside of roof decks less than ¾ of an inch thick.

1/8 inch
3/4 inch
1/2 inch
1/4 inch

A minimum distance of _____ inches is recommended between a penetration and valley center.

- 6
- 12
- 16
- 18

The minimum length of 5d box nails to be used on 24 inch taper-split shakes is _____ inches.

- 1 1/4
- 1 3/4
- 2
- 6

Crickets shall be installed at the upslope side of chimneys or curbed roof penetrations when the chimney or curb is more than _____ inches wide.

- 24
- 36
- 48
- 60

15. There are _____ 22 x 12 slates in a square of roofing.

- 98
- 114
- 108
- 126

Drip edge should be nailed at about _____ inches on centers, slightly staggered.

- 6
- 12
- 10
- 8

Metal shingle roof systems may be secured using _____.

- Staples, screws or nails
- Staples, nails or clips and tabs
- Screws, nails or clips and tabs
- Staples, screws or clips and tabs

If a starter course of shakes consists of two layers, joints should be offset between neighboring units in the adjacent courses a minimum of _____ inches.

    3/4
    1
    1 1/4
    1 1/2

_____ is a natural, self-healing metal that weathers to a soft blue-gray patina.

    Stainless steel
    Terne
    Zinc
    Copper

For steep – to low-slope transitions, it is recommended that asphalt shingles be held back a minimum of _____ inches above the transition.

    8
    10
    12
    14

It is suggested that _____ be used when installing slate roofing.

    Galvanized nails
    Stainless steel nails
    A hot glue gun
    Copper-slating nails

When tapering a 16- foot open valley, the bottom of the valley will be _____ inches greater than at the top of the valley.

    4
    1
    2
    3

Water and ice-dam protection should be applied starting at a roof system's eaves and extend upslope to a point corresponding to a minimum _____ inches inside the exterior wall line of a building.

    22
    12
    24
    36

The common dimensions for standard three-tab shingles are _____.

    12" x 36"
    12" x 40"
    11" x 36"
    11" x 40"

It is recommended that valley metal for use with wood shakes or shingles be a minimum of _____ inches wide.

    12
    14
    18
    24

_____ flashings provide a weatherproof transition material where a roof area intersects a head wall.

    Step
    Apron
    Backer
    Counter

Counter-battens should be spaced not more than _____ on center when used with nominal 2-by-2 wood battens.

    12
    16
    18
    24

A type _____ clay or concrete tile has a rise-to-width ratio greater than 1:5.

    I
    II
    III
    IV

_____ is not a recommended to be used as a valley underlayment.

    Heavy weight felt
    Full-width sheet of polymer-modified bitumen
    Base sheet
    Self-adhering polymer-modified bitumen sheet

The minimum nominal thickness recommended for _____ roof shingles is 0.024 inches.

    Asphalt
    Aluminum
    Copper
    Zinc

Where wall cladding counterflashes wall flashing metal, the cladding material and water-resistive barrier should extend past and cover the top edge of the flashing metal a minimum of _____ inches.

    2
    4
    6
    8

_____ is the most common method of fastening tile.

    Nailing
    Screwing
    Clipping
    Mortaring

Each wood shingle should be fastened with _____ fastener (s) located approximately ¾ of an inch to ___ inch from the side edges.

    1
    2
    3
    4

No. 30 asphalt felt is commonly designated Type _____ by ASTM D4869 standards.

    I
    II
    III
    IV

Asphalt shingles classified according to ASTM D7158 as Class _____ are said to pass at a basic wind speed up to and including 150 mph.

    D
    F
    G
    H

1 Exam Prep
Answer Key - NRCA Steep-Slope Roof Systems

2017

1.	B	NRCA Steep-slope Roof Systems	53
2.	A	NRCA Steep-slope Roof Systems	68
3.	D	NRCA Steep-slope Roof Systems	72
4.	A	NRCA Steep-slope Roof Systems	74
5.	A	NRCA Steep-slope Roof Systems	71
6.	D	NRCA Steep-slope Roof Systems	211
7.	D	NRCA Steep-slope Roof Systems	379
8.	B	NRCA Steep-slope Roof Systems	72
9.	B	NRCA Steep-slope Roof Systems	586
10.	B	NRCA Steep-slope Roof Systems	73
11.	A	NRCA Steep-slope Roof Systems	70
12.	D	NRCA Steep-slope Roof Systems	104
13.	B	NRCA Steep-slope Roof Systems	576, Fig. 4-3
14.	A	NRCA Steep-slope Roof Systems	77
15.	D	NRCA Steep-slope Roof Systems	471
16.	B	NRCA Steep-slope Roof Systems	210
17.	C	NRCA Steep-slope Roof Systems	372
18.	D	NRCA Steep-slope Roof Systems	578
19.	C	NRCA Steep-slope Roof Systems	363
20.	B	NRCA Steep-slope Roof Systems	78
21.	D	NRCA Steep-slope Roof Systems	472
22.	A	NRCA Steep-slope Roof Systems	74
23.	C	NRCA Steep-slope Roof Systems	55
24.	A	NRCA Steep-slope Roof Systems	57
25.	D	NRCA Steep-slope Roof Systems	584
26.	B	NRCA Steep-slope Roof Systems	76
27.	D	NRCA Steep-slope Roof Systems	187
28.	A	NRCA Steep-slope Roof Systems	200
29.	A	NRCA Steep-slope Roof Systems	72
30.	B	NRCA Steep-slope Roof Systems	362
31.	A	NRCA Steep-slope Roof Systems	78
32.	A	NRCA Steep-slope Roof Systems	206
33.	B	NRCA Steep-slope Roof Systems	580
34.	D	NRCA Steep-slope Roof Systems	50
35.	D	NRCA Steep-slope Roof Systems	60

1 Exam Prep
2018 NRCA Architectural Metal Flashing, Condensation and Air Leakage Control
Questions and Answers

Roof systems designed for low slope applications are used when roof slopes are greater than _____.

- 1:12
- 2:12
- 3:12
- 4:12

_____ has a substantially higher coefficient of expansion than any other roofing metal except zinc.

- Copper
- Aluminum
- Lead
- Zinc

The use of _____ in roof system applications is limited because of the vulnerability of cut edges.

- Aluminized steel
- Copper
- Stainless steel
- Galvanized steel

Which metal is not one of the more common metal types used for copings?

- Copper
- Galvanized or Galvalume
- Zinc
- Extruded aluminum

NRCA recommends valley metal for use with wood shakes or shingles be a minimum of _____ wide.

- 10 inches
- 12 inches
- 14 inches
- 24 inches

Weatherproofing is the ability of a membrane or roof covering to prevent the passage of water with a limited amount of _____ pressure.

- Hydrokenesis
- Hydrostatic
- Non-hyrdostatic
- hydropulsive

The thermal conductance of asphalt shingles is _____ Btu/h•ft•^{2}F.

- 1.06
- 2.27
- 3.00
- 4.76

8. According to NRCA, a vapor retarder should be used when the coldest month is below 40° and the expected interior winter relative humidity is _____.

- 45% or greater
- 55% or greater
- 65% or greater
- 75% or greater

All of the following metals are solderable except for _____.

- Copper
- Lead
- Stainless Steel
- Galvalume

The minimum metal thickness of stainless steel drip edge metal to be used with a _____ roofing system is 24 gauge prefinished galvanized steel.

- Metal Shingle
- Asphalt Shingle
- Clay and Concrete Tile
- Wood Shake and Wood Shingle

Moisture in the form of water vapor can enter into buildings via _____ through the building envelope materials.

- Condensation
- Permeability
- Conductance
- Overflow drainage

12. _____ provide a hidden method for the anchorage of sheet metal components.

Copings
Cleats
Clips
Fasteners

13. Which of the following statements is not true when describing a scupper?

They can be the primary or secondary source of drainage.
They are typically installed at roof edges.
They may be used to direct drainage from one roof to another.
They should be a minimum of 1/2" thick.

14. Many low slope roof assemblies are _____.

Self-drying
Water shedding
Undesirable in humid climates
Always installed with a vapor barrier

15. When selecting vapor retarder materials, the following information should be considered.

Insulation type
Roofing system
Type of adhesives used
The winter relative humidity

16. The design winter dry bulb temperature for West Palm Beach, Florida is _____.

A. 0° F
   43° F
   32° F
   78° F

17. When metal counterflashing is used at wall, _____.

The reglet is inset into a raggle
The Raggle is set in the reglet
The raggle only is used
The reglet only is used

18. Plastic sheet vapor retarder perm ratings generally range from ____ to _____ perms.

A. .5 to .6
B. .05 to .70
C. .08 to .10
D. .12 to .14

Flashing on the front, or downslope, side of a dormer or chimney is called _____ flashing.

- Step
- Apron
- Counter
- Base

The use of a vapor retarder is recommended when temperatures are expected to be below _____ for the average temperature during the coldest month.

- 32 degrees °F
- 40 degrees °C
- 40 degrees °F
- 32 degrees °C

Which one of the following is not classified as an insulation board?

- Fiberglass
- Vermiculite
- Cellular glass
- Perlite

Carbon steel, _____, and electroplated galvanized steel fasteners and connectors should not be used in contact with treated wood.

- Zinc
- Aluminum
- Copper
- Terne

A Class II vapor retarder has a permeance of _____.

- 1.0 perm or less and greater than 0.1 perm

- 1.0 perm or less and greater than 1.0 perm
- Greater than 1.0 perm

24. Asphalt shingles have an R-value of _____.

- A. .17
- B. .06
- C. .78
- D. .44

_____ fasteners are recommended for use on treated wood for maximum corrosion resistance.

- Copper
- Galvanized steel
- Aluminum
- Stainless steel

Miami-Dade county in Florida is located in US Climate zone _____ .

- 1A
- 2A
- 3A
- 4A

The time rate of vapor transmission through a material is measured in _____.

- Bulk ratings
- Perms
- Degrees
- Grains

According to NRCA, a gutter bracket made of galvanized steel should measure _____

- 1/8 inch by 1 inch
- 3/16 inches by 1 inch
- 3/8 inch by 1 inch
- 1/4 inch by 1 1/2 inches

End-lap joining of A-type edge metal can be accomplished by one of the following methods.

- Cover plates
- Overlap joint
- Membrane coated metal joint
- All of the above

The outside dimension of the outlet tube is typically _____ of an inch less than the inside dimension of the downspout.

- 1/8
- 3/8
- 5/8
- ½

Please see answer key on the following page

1 Exam Prep
2018 NRCA Architectural Metal Flashing, Condensation and Air Leakage Control
Answers

1. C 195
2. B 20
3. A 21
4. C 47
5. D 97
6. B 329
7. B 273
8. A 198
9. D 44
10. C 86
11. B 185
12. B 36
13. D 71
14. B 197
15. A 211
16. B 279
17. A 69
18. B 210
19. B 97
20. C 198

B328, 299, 306, 315

22.	B	107
23.	A	190
24.	D	220
25.	D	39
26.	A	262
27.	B	190
28.	A	79
29.	D	57
30.	A	92

1 Exam Prep

NRCA Waterproofing Manual

1. Butyl rubber waterproofing membranes consist of _____

    Factory-fabricated sheets of standard grade butyl rubber
    Factory-fabricated sheets of high grade butyl
    Factory-fabricated sheets of reinforced grade butyl rubber
    Factory-fabricated sheets of grade butyl rubber

During extremely hot weather, installation of the protection course and backfilling should be done within how many hours?

8
12
24
48

When applying the protection course of PVC membrane avoid all _____

Evidence of moisture
Excessive heat
Cold weather below 50 degrees
Unnecessary traffic

Fluid-applied elastomer shall comply with _____

OSHA
FBC 2001
ASTM C 836
NRCA 2003

Water exerts a pressure of _____ per foot of depth?

8.33 pounds per square foot
8.33 pounds per cubic foot
62.4 pounds per square foot
62.4 pounds per cubic foot

According to the NRCA to resist 20 feet of head, the number of coal-tar plies required is _____

- 1
- 2
- 3
- 4

Coal tar used in waterproofing differs from coal tar used in roofing in which way?

- lower softening point temperature
- lower flash point temperature
- different physical properties
- All of the above

Marine grade plywood is made entirely of _____.

- Birch and Douglas-Fir
- Douglas-Fir and Western Larch
- Western Larch and Pine
- Pine and Birch

Compacted earth or drainage rock should be compacted by _____.

- 35% - 40%
- 50% - 60%
- 85% - 90%
- None of the above

Which of the following waterproofing materials are appropriate for use beneath slabs below grade where an appropriate substrate (e.g. compacted earth, nonreinforced concrete slab) is in place before the installation of the waterproofing membrane:

- Bentonite
- Cementitous waterproofing
- Crystalline waterproofing
- Fluid-applied elastomeric materials

ANWSER KEY

1	C	NRCA Waterproofing Manual, 2005	44
2	C	NRCA Waterproofing Manual, 2005	45
3	A	NRCA Waterproofing Manual, 2005	45
4	C	NRCA Waterproofing Manual, 2005	46
5	C	NRCA Waterproofing Manual, 2005	32
6	D	NRCA Waterproofing Manual, 2005	40
7	D	NRCA Waterproofing Manual, 2005	41
8	B	NRCA Waterproofing Manual, 2005	39
9	C	NRCA Waterproofing Manual, 2005	39
10	A	NRCA Waterproofing Manual, 2005	37

1 Exam Prep
Roofing Construction and Estimating Questions

Note: Some questions may need to reference the diagrams at the end of the test.

The roof is 60 feet by 30 feet measured eave to eave. The height of the gable is 5 feet. The squares of shingle required to roof the residence is? (Refer to Diagram 1 on last page)

- 16
- 17
- 18
- 19

Eave to eave measurement is 40 feet. The gable is 8 feet high. The rise and run is?

- 3
- 4
- 5
- 8

In high wind areas the drip edge should be nailed on centers

- 8 inch
- 10 inch
- 6 inch
- 4 inch

When more than one piece is required to cover the eaves the lap should be how many inches?

- 12
- 8
- 6
- 3

If a roof leaks it is most likely to leak

- At the perimeter
- At a flashing point
- Under the membrane
- At a valley

There should be no fasteners within how many inches of a woven valley centerline?

- 12
- 10
- 8
- 6

Shingles can be installed on roofs as steep as

    5:12
    18:12
    21:12
    20:12

The minimum pitch for all shingle applications is

    2:12
    1/6
    1/12
    2:12

When installing a 6-inch pattern, remove how many inches from the second course?

    12
    8
    6
    4

When installing closed-cut valleys care should be taken to make sure shingle end joints are at least how many inches from the centerline of the valley?

    12
    10
    8
    6

Application of shingles in a closed-cut valley requires shingles extend at least how many inches beyond the valley centerline?

    12
    10
    8
    6

The minimum tons of mission tile to cover 2,000 square feet of roofing area is

    Less than 10
    Between 10 and 14
    Between 14 and 18
    More than 18

On roof slopes from 4:12 to 6:12 the tile requires

    Nailing with 2 nails and bulling
    Nailing with one nail only
    Fastening only
    Nailing with one nail in addition to using mortar

Before applying roofing over prestressed concrete decks many manufacturers recommend the installation of

2,500 psi concrete fill
1/2 inch thick protection board
3 inches of 2,500 psi concrete
2 inches of 2,500 psi concrete

Type IV asphalt on smooth surfaces lacks which of the following?

    Viscosity
    Self-healing properties
    Good adhesion in cold weather
    Good melt rates

Cold applied bitumens should be applied at a rate of how many gallons per square?

    1
    2
    3
    4

Over a non-nailable deck the recommended plies of 15-pound tar saturated felts in solid moppings of coal-tar bitumen is

    1
    2
    3
    4

The lack of expansion joints will cause roofing felt to

    Slip
    Split
    Blister
    Bubble

Expansion joints may be installed in all of the following except?

    The first third of the roof
    The last third of the roof
    In a valley
D   In the middle of the roof

20. Oakum applied prior to caulking is called

    Backer rod
    Filler
    Gapping
    Sealing

When temperatures do not exceed 125 degrees the type of asphalt to be used below grade is

    1
    2
    3
    4

To prevent chimneys from leaking the contractor should apply which of the following?

    A generous amount of roofing cement
    A small amount of roofing cement
    A flue collar
    A flue cap

23. A roof with a rake factor of 1.302 has a _____ slope in inches per foot.

    6
    8
    10
    11

A roof with a 5:12 slope has a hip factor of

    1.452
    1.474
    1.524
    1.732

Roofing nails should penetrate into deck lumber at least how many inches?

    1 1/2
    1/2
    12
    3/4

26. Drip edges should be made of corrosion resistant material and extend _____ inches back from the roof edge.

    A   3
    B   6
    C   9
    D   36

27. Flashing against a vertical sidewall is called

    Good practice
    Expensive
    Flashing shingles
    Step flashing

28. When applying roll roofing on the first course parallel to the eaves, end laps should be a minimum of _____ inches wide.

    6
    4
    2
    8

The first thing a professional roofer measures is

    Ridge
    Valley
    Shingle area
    Eaves

Placing nails in an area that will be covered by roofing materials is called

    Good practice
    Unusual
    Conceited nailing
    Blind nailing

31. When installing shingles using a 6" pattern, you must start the first course with a _____ shingle.

    A   Full
    B   Half
    C   Quarter
    D   Third of a

32. When trimming open valley shingles, leave _____ inches on each side of the valley for the water trough.

    1
    3
    5
    8

33. Trimming of a sharp valley corner is known as

    Good to do if the boss is watching
    Dubbing
    Clipping
    Expensive

34. On a new shingle roof, nails should be _____ inches long.

    1
    1 1/4
    1 1/2
    2 1/2

35. When reroofing over asphalt shingles, nails should be _____ inches long.

    2 1/2
    3
    1 1/2
    1

36. When roofing, use _____ penny nails for 24" shingles.

    3
    4
    5
    6

37. Wood shingles and shakes have wind uplift ratings up to _____ miles per hour.

    63
    80
    90
    130

Shakes 24" x 3/4" handsplit and resawn with 7 1/2" exposure will cover approximately _____ square feet per square.

    75
    65
    85
    100

39. Application of Spanish clay tile takes between _____ hours per square.

    1 - 2
    2 - 3
    3 - 4
    4 - 5

A roof 76 feet long, 152 feet wide has a ridgeline perpendicular to the 76-foot side. The height of the ridge is 19 inches above the roof edge. The slope of the roof is

    1/8 in 12
    IA in 12
    1/2 in 12
    1 in 12

Areas of loose membrane should be cut, heated and bonded to the substrate. An additional piece of the same material shall be installed beyond the area to be repaired extending a minimum of how many inches over the cut in all directions?

    6
    7
    8
    4

The removal of the corner of a shingle in a valley is called

    Bad practice
    Common practice
    Cropping
    Dubbing

43. No nail should be located closer than _____ inches to the valley center line.

    6
    12
    18
    24

Usually the maximum layers of shingles a roof can support is

    2
    3
    4
    9

45. Existing gypsum decks when re-roofed require _____ fasteners.

    Self-locking
    Cap or Tape
    Annular shank
    Nail-tite Type A

46. Fasteners should be long enough for the shank to penetrate through the roofing materials and at least _____ inch into the deck.

- 7/8
- 1
- 3/4
- 1/2

Corrosion resistant drip edges should extend how many inches back from the edge?

- 1
- 2
- 3
- 4

Roof planes butting against walls at the end of shingle courses should be protected by metal shingles called _____ flashing.

- Stop
- Step
- 5 x 5
- Bull

49. Drip edge should be fastened with nails a maximum of _____ inches on center.

- 12
- 10
- 8
- 6

50. A good roofer should always _____ when estimating a roof?

- Measure the roof
- Sketch the roof
- Secure the ladder
- Photograph the roof

51. The alignment of the top edge of the new shingles with the butt edge of the old shingles is known as

- Butt-up
- Butt-down
- Button-up
- Button-down

52. The placing of asphalt shingles over built-up roofing is

    Not allowed
    Allowed only in cold climates
    Allowed for less than 2 in 12
    Allowed

53. Shingling up the rakes followed by shingling across the roof is known as the _____ method.

    Hexagonal
    Octagonal
    Vertical
    Diagonal

The most common pitch for corrugation is

    3
    4
    5
    6

Vertical front wall flashing should extend up the wall a minimum of how many inches?

    3
    4
    5
    6

56. Prefabricated roof panels have a standard width of _____ inches?

    18
    24
    36
    42

57. The _____ penny nail is usually adequate for handsplit shakes.

    2
    4
    6
    8

A suggested valley flashing for metal roofs is

    Aluminum
    Terne
    Stainless steel
    Galvanized iron

One square of 18 inch X 3/8-inch straight shakes with 10 inches laid to weather will cover approximately _____ square feet.

  A   94
  B   135
  C   110
  D   118

60. All metal sheets heavier than 30 gauge are called _____ metal

  .   Flat
  A.   Round
  B.   Coil stock
  C.   Sheet

A The best way to apply a glass fiber-reinforced asphalt emulsion roof system is to

  A   Spray
  B   Rock
  A.   Roll
  B.   Mop

1 A type of glass fiber-reinforced asphalt emulsion roof is Type

  A   V
  B   IV
  C   III
  D   AB negative

63. Concealed roll roofing ridge nailing requires 2 nails _____ inches from the top of the strip.

  2.   6
  3.   8
  4.   5 3/4
  5.   5'/2

64. Corrosion resistant _____ should be used when blocking is not used.

  A   Staples
  B   Galvanized nails
  C   Edge clips
  D   Termination bars

7. When hot-mopping 90-pound material along the eaves, the top of the sheet should be

  A   Held in place
  B   Nailed
  C   Double mopped
  D   Ribbon mopped

66. Alignment of the top edge of new shingles with the butt edge of the old shingles is

    1   Butt up
    2   Butt out
    3   Butt in
    4   Butt down

67. A new 3-tab roof using a 6-inch pattern will require a full shingle on the _____ course.

    A   Third
    B   Fifth
    C   Sixth
    D   Seventh

68. According to Roofing Construction and Estimating, on new roll roofing work, use nails _____ inch/es long.

    A   7/8
    B   1
    C   1/4
    D   i/2

18. Roofing and Construction Estimating states the gage nail usually adequate for tile is

    A.   6
    B.   8
    C.   10
    D.   12

70. Ballast normally adds _____ pounds per square foot of dead load.

    7.   5
    8.   10
    9.   15
    10.   25

71. One square of 18-inch X 3/8ths inch True Edge shakes with 8 inches laid to weather will cover approximately _____ square feet.

    A.   56
    B.   53
    C.   70
    D.   80

72. Commercial standard slates up to 18 inches long should normally be fastened with _____ penny nails.

   15. 12
   16. 10
   17. 6
   18. 3

73. When trimming valley shingles, leave _____ inches on each side of the valley centerline.

   A. 1
   B. 3
   C. 5
   D. None of the above

A. On a new slate roof, nails should be how many inch/es longer than twice the thickness of the slate?

   1
   1 1/4
   1 1/2
   2

B. The weather check nearest the butt of the tile is called a

   Drain hole
   Bird's relief
   Air plug
   Nose lug

C. Roll roofing material used for valley flashing shall be installed with

   An 18 inch strip face down and a 36 inch strip face up
   A 36 inch strip face up
   A 36 inch strip face down and an 18 inch strip face down
   An 18 inch strip face up and a 36 inch strip face down

D. The first strip of mineral surfaced roll roofing used in open valley construction should be no wider than

   1.5"
   1.5'
   3.0'
   3.6"

E. For APA 48/24 sheathing the number of required panel clips between supports is?

   1
   2
   3
   4

79. The clipping of shingles at a 45-degree angle is

    C.   Smart
    D.   Code
    E.   Flubbing
    F.   Dubbing

2. When flashing soil stacks it is permissible to

    A.   Cut a lead sleeve flush with the top of the vent pipe
    B.   Cut a lead sleeve 4 inches longer than the vent pipe
    C.   Cut the lead sleeve below the vent pipe
    D.   Install a counterflashing lead cover with a hole no less than one inch smaller than the vent opening

3. Reroofing over old wood shingles requires nails how long?

    A.   1 inch
    B.   2 inches
    C.   1 1/2 inches
    D.   8 inches

4. The number of bundles per square for straight-split red cedar shakes measuring 18 inches by 3/8 inches is

    A.   4
    B.   5
    C.   19
    D.   16

5. The number of bundles of shakes required per square with 1/2 inch spacing, 11 V2 inch exposure use number one straight split true edge shakes is

    4.35
    4.94
    3.7
    4.24

A. The type of mortar to be used when setting tile is

    M
    N
    S
    0

85. The masonry trowel recommended for tile installation is

        12 inches
        10 inches
        8 inches
6 inches

A. The maximum wind velocity is not greater than 100 mph. The roof height is 30 feet to the ridge. The eaves course which of the following?

        Nail and clip
        Nail only
A.   Clip only
B.   2 12d nails

1. The required depth of ribs when using metal decking for a BUR substrate is

        1 inch
        1/2 inch
        1 1/2 inches
        2 inches

2. Tile installation on slopes 2 1/2 in 12

        Are not allowed
        Require mortar
        Require nails and clips
        Require 2 ply sealed underlayment

3. Taper-sawn 24-inch shakes on a new roof system require what type of nails?

        3d
        4d
        5d
        6d

4. A rafter extending diagonally from an outside corner of a building to a ridge board is a

        Valley rafter
        Hip rafter
        Jack rafter
        Support rafter

5. In high wind areas the drip edge should be nailed on center how many inches apart?

        2
        6
        8
        12

92. In high wind areas joints should be lapped at least how many inches?

    2
    3
    4
    6

243. Valley centerlines should be increased to widen how many inches per foot going down the valley?

    1/8
    1/4
    2
    6

244. Widening of valley centerlines is helpful because it

    Gives a better appearance increasing your chances of getting paid
    Lets ice free itself
    Allows rainwater to move freely
    Does not allow the accumulation of leaves

245. Asphalt shingles may be installed with roof slopes as low as

    2 in 12
    2½ in 12
    3 in 12
    4 in 12

246. Asphalt shingles require

    A solid deck
    A bottom layer
    Sunny climates
    Heat index factors

97. The most widely used type of asphalt shingle is the

    Strip
    3-tab
    Architectural
    Fiberglass

1. Closed-cut valley work requires the end shingle

    Be dubbed
    Be laced
    Extend beyond the valley centerline 12 inches
    Be woven

3. Number 1 straight-split 18 inch long shakes with 7 1/2 inch exposure requires how many bundles per square?

       3
       4
       5
       6

4. Hip and ridge bundles contain how many units per bundle?

       30
       40
       50
       60

5. When using the mortar-set method on roof slopes of 5 in 12 each eave tile requires how many nails in addition to using mortar?

       1
       2
       3
       Nails are not required

6. The minimum softening point for Type IV asphalt is

       205 degrees
       225 degrees
       275 degrees
       215 degrees

7. When re-roofing over wood, install shingles using the

       End to end method
       The butt-up method
       The toe to toe method
       The overlap method

8. Leaks often occur

       Around the house
       Around the chimney
       Along the roof edge
       Along the roof ridge

105. When re-roofing the Butt-up method means

   The roofers should be as close together as possible
   The tops of the old shingles are installed flush against the butts of the new shingles
   The tops of the new shingles are installed flush against the butts of the old shingles
   The new shingles butt the old shingles

451 The maximum width of plastic-bitumen composites is

   3 feet
   3 feet 7 inches
   4 feet
   33 feet

452 PVC is incompatible with which of the following?

   Bituminous material
   Polyvinyl chloride
   Chlorosulfonated polyethylene
   Chlorinate polyethylene

453 Mechanically fastened EPDM systems must penetrate how far into concrete decks?

   1 foot
   6 inches
   1 inch
   3/4 inch

- The maximum width of EPDM flashings is

   1/2 foot
   2 feet
   3 feet
   4 feet

- Edge flashing on slopes less than 1 in 12 requires priming on

   The bottom side only
   Both sides
   The top side only
   The contact side only

- Cold-applied bitumen emulsions should be applied at a rate of how many gallons per square?
   1
   2
   3
   4

112. Type IV asphalt has a softening temperature of

   7. 205 to 225 degrees
   8. 200 to 220 degrees
   9. 158 to 176 degrees
   10. 135 to 151 degrees

113. When flashing at vertical walls, the roofer should do which of the following?

   A   Lap the pan flashing over a lead apron to send the water runoff underneath the field tile
   Lap the pan flashing under a lead apron to send the water runoff back unto the field tile
   Lap the lead apron under the field tile to send the water runoff over the pan unto the flashing
   Lap the pan flashing over a lead apron to send the water runoff back unto the field tile

1. When installing battens on roof slopes of less than 6 in 12, the roofer should use

   4 foot long battens
   6 foot long battens
   4 foot long battens with 1/2 inch drain slots
   8 foot long battens with 1/2 inch drain slots

2. Open valleys require shingles be installed no closer than how many inches each side of centerline?

   3
   6
   12
   18

3. Given number one handsplit shakes with 22 inch exposure, the number of bundles required per square is

   9.09
   2.27
   4.17
   2.78

4. The vent jack should have skirting of

   2.25 square feet
   18" X 24"
   24" X 24"
   4 square feet

5. During the application of slate care should be taken to ensure proper jointing

   4. During the transit stage of the job
   5. Between 3 and six inches as near the bottom as possible
   6. Between 3 and six inches as near the top as
   7. Not less than 3 inches and as near the center as possible

119. Steel purlins are normally spaced

    2 feet on center
    2 feet edge to edge
    3 feet on center
    4 feet on center

1. Special steep asphalt softens at

    205 to 225 degrees
    180 to 205 degrees
    158 to 176 degrees
    135 to 151 degrees

2. The minimum parapet flashing where the deck is supported by the wall is

    4 inches
    6 inches
    8 inches
    12 inches

3. On roof slopes of less than 1 in 12 the roofer should

    Wear tennis shoes with self-gripping soles
    Wear a shoulder harness
    Prime the facing side of the flashing
    Prime both sides of the flashing

4. The minimum elevation of the expansion joint above the finished roof is

    .33 inches
    .33 feet
    6 inches
    8 inches

5. The test cut of the BUR system should be

    10 by 42 inches to the length of the felts
    12 by 36 inches at right angles to the felts
    24 by 10 inches at right angles to the felts
    42 by 10 inches at right angles to the felts

6. Mechanical fasteners should penetrate concrete decks at least

    1
    2
    3
    4

126. Mechanical fastening of the membrane installed over treated wood nailers should be

> 24 inches on center
> 16 inches on center
> 112 inches on center
> 8 inches on center

5. Tapered rigid insulation usually comes in lengths of how many feet?

> 2
> 3
> 4
> 8

6. The exposure width to the old shingles should be how many inches?

> 4
> 5
> 6
> 8

7. Flashing must be primed on both sides when the roof slope is less than

> 1:12
> 2:12
> 3:12
> 6:12

(b) Type IV asphalt softens at how many degrees?

> 210
> 225
> 158
> 135

(c) Which is not a type of downspout?

> Plain rectangular
> Corrugated rectangular
> Plain round
> Ogee

(d) The difference between gravel stop and eave drip is

- (b) There is no difference
- (c) Eave drip is usually a heavier gage
- (d) Gravel stop has a more pronounced lip
- (e) Gravel stop is usually a heavier gage

133. Tapered rigid insulation usually comes in widths of

    18 inches
    24 inches
    36 inches
    4 feet

1. Which of the following is especially vulnerable to leakage?

    Chimneys
    Eaves
    Valleys
    Counterflashing

2. On a wood roof, all may have a sheet metal patch except?

    Knots
    Large cracks
    Rotted wood
    Resinous areas

3. Who is responsible for fire equipment at the kettle?

    Employer
    Fire marshal
    Kettle worker
    Home owner

4. Polyvinyl chloride roofing material should not be exposed to

    Ozone
    Hydrogen
    Carbon products
    Ultraviolet light

5. Where a sloping roof meets a vertical wall, flashing must be at least how many inches high?

    8
    10
    12
    5

6. The percentage of roofing injuries attributable to hot bitumen work is

    10
    23
    44
    51

9. Roll roofing is to be installed over existing roofing materials. The insulation is damp. The roofer should

    A   Remove the damp insulation
    B   Install a roof vent every 100 square feet
    C   Run a fan over the wet areas for 24 hours
    D   Cut 2 foot by 2 foot squares in the roof

2. In damp areas where good ventilation is important clay tile roofs should have

    A   Double selvage
    B   A hot mop application
    C   A ballast system
    D   A counter batten system

3. For slate tile installed over copper crickets, the slate should lap the copper at least how many inches?

    A   2
    B   4
         6
         8

Which should not be soldered according to Roofing and Construction Estimating?

    Aluminum
    Copper
    Lead
    Nickel alloys

Coal tar is not recommended for roof slopes greater than

    1:12
    2:12
    3:12
    4:12

When checking for leaks on a tile roof, look for

    Broken or missing tiles
    Improper valley installation
    Excessively high ridge caps
    Worn downspouts

The flange under the tile course should extend immediately

    Above the pipe
    Below the pipe
    Around the pipe
    Adjacent to the pipe

147. Two joints of shakes should never line up in how many courses?

    1
    2
    3
    4

The exposure required for a 24 inch slate using a 5:12 installation is how many inches?

    7
    7 1/2
    8
    10

Nails used for roll roofing should be spaced how far apart?

    1 inch
    2 inches
    3 inches
    4 inches

A counter batten system of 1 X 2's should be mounted vertically

    Every 3 feet
    24 inches on center
    32 inches on center
    16 inches on center

The roofer **should allow no less than how** many inches for expansion when installing wood shingles?

    3/8
    1/2
    1/4
    5/8

According to Roofing and Construction Estimating, valley flashing metal shall

    Extend beyond the ridge
    Extend 12 inches beyond the ridge
    Extend 18 inches beyond the ridge
    Extend 24 inches beyond the ridge

153. **To construct an open valley, shingles at the upper end of an open valley should be** inches **apart at the centerline.**

    A   3
    B   6
    C   **9**
    D   12

Jimmy Joe is trimming the upper corner of shingles along the valley centerline at a 45 degree angle. The process of trimming the shingles is known as

    Trimming the shingles
    Dubbing
    Cropping
    Serration

The end lap when applying roll roofing parallel to the eaves using the concealed nail method should be how many inches?

    2
    4
    6
    8

Billy Ray is installing 24 inch tapersplit shakes. Billy Ray should use

    Stainless steel 5d box nails 1 3/4 inches long
    Blue 5d box nails 1 3/4 inches long
    Steel wire 5d common nails 1 3/4 inches long
    Bright 5d box nails 1 3/4 inches long

The slope of a woven valley should be limited to slopes of at least

    3 in 12
    4 in 12
C5 in 12
    6 in 12

In single layer applications, all felts should be lapped

    Vertically in shingle fashion a minimum of 2 inches
    Horizontally in shingle fashion a minimum of 3 inches
    Vertically in shingle fashion a minimum of 4 inches
    Horizontally in shingle fashion a minimum of 2 inches

When installing gravel stops Bobby Ray should

    Nail the gravel stop 4 inches on center
    Prime the face side of the gravel stop
    Prime both sides of the gravel stop on slopes of 1 in 12 or less
    Prime both sides of the gravel stop on slopes of less than 1 in 12

160. Test cuts for **BUR** systems should be at least

    10 X 24 inches
    12 X 24 inches
    12 X 36 inches
    10 X 42 inches

Tapered rigid insulation usually comes in

    2 foot by 2 foot dimension with a taper across the 2 foot dimension
    2 foot widths with a taper across the 2 foot dimension
    2 foot lengths with a taper across the 2 foot dimension
    2 foot and even increments to ten feet

Jimmy Joe installed the insulation using dead-level asphalt. Jimmy Joe is going to apply an **EPDM** roof membrane system. Jimmy Joe should

    Install a slip sheet between the membrane and the incompatible substrate
    Know that is not a recommended roofing application
    Never mix EPDM systems with any type of asphalt application
    Insure the dead-level asphalt is completely dry before installing the EPDM roof membrane system

A slip sheet is going to be used. PVC is compatible with all of the following except

    Bituminous material
    Foamed glass insulation
    Fully adhered modified bitumen
    Polystyrene insulation

According to Roofing and Construction Estimating, when installing a woven valley, the contractor should

    Use double underlayment
    Use 50 pound or heavier roll roofing
    Overlap the shingles at least 36 inches
    Nail the shingles 12 inches on center

According to Roofing and Construction Estimating, when installing a woven valley, the contractor should

    Extend the shingle 36 inches beyond the centerline
    Extend the shingle 12 inches beyond the hip line
    Use double underlayment 30 pound felt or higher
    Extend the shingle 12 inches beyond the valley centerline

166. When installing battens, the contractor can

- Nail the battens every 4 feet on center
- Use 4-foot long battens with 3/4 inch drain slots
- Shim the battens every 4 feet with 1/2 inch moisture-resistant lath strips
- Shim the battens every 4 feet with 1/4 inch moisture-resistant lath strips

When completing a T-lock shingle reroof, install the shingles

- 174 inch higher than the old shingles
- 1/4 inch lower than the old shingles
- 1/2 inch higher than the old shingles
- 1/2 inch lower than the old shingles

Roof tile is being installed in a valley using a two-ply underlayment system. Bobby Jo could use a

- 24 inch by 16 inch stainless steel skirt at the end of the valley
- 24 inch by 18 inch lead skirt at the end of the valley
- 24 inch by 16 inch lead skirt at the top of the valley
- 24 inch by 16 inch lead skirt at the end of the valley

The most common wood purlins used for corrugated steel panels are

- 1 x 4's or 2 x 4's spaced 24 to 48 inch on center
- 1 x 4's or 2 x 4's spaced 16 to 48 inch on center
- 2 x 4's or 2 x 6's spaced 16 to 48 inch on center
- 1 x 2's or 2 x 2's spaced 16 to 48 inch on center

The maximum slope of a BUR depends on

- The interply, surface bitumen and the roofing surface
- The slope, type of bitumen and the temperature
- The temperature, type of bitumen, local codes and common roofing practices
- The type of bitumen, roofing surface and insulation

According to Roofing and Construction Estimating, do not install pitch bitumen over roof slopes more than

- 1/8 in 12
- 14 in 12
- 1/2 in 12
- 1 in 12

According to Roofing and Construction Estimating, never install lightweight concrete decks on roofs with slopes greater than

- 1/8 in 12
- 1/4 in 12
- 1/2 in 12
- 1 in 12

The flash point of asphalt is

- When yellow smoke is emitted from the kettle
- The lowest temperature at which the asphalt gives off enough vapor to form an ignitable concentration
- When the kettle man turns red and starts choking, coughing and gagging
- When the kettle is opened too quickly thereby introducing excess oxygen to the surface of the asphalt

Cover all large cracks and resinous areas with

- Sheet metal
- 30 pound felt
- 90 pound felt
- 2 layers of 30 pound felt

In a closed valley

- The felt underlayment must be doubled in the valley area
- Flash the valley with a 36 inch-wide layer of mineral or smooth surfaced roll roofing (50 pounds or heavier)
- Metal flashing is the best choice
- Do not use asphalt plastic cement

No fasteners may be used within how many inches of centerline when flashing a closed-cut valley?

- 3
- 4
- 5
- 6

177. Shingles must extend at least _____ inches on each side of a woven valley.

- 6
- 8
- 10
- 12

178. Woven valleys should only be used when the roof slope is _____ or steeper.

       2 in 10
       4 in 10
       3 in 12
       4 in 12

To install shingles in a woven valley

       Trim the shingles two inches back from the valley centerline
       The felt underlayment must be doubled in the valley area
       Extend the shingles across the valley
       Shingle end joints should be at least 12 inches from valley centerline

180. No fasteners may be used within _____ inches of centerline in a woven.

       6
       5
       4
       3

Use a box nail to install a 24-inch tapersplit shake on a new roof.

       6d
       5d
       4d
       3d

182. Dead level asphalt or pitch can be heated safely to _____ degrees.

       400
       450
       475
       500

183. The slates are installed at the upper end of the valley to within two inches of each side of the valley centerline when installing a(n) _____ (slate) valley.

       Canoe
       Round
       Closed
       Open

Given four bundles of single-coursing No. 1 grade 16-inch wood shingles, the maximum recommended weather exposure for sidewall application is

    140 square feet applied at a 7-inch exposure
    150 square feet applied at a 7 1/2-inch exposure
    160 square feet applied at a 8-inch exposure
    170 square feet applied at a 8 1/2-inch exposure

185. Flat and steep asphalts can be heated safely to _____ degrees Fahrenheit.

    400 and 437
    437 and 450
    450 and 475
    475 and 500

186. Do not heat asphalt to within _____ degrees Fahrenheit of the flash point.

    50
    40
    35
    25

187. Mineral granules applied over mastic as roof surfacing should be deposited at the rate of _____ pounds per square.

    40 to 50
    50
    50 to 60
    60

188. Aluminum coating on a roof reduces the heat load by _____ percent, compared to dark-surfaced roofing.

    A   35
    B   40
    C   45
    D   50

189. Aluminum coating is applied at the rate of about _____ gallon(s) per square.

    1
    1 to 2
    2
    2 to 3

190. Aluminum coating can be _____ onto the roof surface.

      Brushed
      Cemented
      Nailed
      Rolled

When applying elastomeric roofing, brush-apply lap cement at the rate of one gallon per _____ linear feet for a three inch lap.

      175 to 225
      150 to 200
      125 to 175
      100 to 150

Before re-roofing, all large cracks, knotholes, loose knots and resinous areas in the deck should be?

      Covered with sheet metal patches nailed to the deck
      Filled and sealed
      Cleaned out and sealed
      Addressed

193. Type IV (special steep) asphalt softens at _____ degrees Fahrenheit.

      135 to 151
      158 to 176
      180 to 205
      205 to 225

One of the advantages of mineral surfaced roll roofing is

      It is inexpensive
      It will not buckle
      It will last a long time
      The variety of colors available

Application of step flashing against a vertical side requires underlayment to be carried up onto the sidewall at least

      2 to 3 inches
      3 to 4 inches
      4 to 6 inches
      6 to 8 inches

On closed-cut valleys, make sure the shingle end joints are at least **how many inches from the centerline of** a closed-cut or woven valley?

- 6
- 8
- 10
- 12

Eave tile should be set in

- Adhesive
- Mortar
- Grout
- Asphalt

The average weight of one square of mission tile is how many pounds?

- 1,250 to 1,350
- 1,100 to 1,200
- 800 to 1,600
- 900 to **1,000**

To pass the test, the weight of the test-cut components must be within what percent plus or minus of the specified requirements?

- 10
- 15
- 25
- 50

When applying double coverage underlayment on low slopes where icing along the eaves is anticipated, courses should be cemented to a point at least how many inches beyond the interior wall line?

- 6
- 12
- 18
- 24

The maximum length of roof battens without shimming is how many feet?

- 2
- 4
- 6
- 8

202. To allow for expansion and contraction, install a loose 4-inch glass fiber strip covered with?

> Type III asphalt
> A 16-inch Tedlar sheet
> Concrete or mortar barrier
> Lead slip sheet

Narrow EPDM sheets are usually

> Less than 3 feet wide
> 5 feet 6 inches wide
> 4 feet 8 inches wide
> More than 5 feet wide

Shingles applied in a closed cut valley require the shingle end to extend at least how many inches beyond the valley centerline?

> 3
> 6
> 8
> 12

Mineral surfaced roll roofing should be installed when the temperature is above how many degrees?

> 40
> 45
> 50
> 60

When shingling a woven valley, no fasteners should be within how many inches of the valley centerline?

> 3
> 6
> 8
> 12

Continuous flashing over unsealed underlayment requires

> A mortar installation at the eaves
> Flashing over unsealed underlayment
> Flashing under unsealed underlayment
> Asphalt barriers be installed with lead skirts

208. Slate headlap should be a constant

        3 inches
        6 inches
        1 foot
        18 inches

To ensure a snug fit it is good practice to

        Order pre-cut materials
        Hire a professional carpenter
        Miter the rake tiles
        Use lead soakers

The coverage for Number 1 handsplit and resawn 24 inch by 3/8ths inch shakes with 7 1/2 inch exposure is how many square feet per square?

        75
        80
        53
        65

According to Roofing Construction and Estimating, if battens are not raised or kerfed to allow drainage, they should not be longer than how many feet?

        4
        6
        8
        10

Leaks normally occur around counterflashing during blowing rain because?

        There is not enough asphalt sealer at the joint
        The counterflashing doesn't lap far enough over the base flashing
        The shingles are not dubbed in cement
        The nails do not penetrate the substrate far enough

According to Roofing Construction and Estimating, Type IV special steep asphalt softens at how many degrees Fahrenheit?

        135 to 151
        158 to 176
        180 to 205
        205 to 225

214. For open valleys, flash the valley with metal that's wide enough to extend at least

    A   4 inches under the slate
    B   6 inches under the slate
    C   8 inches under the slate
    D   12 inches under the slate

215. When the horizontal width of a chimney is greater than _____ feet, install a fabricated galvanized metal saddle flashing or a wooden cricket above the chimney.

    2
    2.5
    3
    3.5

When fabricating the flashing with water guards, the flashing should be anchored to the sheathing with

    Metal clips
    Tin clips
    Mortar
    Adhesive sealant

Ridge caps over standing-seam roofs are often installed over

    2 X 4 wood battens
    1 X 2 wood battens
    Double selvage
    Hot mop base sheathing

The maximum recommended exposure for a 4 in 12 roof using 16 inch Number 1 Blue Label wood shingles is how many inches?

    3
    5
    4
    6

According to Roofing Construction and Estimating when installing metal roofing flashing at a vertical wall, the pan should be bent how many degrees?

    90
    45
    30
    15

When shingling a woven valley, the end shingle should extend beyond the valley centerline at least how many inches?

- 3
- 6
- 8
- 12

The rule of thumb for adequate attic ventilation is

- 1 square foot of net free vent for each 150 square feet of vertical attic surface
- 1 square foot of net free vent for each 300 square feet of vertical attic surface
- 1 square foot of net free vent for each 150 square feet of horizontal attic surface
- 1 square foot of net free vent for each 300 square feet of horizontal attic surface

Cap flashing should extend into the mortar joint a minimum of how many inches?

- 1
- 1.5
- 2
- 2.5

When installing tile and flashing along the vertical wall

- Start at the low end and work up the slope lapping the upper piece at least 4 inches
- Start at the high end and work down the slope lapping the upper piece at least inches
- Start at the low end and work up the slope lapping the upper piece at least 6 inches
- Start at the low end and work up the slope lapping the upper piece at least 8 Inches

A vapor retardant base sheet should be installed when the outside winter temperature is how many degrees or less?

- 32
- 40
- 45
- 50

When measuring from the apex of the roof to the face edge of the first batten, the heads of the two tiles should not be more than how many inches apart?

- 1
- 2
- 3
- 4

226. Given a roof slope of 10 in 12 and a hip run of 12 feet, the actual length of any hip for the roof will be

    10 feet
    12 feet
    15.62 feet
    19.7 feet

Random wood shake patterns will require

    Nothing, use conventional pattern calculations
    Cut shakes
    Selecting thicker shakes
    Selecting thinner shakes

According to Roofing and Construction Estimating, it is a good practice when installing Stab shingles to use which material to flash valleys?

    Modified bitumen
    Mineral surfaced roll roofing
    Double 30 pound felt
    Metal flashing

The required test cut area should be

    12 inches by 12 inches
    12 inches by 18 inches
    10 inches by 42 inches
    18 inches by 36 inches

The roofer should allow how many inches of overhang along the rake fascia for the installation of wood shakes according to Roofing Construction and Estimating?

    .5
    1
    2
    3

When installing tile roofs according to Roofing Construction and Estimating, on slopes steeper than 6 in 12, you can use

    Double selvage
    Battens
    Ridge vents
    1-ply non-sealed system

232. Which is not a factor regarding end laps?

    Local code requirements
    Severity of the climate
    Slope of the chimney cricket
    The type of underlayment

When installing wood shingles over space sheathing, adjacent courses should be offset a minimum of how many inches?

    1
    1.5
    2
    3

When installing gravel stops over PVC flashing on roof slopes of less than 1 in 12

    Nail the flashing every 3 inches
    Prime the bottom side of the flashing
    Prime the top side of the flashing
    Prime both sides of the flashing

Number 1 Straight-split 18 inch by 3/8 inch shingles with an 8 inch exposure has an approximate coverage of how many square feet per square?

    100
    94
    80
    75

When flashing a valley according to Roofing and Construction Estimating, the contractor should install which of the following in the valley centerline?

    36 inch wide roll roofing, 50 pound or heavier
    18 inch wide 26 gage galvanized metal
    2 layers of 30 pound asphalt-saturated felt
    18 inch wide roll roof mineral side up

According to Roofing and Construction Estimating, the drip edge should be installed

    Under the felt along the eaves and under the underlayment along the rakes
    Over the felt along the eaves and under the underlayment along the rakes
    Over the felt along the eaves and over the underlayment along the rakes
    Under the felt along the eaves and over the underlayment along the rakes

238. The sealing out of water under pressure is called

       Hydrostatic head
       Hydrokenisis
       Blocking head
       Force majeure

To pass the test, the weight of the test-cut components must be within what percent plus or minus of the specified requirements?

       10
       15
       20
       25

The starter course for wood shingles according to Roofing and Construction Estimating should overhang beyond the eaves fascia

       1 inch
       1.5 inches
       1.75 inches
       2 inches

Ballasted EPDM systems are limited to a height of

       32 feet
       48 feet
       60 feet
       80 feet

A gutter is 3 inches by 4 inches. The total cross-sectional area is

       14 inches
       12 inches
       7 inches
       49 inches

When installing random-width slates, offset joints in adjacent courses at least

       1/2 foot
       3 inches
       2 inches
       1 inch

244. When test cutting BUR systems, test cut an area at least

        12 inches by 24 inches
        24 inches by 36 inches
        36 inches by 42 inches
        10 inches by 42 inches

Roofing and Construction Estimating recommends when a chimney is over two feet, install a

        Fabricated galvanized metal saddle
        5 X 5 metal pan flashing strip
        Wooden dormer extending at least 6 inches either side of the chimney
        26 gage metal apron

CPE roofing may be used with all of the following except

        Mechanical screws
        Heat-welds
        Coal-tar pitch
        Stainless steel nails

Termination bar should be mechanically fastened to the deck every

        6 inches
        12 inches
        24 inches
        3 feet

Which of the following may be used with EPDM systems?

        Seam caulk
        Coal tar
        Asphalt
        Oil-based roofing cement

Battens are required on roof slopes of

        6 in 12 and less
        8 in 12 and greater
        10 in 12
        7 in 12 and greater

A plywood index number of 32/16 means

        The plywood is 32 inches by 16 inches
        The plywood will span 32 inches between rafters and 16 inches between floor joists
        The plywood will span 16 inches between rafters and 32 inches between floor joists
        The plywood will hold 32 pounds and 16 ounces

251. EPDM membranes should never be installed with which of the following?

> Cold process
> Heat seal
> Plastic cement and dead level
> Ballast

Weepholes should be what size in diameter?

> 1/8 inch
> 1/4 inch
> 1/2 inch
> 3/4 inch

One of the drawbacks to using mineral surfaced roll roofing is

> The sun will cause deterioration problems after 3 years
> The granules will wash away over time
> Tears and rips are hard to repair
> A small tear will affect a large deck area

According to Roofing Construction and Estimating, a 54 inch horizontal wide chimney requires

> A wood saddle at the upper side of the chimney
> A copper flash at the low side of the chimney
> A galvanized iron cricket at the upper side of the chimney
> A metal apron on the terminal side of the cricket

Which of the following is not a single-ply roofing system?

> CPE
> PVC
> CSPC
> PIB

As a general rule, most gutters are usually any of the following inches wide except

> 2
> 4
> 5
> 6

The number of plies required for 20 feet of head is

> 1
> 2
> C3
> D4

258. The linear expansion for mild steel per 100 degrees is

    .00065
    .00128
    .00006
    .00173

According to Roofing Construction and Estimating, 1 X 2 wood battens 4 feet long should have ends separated by how many inches?

    1 inch
    2 inches
    1/2 inch
    3/4 inches

260 When installing wood shingles over spaced sheathing, the drip edge should extend

    1/2 inches
    3/4 inches
    1 inch
    1.5 inches

Type II flat asphalt may be used on slopes up to

    .5 in 12
    1 in 12
    1 1/2 in 12
    2 in 12

Roof slopes of less than 6 in 12 use

    8 foot battens with 1/2 inch drain slots
    4 foot double battens with drain slots every 4 feet
    8 foot battens with 1/2 inch drain slots
    4 foot battens with 1/2 inch drain slots between ends

Mission tile weighs approximately how many pounds per square?

    800
    900
    1,000
    1,300

What pattern is normally used for a hip roof when using three tab shingles?

    4 inch
    5 inch
    6 inch
    Straight-Up

265. The top thin edge of a wood shake shingle is called the

    tab
    toe
    tail
    butt

266. When re-roofing over wood or asphalt shingles always use the _____ method to assure a smooth roof.

    straightly
    stair-step
    diagonal
    butt-up

267. The best type o contract, according to Roofing Construction and Estimating, for gravel tear-off is a _____ contract.

    cost plus
    lump sum
    unit price
    open-end

According to Roofing Construction & Estimating, T-Lock shingles require two nails per shingle: They should be located _____ inches from the edge and _____ inches above the cutout.

    2 - 2
    1 - 2
    3 - 1
    1 - 1

269. Any time the width of a chimney exceeds _____ feet a metal saddle flashing should be installed.

    2
    3
    4
    6

According to Roofing Construction & Estimating, nails placed in an area that will be covered by a shingle is called

    blind nailing
    face nailing
    butt nailing
    edge nailing

According to Roofing Construction & Estimating, the term given to a triple layer of shingles used for visual distinction is called a

    ribbon or shadow course
    pattern line
    saddle flashing
    starter course

According to Roofing Construction & Estimating, metal flashing for fireplaces and chimneys should extend out onto the shingles at least _____ inches.

    3
    4
    5
    6

273. Roofing Construction & Estimating, the full face or woven valley method can be used on most roofs that have a pitch of _____ or steeper.

    2 in 12
    3 in 12
    4 in 12
    5 in 12

According to Roofing Construction & Estimating, when using 'W' shaped formed metal valleys on asphalt shingle roofs, trim the shingles to leave about _____ on each side of the hump for the water trough.

    1 inch
    1 - 1/2 inches
    2 inches
    2 - 1/2 or 3 inches

Roofing Construction & Estimating, on a new roof, the nails used to install strip or individual shingles should be _____ long.

    7/8"
    1"
    1 - 1/4"
    1 - 1/2"

One square of 18" x 1/2" to 3/4" handsplit and resawn cedar shakes installed with a 6-1/2" weather exposure will cover approximately _____ square feet of roof area. Select the closest answer.

    55
    65
    75
    100

277. According to Roofing Construction & Estimating, when applying shakes with a 10 inch exposure, nails should be driven about _____ inches above the butt line of the next course.

    7-1/2 to 8 inches
    10 to 12 inches
    1-1/2 to 2 inches
    3/4 to 1 inch

Roofing Construction & Estimating, one roofer and one laborer can install one square of field tile at the rate of _____ hours.

    1 to 2
    2 to 3
    3 to 4
    4 to 5

279. For BUR construction, plywood should be a minimum of _____ thick, for rafters spaced 24 inches on center.

    A. 13/32"   B. 7/16"   C. 15/32"   D. 1/2"

280. The roof should be loaded by stacking bundles of shingles

    A. Along the edges   B. Anywhere on the roof
    C. Along the ridge   D. Along any horizontal space

281. Per RCE, asphalt on fiberglass shingles should never be used on a roof with a pitch of _____ or under.

    A. 5/12   B. 4/12   C. 3/12   D. 2/12

282. The drip edge should run beyond the corner of the roof _____ inches.

    A. 1-2   B. 2-3   C. 3-4   D. 4-6

283. _____ are the most vulnerable areas of shingle and shake roofs and should receive the most care.

    A. Dormers   B. Valleys   C. Fascias   D. Flashings

284. _____ is one of the least expensive metal valley flashing materials and therefore, most often used.

    A. Aluminum   B. Copper   C. Zinc   D. Tin

285. The most widely used type of asphalt shingle is

    A. Two tab strip   B. Three tab strip
    C. Individual American   D. Two tab hexagonal

How many three-tab shingles that carry a 15 year warranty and measure 36" long x 12" wide are there in are there in a square?

   A. 64 — 90   B. 65 — 80   C. 65 — 95   D. 72 —120

287. A term for applying shingles diagonally is the _____ method.

   A. Stair — step   B. Straight up   C. Laced   D. Drift — down

288. For open valley application trimming off corners of shingles is referred to as

   A. Skimping   B. Chalking   C. Dubbing   D. Sizing

289. A full lace valley can be used on roofs that have a pitch of or _____ steeper.

   A. 2/12   B. 3/12   C. 4/12   D. 5/12

290. A water diverter used on the high side of a chimney, usually metal, is

   A. Counter flashing   B. Saddle flashing
   C. Standard flashing   D. Simple flashing

291. On new shingle roofs use nails, _____ inch(es) long.

   A. 1   B. 1-1/4   C. 1-1/2   D. 1-3/4

292. According to the NRCA. when applying roll roofing using the concealed nail method; _____ inch strips of asphalt material should be installed along the eaves and rakes.

   A. 4   B. 9   C. 12   D. 18

293. Placing nails in an area to be covered by shingles is _____ nailing.

   A. Laced   B. Counter   C. Nee   D. Blind

Selvage double coverage roll roofing is produced as a inch wide sheet and may be used on slopes down to inches per foot.

   A. 17-2   B. 19-1   C. 34-2   D. 36-1

295. Fire retardant shakes must be installed over a solid deck of _____ inch thick minimum ply-wood or equivalent materials to earn a class "B" fire rating.

   A. 1/4   B. 1/3   C. 1/8   D. 1/2

296. When applying the first row of shakes on top of the starter shakes, select only shakes that will permit you to offset the joints of the starter at least _____ inch(es)

   A. 1   B. 1-1/4   C. 1-1/2   D. 1-3/4

According to the NRCA, when applying wood shingles, spacing between adjacent shingles should be no more than

    A. 1/4"   B. 3/8"   C. 1/2"   D. 3/4

298. On wood shingles with a 5 inch exposure, nail about _____ inches from the bottom edge of the shingle.

    A. 2   B. 5   C. 7   D. 10

299. On wood shingles drive the nail about _____ inches above the butt of the succeeding course.

    A. 1/2-1   B. 1-1 1/2   C. 1 1/2-2   D. 2-2 1/2

300. 18" x 3/4" no. 1 handsplit and resawn shakes with a 7'/2" weather exposure have a _____ square foot coverage per square of shakes.

    A. 60   B. 65   C. 70   D. 75

301. When installing hip and ridge tiles, the tiles should lap at least _____ inches.

    A. 1 1/2   B. 2   C. 2-1/2   D. 3

302. Spanish clay roof tile should take an average of _____ man-hours per square to install, on an average roof, per the National Construction Estimator.

    A. 2 to 3   B. 1 to 2   C. 3 to 4   D. 5 to 6

303. The total number of pieces of 14" x 8" slate needed per square when laid with a 3 inch head lap is _____ pieces.

    A. 290   B. 327   C. 374   D. 654

304. On roofs that slope more than 1/2 in 12, seal joints of flat seams of most metals with

    A. Solder   B. Spiral bending tools
    C. Caulking compound   D. Folding and nailing

305. Which of the following has the greatest coefficient, of thermal expansion?

    A. Steel   B. Copper
    C. Aluminum   D. Zinc

306. Don't apply aggregate surfacing to roofs with slopes over _____ inches per foot.

    A. 2   B. 3   C. 4   D. 5

307. According to the NRCA, it is essential that positive drainage be designed into a surface that is to be waterproofed. A minimum slope of _____ per foot is recommended.

    A. 1/16 inch   B. 1/8 inch   C. 1/4 inch   D. 1/2 inch

308. Steel decks shall be a minimum of _____ gage steel.

    A. 26   **B. 24**   C. 22   D. 20

309. Poured gypsum concrete decks should have a minimum thickness of _____, not including the formboard.

    A. 1"   **B. 1-1/2"**   C. 2"   D. 3"

A should be mechanically fastened over all structural cement fiber panel roof deck prior to **installation of insulation board.**

    A. a layer of sheet metal   B. fiberglass membrane
    C. layer of fiberboard   **D. base sheet**

311. The softening **point of type III asphalt used in roofing should be** _____ degrees Fahrenheit maximum.

    A. 135-151   **B. 158-176**   C. 180 205   D. 210 225

312. The EVT is the temperature at which asphalt will attain optimum viscosity for **mechanical spreader application. Apply the roofing bitumen** within _____ degrees Fahrenheit of the **EVT.**

    A. 10   B. 15   **C. 20**   D. 25

313. The least common aggregate for the surfacing of built-up roofs is

    A. **Gravel**   B. Slag   C. Limerock   **D.** Crushed rock

The **roof expansion joints are necessary in order to**

    To assist in distribution of superimposed loads.
    To accommodate movement of roof assemblies due to thermal movement.
    To control possible leakage.
    None of the above.

315. **When repairing splits, blisters, alligatoring & fishmouths, the patch should be** _____ inches wider than the area **you are repairing.**

    A. 2   **B. 4**   C. 6   **D. 7**

316. Lightweight insulated concrete roof decks must have a minimum thickness of _____ inches.

    A. 1   B. 1 1/4   C. 2   **D. 3**

317. Lightweight insulates concrete decks must have a minimum compressive strength of _____ pounds per square inch.

    A. 50-75   B. 75-100   C. 100-125   D. 125-500

318. Special Kraft-faced fiberglass balls come in 2 thickness and are _____ inches wide and _____ inches long.

    A. 12-24   B. 24-36   C. 30-40   D. 24-48

319. A U-Value of 0.17 will equal _____ R Value.

    A 6.25   B. 5.88   C. 5.56   D. 5.26

320. Given: A roof system has the following "R" values:
    Outside Air   0.17
    Built-up Roof   0.33
    Insulation   8.33
    Dead Air Space   0.94
    Ceiling Tile   1.62
    Inside Air Film   0.61

The overall "U" factor of the above roof system is

    A. 0.008   B. 0.08   C. 0.12   D. 0.80

Most leaks occur around vents in about every type of roof, usually because of

    Inadequate shingling around a vent
    Improper flashing
    Vent flashing not as wide as it should be
    All of the above

322. Normally _____ shingle roofs are the maximum allowed on any structure.

    A. 1   B. 2   C. 3   D. 4

323. The roofing RCE book recommends that the first shingle course of a "butt — up" roof have _____ inches cut off the top of the shingle for 5 inch shingle exposure.

    A. 0   B. 1   C. 2   D. 3

Is it permitted to reroof a home with wood shingles over wood shingles?

    No
    Yes
    In all areas except wet climates
    In southern states only

325. At least a _____ gauge metal should be used for gutters and downspouts.

    A. 26   B. 28   C. 24   D. 30

Reference Diagram 2 at end of test for questions 326 - 332

326. The total length of the ridge is _____ feet.

    A. 120   B. 150   C. 180   D. 210

327. The total length of the valleys is

    A. 45.9   B. 89.4   C. 90.0   D. 91.8

328. The total net area of the roof is _____ squares.

    A. 59.5   B. 62.5   C. 65.5   D. 68.5

329. The total length of the rake required is _____ feet.

    A. 60.0   B. 69.5   C. 90.0   D. 120.0

330. The total length of hips is _____ feet.

    A. 23.3   B. 30.4   C. 91.8   D. 123.8

331. The total length of the drip edge required for the building is _____ feet.

    A. 420   B. 430   C. 440   D. 450

What is the surface area of the roof portion bordered by the valleys (between the wings)? Select the closest answer.
    A. 2250 sf   B. 2425 sf   C. 2600 sf   D. 2275 sf

The following questions are not multiple choice. Test your knowledge

What is the formula for figuring the slope of a roof?

The roof slope factor for a 5/12 roof slope is:

It is recommended that you install shakes or wood shingles over solid sheathing when the average expected low temperature will be below:

What is the widest board recommended for solid roof sheathing?

What is the proper spacing of wood shingles when installed on non-continuous 1 x 4 sheathing?

The purpose for underlayment for sloping roofs:

What is drip edge attached to?

How is drip edge installed at an eave end?

The underlayment should lap:

When water backs up under shingles and begins leaking into ceilings as a result of freeze/thaw cycles of snow, this is known as:

What is not a method used for ice protection of asphalt and fiberglass roofing?

What is the name of the agency that determines the fire rating for asphalt roofing?

How many nails are typically required for a three-tab asphalt shingle?

When nailing down asphalt shingles: Always drive the nail straight.

Approximately how many pounds of nails are required per square for asphalt shingles?

If the exposure for three-tab fiberglass shingles is five inches, the head lap would normally be how many inches.

What is the recommended procedure for installing roll roofing?

How many bundles are in a square of Blue Label cedar shingles?

The side lap or offset for wood shingles or shakes should be how many inches?

Concrete tiles weigh how much per square?

What is the overlap for a metal cap overlap over a field tile?

What type of flashing is used for open valleys on a slate roof?

The weight of a coated vapor retarder for a built-up roof is usually between:

The life expectancy of properly installed aggregate-surfaced BUR system is:

What type of flashing is used for open valleys on a slate roof?

How many lbs of asphalt bitumen are required per square between felts with an application tolerance of plus or minus 15 percent?

What is the most common type of asphalt for roofing?

What is the maximum temperature to which you can heat TYPE III asphalt?

What is the flash point for asphalt roofs?

An asphalt emulsion is applied to a bitumen roof with a slope of 4:12. How many be used to cover 1 square?

A properly installed aggregate-surfaced BUR system has a life expectancy of how

The purpose of surface aggregate for BUR system is all of the following except:

In built up roofs, cant strips shall extend how many inches up the vertical surface?

Do you have to insulate under a wood frame floor?

The best way to identify a roof leak is to:

What is the correct way to repair an asphalt shingle?

What is the major cause of a leaky vent pipe?

To repair an asphalt shingle:

Warm weather is the best time to repair asphalt shingles because:

Where is a leak most likely to occur on a roof? Around a vent pipe.

What area are leaks most likely to occur with a wood shingle roof?

gallons of material will

many years?

The best time to repair asphalt shingles is during warm weather because:

What is the correct procedure to replace a broken roof slate?

At what point is a wood shake or shingle roof is considered beyond repair?

What is the most common type of venting for a hip roof?

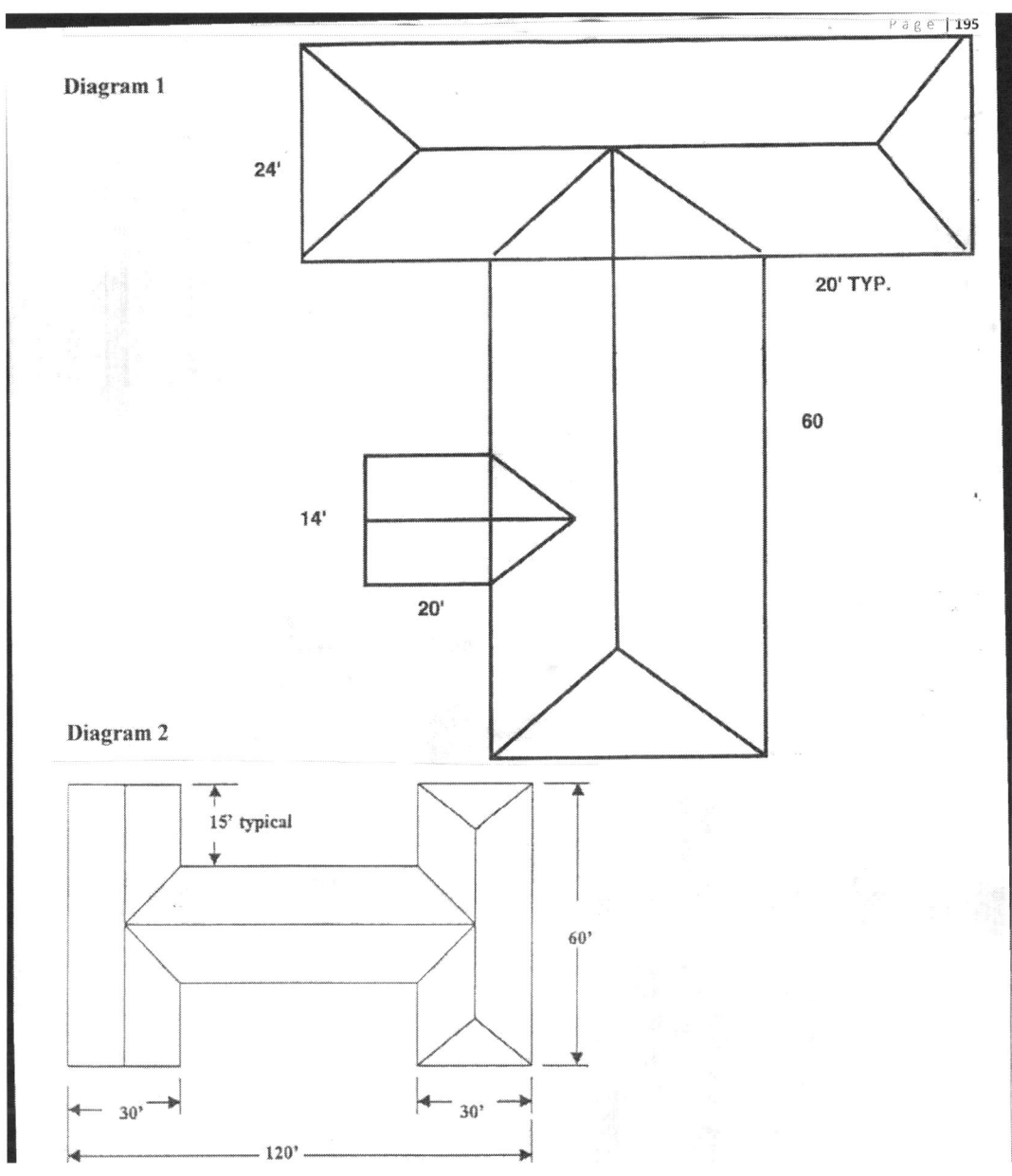

ROOF PLAN WITH A UNIFORM 7 IN 12 RISE AND RUN

ANSWER KEY

#	Ans	Topic	Page
1.	D	Roofing and Construction Estimating	11

Step 1.   Height ÷ Common Run X   12 = Rise to Run
         5   ÷   15   X   12 = 3.9 = 4 to 12

Step 2   Length X Width X Flat Area Factor ÷ 100 = Squares
         60   X 30   X   1.054   ÷ 100 = 18.97

#	Ans	Topic	Page
2.	C	Roofing and Construction Estimating	11

         Height ÷ Common Run X 12 = Rise to Run
         8   ÷   20   X 12 = 5 in 12

#	Ans	Topic	Page
3.	D	Roofing Construction and Estimating	40
4.	D	Roofing Construction and Estimating	40
5.	D	Roofing Construction and Estimating	64
6.	D	Roofing Construction and Estimating	67
7.	C	Roofing Construction and Estimating	76
8.	B	Roofing Construction and Estimating	77
9.	C	Roofing Construction and Estimating	82
10.	B	Roofing Construction and Estimating	90
11.	A	Roofing Construction and Estimating	91
12.	B	Roofing Construction and Estimating	198
13.	D	Roofing Construction and Estimating	204
14.	D	Roofing Construction and Estimating	296
15.	B	Roofing Construction and Estimating	304
16.	C	Roofing Construction and Estimating	305
17.	D	Roofing Construction and Estimating	315
18.	B	Roofing Construction and Estimating	319
19.	C	Roofing Construction and Estimating	321
20.	A	Roofing Construction and Estimating	369
21.	B	Roofing Construction and Estimating	373
22.	D	Roofing Construction and Estimating	382
23.	C	Roofing Construction & Estimating	15
24.	B	Roofing Construction & Estimating	15
25.	D	Roofing Construction & Estimating	106
26.	A	Roofing Construction & Estimating	40

#	Ans	Reference	Page
27.	D	Roofing Construction & Estimating	99
28.	A	Roofing Construction & Estimating	135
29.	D	Roofing Construction and Estimating	6
30.	D	Roofing Construction and Estimating	137
31.	A	Roofing Construction and Estimating	82
32.	B	Roofing Construction and Estimating	89
33.	B	Roofing Construction and Estimating	89
34.	B	Roofing Construction and Estimating	106
35.	C	Roofing Construction and Estimating	106
36.	B	Roofing Construction and Estimating	167
37.	D	Roofing Construction and Estimating	160
38.	A	Roofing Construction and Estimating	175
39.	C	Roofing Construction and Estimating	229
40.	B	Roofing and Construction Estimating	11

Height in feet ± Common Run X 12 = Rise

1.583 ±   76   X 12 = .25

#	Ans	Reference	Page
41.	A	Roofing Construction & Estimating	330
42.	D	Roofing Construction & Estimating	89
43.	A	Roofing Construction & Estimating	67
44.	B	Roofing Construction & Estimating	394
45.	D	Roofing Construction & Estimating	294
46.	C	Roofing Construction & Estimating	106
47.	C	Roofing Construction & Estimating	40
48.	B	Roofing Construction & Estimating	99
49.	B	Roofing Construction & Estimating	40
50.	B	Roofing Construction and Estimating	6
51.	A	Roofing Construction and Estimating	395
52.	D	Roofing Construction and Estimating	398
53.	D	Roofing Construction and Estimating	83
54.	A	Roofing Construction and Estimating	271
55.	C	Roofing Construction and Estimating	101
56.	D	Roofing Construction and Estimating	277
57.	C	Roofing Construction and Estimating	167

58.	D	Roofing Construction and Estimating	261
59.	D	Roofing Construction and Estimating	175
60.	D	Roofing Construction & Estimating	255
61.	A	Roofing Construction & Estimating	305
62.	A	Roofing Construction & Estimating	305
63.	D	Roofing Construction & Estimating	139
64.	C	Roofing Construction & Estimating	29
65.	B	Roofing Construction & Estimating	48
66.	A	Roofing Construction and Estimating	395
67.	D	Roofing Construction and Estimating	82
68.	B	Roofing Construction and Estimating	106
69.	C	Roofing Construction and Estimating	205
70.	B	Roofing Construction & Estimating	337
71.	A	Roofing Construction and Estimating	175
72.	D	Roofing Construction and Estimating	245
73.	B	Roofing Construction and Estimating	89
74.	A	Roofing Construction and Estimating	245
75.	D	Roofing Construction and Estimating	198
76.	A	Roofing Construction and Estimating	68
77.	B	Roofing Construction and Estimating	68
78.	B	Roofing Construction and Estimating	28
79.	D	Roofing Construction and Estimating	89
80.	A	Roofing Construction and Estimating	101
81.	B	Roofing Construction and Estimating	106
82.	B	Roofing Construction and Estimating	163
83.	B	Roofing Construction and Estimating	175
84.	A	Roofing Construction and Estimating	206
85.	B	Roofing Construction and Estimating	206
86.	A	Roofing Construction and Estimating	205
87.	C	Roofing Construction and Estimating	293
88.	D	Roofing Construction and Estimating	200
89.	D	Roofing Construction and Estimating	167
90.	B	Roofing Construction and Estimating	14

91.	A	Roofing Construction and Estimating	40
92.	B	Roofing Construction and Estimating	40
93.	A	Roofing Construction and Estimating	89
94.	B	Roofing Construction and Estimating	89
95.	A	Roofing Construction and Estimating	76
96.	A	Roofing Construction and Estimating	76
97.	B	Roofing Construction and Estimating	78
98.	C	Roofing Construction and Estimating	91
99.	D	Roofing Construction and Estimating	175
100.	B	Roofing Construction and Estimating	178
101.	A	Roofing Construction and Estimating	204
102.	A	Roofing Construction and Estimating	304
103.	B	Roofing Construction and Estimating	395
104.	B	Roofing Construction and Estimating	382
105.	C	Roofing Construction and Estimating	395
106.	B	Roofing Construction and Estimating	344
107.	A	Roofing Construction and Estimating	343
108.	C	Roofing Construction and Estimating	340
109.	D	Roofing Construction and Estimating	344
110.	B	Roofing Construction and Estimating	317
111.	C	Roofing Construction and Estimating	305
112.	A	Roofing Construction and Estimating	304
113.	D	Roofing Construction and Estimating	217
114.	C	Roofing Construction and Estimating	200
115.	A	Roofing Construction and Estimating	89
116.	B	Roofing Construction and Estimating	175
117.	A	Roofing Construction and Estimating	220
118.	D	Roofing Construction and Estimating	234
119.	D	Roofing Construction and Estimating	256
120.	A	Roofing Construction and Estimating	304
121.	C	Roofing Construction and Estimating	312
122.	D	Roofing Construction and Estimating	317
123.	B	Roofing Construction and Estimating	321

124.	D	Roofing Construction and Estimating	327
125.	A	Roofing Construction and Estimating	340
126.	D	Roofing Construction and Estimating	340
127.	A	Roofing Construction and Estimating	354
128.	B	Roofing Construction and Estimating	396
129.	A	Roofing Construction and Estimating	317
130.	A	Roofing Construction and Estimating	99
131.	D	Roofing Construction and Estimating	408
132.	C	Roofing Construction and Estimating	41
133.	B	Roofing Construction and Estimating	354
134.	C	Roofing Construction and Estimating	382
135.	C	Roofing Construction and Estimating	392
136.	A	Roofing Construction and Estimating	426
137.	C	Roofing Construction and Estimating	343
138.	D	Roofing Construction and Estimating	100
139.	B	Roofing Construction and Estimating	334
140.	A	Roofing Construction and Estimating	330
141.	D	Roofing Construction and Estimating	202
142.	B	Roofing Construction and Estimating	246
143.	A	Roofing Construction and Estimating	268
144.	A	Roofing Construction and Estimating	303
145.	A	Roofing Construction and Estimating	382
146.	A	Roofing Construction and Estimating	220
147.	C	Roofing Construction and Estimating	165
148.	D	Roofing Construction and Estimating	237
149.	C	Roofing Construction and Estimating	136
150.	D	Roofing Construction and Estimating	202
151.	C	Roofing Construction and Estimating	165
152.	A	Roofing and Construction Estimating	69
153.	B	Roofing and Construction Estimating	89
154.	B	Roofing and Construction Estimating	89
155.	C	Roofing and Construction Estimating	138
156.	A	Roofing and Construction Estimating	167

157.	A	Roofing and Construction Estimating	92
158.	D	Roofing and Construction Estimating	43
159.	D	Roofing and Construction Estimating	317
160.	D	Roofing and Construction Estimating	327
161.	B	Roofing and Construction Estimating	354
162.	A	Roofing and Construction Estimating	339
163.	C	Roofing and Construction Estimating	343
164.	B	Roofing and Construction Estimating	67
165.	D	Roofing and Construction Estimating	67
166.	D	Roofing and Construction Estimating	200
167.	D	Roofing and Construction Estimating	399
168.	D	Roofing and Construction Estimating	216
169.	B	Roofing and Construction Estimating	256
170.	A	Roofing and Construction Estimating	292
171.	B	Roofing and Construction Estimating	292
172.	D	Roofing and Construction Estimating	295
173.	B	Roofing and Construction Estimating	304
174.	A	Roofing and Construction Estimating	392
175.	B	Roofing Construction and Estimating	67
176.	D	Roofing Construction and Estimating	67
177.	D	Roofing Construction and Estimating	92
178.	C	Roofing Construction and Estimating	92
179.	C	Roofing Construction and Estimating	92
180.	A	Roofing Construction and Estimating	92
181.	B	Roofing Construction and Estimating	167
182.	A	Roofing Construction and Estimating	304
183.	D	Roofing Construction and Estimating	242
184.	B	Roofing Construction and Estimating	176
185.	C	Roofing Construction and Estimating	304
186.	D	Roofing Construction and Estimating	304
187.	C	Roofing Construction and Estimating	308
188.	C	Roofing Construction and Estimating	310
189.	B	Roofing Construction and Estimating	310

190.	A	Roofing Construction and Estimating	310
191.	B	Roofing Construction and Estimating	341
192.	A	Roofing Construction and Estimating	392
193.	D	Roofing Construction and Estimating	304
194.	A	Roofing Construction and Estimating	131/133
195.	B	Roofing Construction and Estimating	99
196.	C	Roofing Construction and Estimating	90
197.	B	Roofing Construction and Estimating	204
198.	A	Roofing Construction and Estimating	198
199.	B	Roofing Construction and Estimating	327
200.	D	Roofing Construction and Estimating	43
201.	B	Roofing Construction and Estimating	200
202.	B	Roofing Construction and Estimating	329
203.	B	Roofing Construction and Estimating	340
204.	D	Roofing Construction and Estimating	91
205.	B	Roofing Construction and Estimating	133
206.	B	Roofing Construction and Estimating	67
207.	B	Roofing Construction and Estimating	218
208.	A	Roofing Construction and Estimating	234
209.	C	Roofing Construction and Estimating	210
210.	A	Roofing Construction and Estimating	175
211.	A	Roofing Construction and Estimating	200
212.	B	Roofing Construction and Estimating	383
213.	D	Roofing Construction and Estimating	304
214.	A	Roofing Construction and Estimating	242
215.	A	Roofing Construction and Estimating	96
216.	A	Roofing Construction and Estimating	66
217.	A	Roofing Construction and Estimating	260
218.	B	Roofing Construction and Estimating	175
219.	A	Roofing Construction and Estimating	262
220.	D	Roofing Construction and Estimating	67
221.	C	Roofing Construction and Estimating	402
222.	B	Roofing Construction and Estimating	99

223.	A	Roofing Construction and Estimating	217
224.	B	Roofing Construction and Estimating	299
225.	B	Roofing Construction and Estimating	201
226.	D	Roofing Construction and Estimating	15/21
227.	A	Roofing Construction and Estimating	185
228.	B	Roofing Construction and Estimating	65
229.	C	Roofing Construction and Estimating	327
230.	A	Roofing Construction and Estimating	164
231.	D	Roofing Construction and Estimating	199
232.	C	Roofing Construction and Estimating	45
233.	B	Roofing Construction and Estimating	164
234.	D	Roofing Construction and Estimating	317
235.	B	Roofing Construction and Estimating	175
236.	A	Roofing Construction and Estimating	67
237.	D	Roofing Construction and Estimating	40
238.	A	Roofing Construction and Estimating	371
239.	B	Roofing Construction and Estimating	327
240.	B	Roofing Construction and Estimating	164
241.	D	Roofing Construction and Estimating	337
242.	B	Roofing Construction and Estimating	408
243.	B	Roofing Construction and Estimating	237
244.	D	Roofing Construction and Estimating	327
245.	A	Roofing Construction and Estimating	96
246.	D	Roofing Construction and Estimating	342
247.	B	Roofing Construction and Estimating	340
248.	A	Roofing Construction and Estimating	342
249.	D	Roofing Construction and Estimating	200
250.	B	Roofing Construction and Estimating	27
251.	C	Roofing Construction and Estimating	337
252.	A	Roofing Construction and Estimating	212
253.	D	Roofing Construction and Estimating	131
254.	C	Roofing Construction and Estimating	220
255.	C	Roofing Construction and Estimating	336

#	Ans	Reference	Page
256.	A	Roofing Construction and Estimating	408
257.	D	Roofing Construction and Estimating	376
258.	A	Roofing Construction and Estimating	277
259.	C	Roofing Construction and Estimating	200
260.	D	Roofing Construction and Estimating	164
261.	A	Roofing Construction and Estimating	304
262.	D	Roofing Construction and Estimating	200
263.	D	Roofing Construction and Estimating	198
264.	B	Roofing Construction and Estimating	84
265.	C	Roofing Construction and Estimating	
266.	D	Roofing Construction and Estimating	396
267.	A	Roofing Construction and Estimating	401
268.	D	Roofing Construction and Estimating	106
269.	A	Roofing Construction and Estimating	96
270.	A	Roofing Construction and Estimating	137
271.	A	Roofing Construction and Estimating	124
272.	B	Roofing Construction and Estimating	97
273.	B	Roofing Construction and Estimating	92
274.	D	Roofing Construction and Estimating	89
275.	C	Roofing Construction and Estimating	106
276.	B	Roofing Construction and Estimating	175
277.	C	Roofing Construction and Estimating	167
278.	C	Roofing Construction and Estimating	229
279.	D	Roofing Construction and Estimating	29
280.	C	Roofing Construction and Estimating	32
281.	D	Roofing Construction and Estimating	38
282.	D	Roofing Construction and Estimating	41
283.	B	Roofing Construction and Estimating	64
284.	A	Roofing Construction and Estimating	65
285.	B	Roofing Construction and Estimating	78
286.	B	Roofing Construction and Estimating	79
287.	A	Roofing Construction and Estimating	83

288.	C	Roofing Construction and Estimating	89
289.	B	Roofing Construction and Estimating	92
290.	B	Roofing Construction and Estimating	96
291.	B	Roofing Construction and Estimating	106
292.	B	Roofing Construction and Estimating	137
293.	D	Roofing Construction and Estimating	137
294.	D	Roofing Construction and Estimating	140
295.	D	Roofing Construction and Estimating	159
296.	C	Roofing Construction and Estimating	165
297.	B	Roofing Construction and Estimating	165
298.	C	Roofing Construction and Estimating	167
299.	C	Roofing Construction and Estimating	167
300.	D	Roofing Construction and Estimating	175
301.	B	Roofing Construction and Estimating	212
302.	C	Roofing Construction and Estimating	229
303.	B	Roofing Construction and Estimating	250
304.	C	Roofing Construction and Estimating	265
305.	D	Roofing Construction and Estimating	277
306.	B	Roofing Construction and Estimating	292
307.	B	Roofing Construction and Estimating	292
308.	C	Roofing Construction and Estimating	293
309.	C	Roofing Construction and Estimating	295
310.	D	Roofing Construction and Estimating	300
311.	C	Roofing Construction and Estimating	304
312.	D	Roofing Construction and Estimating	305
313.	C	Roofing Construction and Estimating	307
314.	B	Roofing Construction and Estimating	319
315.	C	Roofing Construction and Estimating	330
316.	D	Roofing Construction and Estimating	338
317.	D	Roofing Construction and Estimating	338
318.	D	Roofing Construction and Estimating	350
319.	B	Roofing Construction and Estimating	361

B
A
C
C
B
B
C
D
B
B
C
B
C

Rise divided by run

1.083

0 degrees F

6" Page 24

Boards are spaced on center a distance equal the shingle exposure.

IS NOT to be used as a vapor barrier.

The roof deck.

Under the felt.

2" on the edge and 4" at the ends

Ice dam

One layer of 90 lb hot mopped based membrane

UL

4

Always drive the nail straight.

2 1/2 lbs

2 inches

361

384

394

396

400

407

15, Fig. 1-19

15, Fig. 1-19

15, Fig. 1-19

15, Fig. 1-19

15, Fig. 1-19

15, Fig. 1-19

15, Fig. 1-19

10

15

24

30

35

40, Figure 3-5

40

43

61 & 62

62

75

78, Figure 4-6

106

106

112

#	Answer	Reference
349.	Install when temperature is above 45 degrees, if below 45 degrees, cut into shorter lengths and let it warm in the sun.	133
350.	4	161
351.	1 ½"	164, Fig. 6-5
352.	900 lbs.	197
353.	3"	197
354.	15" wide, 16 oz. copper or .0179 zinc coated	242
355.	45 to 80 lbs per square	298
356.	20 years	291
357.	15" copper, Or 0.179 zinc coated.	298
358.	25 lbs	301
359.	Type III	304
360.	475 degrees F	304
361.	437 — 500 degrees	304
362.	3 gallons	305
363.	20 years	307
364.	It causes the roof to sag.	307
365.	5	311
366.	Floors above heated rooms or heated basements require	355
367.	Look for shingles that are worn, curled or damaged.	381
368.	Caulk an area with tar and sprinkle granules onto it.	384
369.	Improper shingling around the flashing.	384
370.	Install metal beneath the shingle and nail the metal into a bed of cement.	385
371.	Asphalt shingles are more pliable as they are warmed.	385
372.	Around a vent pipe.	385
373.	When joints line-up in three adjacent courses.	385

374.	Asphalt shingles become pliable as they are warmed.	385
375.	Insert the new slate underneath the two overlying courses.	386
376.	The cost to repair exceeds 80% of the replacement cost.	390
377.	Eave and ridge vents.	403

ROOFING CONTRACTORS EXAMINATION QUESTIONS

1. As a general rule, how many layers of asphalt shingle roofing will most roof surfaces support?

    1
    2
    3
    4

2. The Residential Asphalt Roofing Manual recommends that the first shingle of a "butt-up" roof have _____ inches cut off the top in addition to cutting off the tabs.

    0
    1
    2
    3

When installing metal flashing shingles where a roof a butts a vertical wall, what is the size of his flashing at the end of the shingles with a five inch exposure?

A. 6" x 7"
B. 6" x 12"
   10" x 7"
   12" x 12"

The first ply of a built-up roof system over a light insulating concrete deck should be installed by

   solid bonding
   mechanical fasteners
   channel mopping
   spot mopping

5. It is not considered good practice to apply roll roofing when the temperature is at or below _____ Fahrenheit.

   30°
   32°
   40°
   45°

Using the NRCA suggested deflection factor, what would be the maximum permissible deflection for a span of 20 feet?

A. 0.083 inches
B. 0.46 inches
C. 0.66 inches
D. 1 inch

7. At _____ is where you begin to tear off a low sloped gravel roof.

A. the bottom and work up.
B. either edge and work across the slope
C. the flashing at valleys
D. the top and work down

8. The NRCA recommends that roof membrane be attached to the roof insulation boards _____ for precast concrete decks.

A. by flood asphalt dip from a tub
B. by mechanical fasteners
C. by solid mopping hot asphalt
D. by strip mopping type II asphalt

9. Asphalt liquid base materials that need softening should be placed

A. over an open fire
B. in an oven with the door open
C. in hot water with cans unopened
D. on an electric burner

10. The softening point of type III asphalt used in roofing should be _____ degrees Fahrenheit maximum.

135 - 151
158 - 176
185 - 205
210 — 225

A _____ should be mechanically fastened over all cement wood fiber panel roof decks prior to installation of insulation board.

layer of sheet metal
fiberglass membrane
layer of fiberboard
base sheet

When applying the second course of roll roofing parallel to the eaves by the exposed nail method, the second course should lap the first course by _____ inches in accordance to NRCA.

2
3
4
6

What should be done to plastic cement to protect it against the elements and prolong its life as a flashing sealant?

Seal it with caulk.
Paint it with all weather paint.
Paint it with aluminum paint.
Nothing, its life cannot be prolonged.

14. Selvage double cover roofing paper is produced as a _____ inch wide sheet and may be used on slopes down to _____ inches.

17- 2
19 -5
34 -2
36 — 1

When reroofing for an existing asphalt shingle roof the first step is to

clean the gutter
install the edging under the shingles
trim the old shingles back from the edge
apply metal edging

16. Low sloped roofs are those roofs having slopes of between _____ and _____ inches per foot.

A. 2 - 6
B. 2 -4
C. 3 - 6
D. 3 -4

17. Precast concrete roof deck should be primed with _____ prior to installation of the insulation boards.

A. concrete surface sealer
B. asphalt cutback
C. elastometric sealer
D. type II asphalt

18. When installing asphalt roll roofing material parallel to the eaves in the exposed nail method, nails should be spaced _____ inches on center according to the NRCA.

2
4
6
8

According to the Roofer's Handbook, where on the slope is the best location to start reroofing operations on a hip roof?

- At the left edge.
- Half way between the left and right edges.
- At the right edge.
- There is no best location.

For two plies of number 15 asphalt saturated (pererated) organic felt on nailable decks, the plies will be lapped _____ inches leaving an exposure of _____ inches.

- 8 - 18
- 13 - 23
- 19 - 17
- 21 — 15

Six inch wide end laps shall be secured after cementing with nails spaced inches on centers when applying roll roofing using the concealed nail method according to the Residential Asphalt Roofing Manual.

- 2
- 3
- 4
- 5

The bottom of plywood used in poured concrete roof decks

- should not be painted.
- may be painted with breather type paint.
- may be painted with a water base interior paint.
- should be painted with oil base paint.

23. The length of roofing nails should be at least _____ inches when applied to strip shingles over new plywood roofs.

- 1
- B. 1 - 1/4
- C. 1 - 1/2
- 1 - 3/4

According to The Roofer's Handbook, the best type of valley to use on a chimney is

- A. smooth
- B. laced
- C. 1/2 laced
- D. VV shaped

25. A full laced valley can be used on most roofs having a pitch of at least

   1 - 12
   2 - 12
   3 - 12
   4 - 12

26. The proper term for applying shingles diagonally is the _____ method.

A. stair - step
B. straight up
   laced
   drift down

27. According to the NRCA, deck deflection should be limited to the _____ of the total span.

A. 1/22
B. 1/240
C. 1/300
D. 1/360

28. You should lap 15 pound felt underlayment _____ inches at the top or head and inches at the lap for a 4 in 12 pitch when applying strip shingles over new deck.

   4-4
   2-4
   4-2
   4-6

When installing asphalt roofing material parallel to the rake, the NRCA recommends the lower end of the sheet shall project _____ over the eaves in the exposed nail method.

   1/8 to 1/4 inches
   1/4 to 3/8 inches
   3/8 to 5/8 inches
   5/8 to 11/16 inches

A _____ should be installed at the back face of chimneys to prevent snow build-up and to divert water flow.

   cricket
   rake
   cart
   curb

QUESTIONS 31 THROUGH 40 REFER TO THE ROOF PLAN SHOWN BELOW:

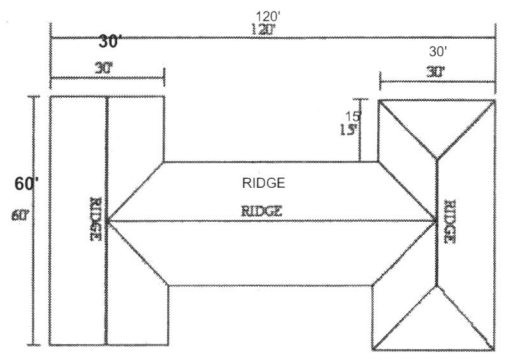

ROOF PLAN WITH A UNIFORM 7 IN 12 RISE AND RUN

31. The total length of the ridge is _____ feet.

    120
    150
    180
    210

32. The total length of the valleys is _____ feet.

    45.9
    89.4
    90.0
    91.8

33. The total net area of the roof is _____ squares.

    59.5
    62.5
    65.5
    68.5

34. The total length of the rake required is _____ feet.

    60.0
    69.5
    90.0
    120.0

35. The total length of hips is _____ feet.

- 23.3
- 30.4
- 91.8
- 123.8

36. The total length of the drip edge required for the building is _____ feet.

- 420
- 430
- 440
- 450

Celotex, Sol-Seal/20 Shingles are specified for this roof. Disregard the effect of ridge or valley or starter shingles and assume no waste factor and five-inch exposure. How many bundles of shingle are required for the roof?

- 812
- 188
- 243
- 249

How many nails are required to fasten the shingles to the roof? Select the closest answer.

- 18,000
- 19,000
- 20,000
- 21,000

How many pounds of 1 - 1/4 inch roofing nails are required for this job? Select the closest answer.

- 125
- 130
- 135
- 140

What is the surface area of the roof portion bordered by the valleys (between the wings)? Select the closest answer.

- 2,250 square feet
- 2,425 square feet
- 2,600 square feet
- 2,775 square feet

ANSWER KEY FOR ROOFING CONTRACTORS EXAMINATION QUESTIONS

1. C
2. C
3. C
4. B
5. D
6. D
8. C
9. C
10. C
11. D
12. A
13. C
14. D
15. C
16. B
17. B
18. A
19. B
20. C

21. 0
22. B
23. B
24. D
25. C
26. A
27. B
28. B
29. B
30. A
31. C
32. D
33. B
34. B
35. C
36. B
37. B
38. C
39. A
40. C

1 Exam Prep
OSHA Code of Federal Regulations Questions
(For Roofing Contractors)

1. All portable ladder side rails shall extend at least _____ inches above the upper landing.

    24
    36
    48
    69

Full thickness undressed lumber with an eight-foot span can have a maximum intended nominal load of _____ P.S.F (lb/ft^2).

    25
    50
    75
    32

A hole is a gap or void _____ inch(es) or more in its least dimension on a roof.

    ½
    1
    2
    3

Toeboards are required on scaffolding above how many feet?

    6
    8
    10
    3

Each portable ladder not self-supporting shall be capable of supporting at least how many times the intended load?

    2
    4
    5
    8

6. A ladder must extend above a roof deck how many feet?

    2
    3
    4
    5

Rob will be working from a ladder. Billy Bob will need fall protection at height _____

    None is required
    6 feet
    8 feet
    10 feet

When nailing roofing nails to 5/8 inch decking, if the air pressure is set at 100 psi or greater, the nailer must be _____

    Held at a slight angle to the decking
    Have a safety device installed at the muzzle
    Regulated not to exceed 110 psi
    Regulated not to have less than 90 psi

When using a hand-tool that is not grounded the user should make sure the tool is _____

    Double insulated
    Dust free
    Newly painted
    Serviced by a three prong adapter

The ladder is against a 20 foot building. The ladder base should be how many feet from the side of the building?

    4
    5
    8
    10

The crane operator should keep the crane how many feet from a 50 Kv power line?

    5
    10
    15
    20

12. Scaffolding must be capable of supporting at least _____

- The weight of the workers, materials, tools and scaffolding itself
- 3 times the intended load
- 4 times the weight of the workers and tools
- 4 times the intended load

Each employee on a scaffold more than _____ feet above a lower level must be protected from falling to that lower level.

- 6
- 8
- 10
- 12

Scaffolding cannot be moved with employees still on it unless the surface on which it is moving is within _____ degrees of level.

- 2
- 3
- 4
- 5

For safety purposes, an employee must place a non-self-supporting ladder at such an angle that the horizontal distance from the top support to the foot of the ladder is approximately _____ of the working length of the ladder.

- One-half
- One-quarter
- Thirty percent
- Forty percent

Ladders must extend how many feet above the upper landing?

- 1
- 2
- 3
- 4

Metal chutes at an angle of more than 45 degrees from the horizontal shall have openings not to exceed how many inches in height?

- 24
- 48
- 60
- 72

When it is not practical to use nails to secure roof bracket scaffolds, brackets shall be secured in place with first-grade manila rope of at least _____.

- ½"
- ¾"
- 1"
- 1.5"

The warning line erected around all sides of the roof area shall not be less than _____ feet from the roof edge when mechanical equipment is not being used.

- 3
- 4
- 5
- 6

On low-sloped roofs of _____ feet or less in width, the use of a safety monitoring system alone as a means of providing fall protection during roofing operations is permitted.

- 40
- 45
- 50
- 60

1 Exam Prep
OSHA Code of Federal Regulations Answers
(For Roofing Contractors)

1.	B	Code of Federal Regulations, (OSHA)	1926.1053(b)(1)
2.	B	Code of Federal Regulations, (OSHA)	Subpart L, Appendix A
3.	C	Code of Federal Regulations, (OSHA)	1926.500(b)
4.	C	Code of Federal Regulations, (OSHA)	1926.451.h.2.ii
5.	B	Code of Federal Regulations, (OSHA)	1926.1053.a.1.ii
6.	B	Code of Federal Regulations, (OSHA)	1926.1053.b.1
7.	B	Code of Federal Regulations, (OSHA)	1926.104(d)
8.	B	Code of Federal Regulations, (OSHA)	1926.302(3)
9.	A	Code of Federal Regulations, (OSHA)	1926.302(a)
10.	B	Code of Federal Regulations, (OSHA)	1926.1053(5)(i)
11.	B	Code of Federal Regulations, (OSHA)	1926.550(15)(i)
12.	D	Code of Federal Regulations, (OSHA)	1926.451(a)(1)
13.	C	Code of Federal Regulations, (OSHA)	1926.451(g)
14.	B	Code of Federal Regulations, (OSHA)	1926.452(w)(6)(i)
15.	B	Code of Federal Regulations, (OSHA)	1926.1053(b)(5)(i)
16.	C	Code of Federal Regulations, (OSHA)	1926.1053(b)(1)
17.	B	Code of Federal Regulations, (OSHA)	1926.852(b)
18.	B	Code of Federal Regulations, (OSHA)	1926.452(h)(2)
19.	D	Code of Federal Regulations, (OSHA)	1926.502(1)(i)
20.	C	Code of Federal Regulations, (OSHA)	1926. & Subpart M, Appendix A

ROOFING STUDY GUIDE
OSHA PRACTICE TEST QUESTIONS

PRACTICE TEST ONE

1. Impact tools, such as drift pins, shall be kept free of _____.

   A. Lint and dust   B. Mushroomed heads
   C. Oil   D. Fungus

2. If an employee wears prescription glasses, OSHA requires that he must be provided with _____ for certain jobs.

   A. Spectacles with protective lenses
   B. Goggles over corrective spectacles
   C. Goggles with lenses that incorporate corrected lenses mounted behind the protective lenses. D. Either A, B, or C

3. When employees are working in an excavation, there can be no more than _____ between them and a means of egress.

   A. 5'   C. 15'
   B. 10'   D. 25'

4. The _____ has the first responsibility for assuring that the required personal protective equipment is worn by workers on a construction site defined by OSHA.

   A. Employee   C. Owner
   B. Employer   D. Prime contractor

5. Lifelines shall be secured above the point of operation to anchorage or structural members capable of supporting a minimum dead weight of _____ pounds.

   A. 1,000   C. 4,000
   B. 2,500   D. 5,400

6. A safety belt lanyard shall be a minimum of one-half inch nylon rope with a maximum length that provides for a fall of no greater than _____.

   A. 6'   C. 12'
   B. 10'   D. 15'

Portable firefighting equipment must be maintained on a job site of 1,500 square feet, at all times during construction.

   False, only required for each 3,000 square feet.
   False in all cases.
   True in all cases.
   True if the job site is "commercial."

8. Electric power operated tools shall be either grounded or _____ type.

    Approved double-insulated
    Approved single-insulated
    #12 Romex
    Three phase

9. Danger signs shall be _____ .

    A. 3   C. 8
    B. 6   D. 10

11. The maximum loading of a medium duty tube and coupler scaffold is _____ per square foot.

    A. 25   C. 35
    B. 30   D. 50

12. First aid kits shall consist of materials approved by the consulting physician in a _____ container.

    A. Water proof   C. Weatherproof
    B. Bulletproof   D. Fireproof

13. Lumber piles stored on a job site shall not exceed _____ in height provided that manually stacked lumber shall not be stacked higher than _____ .

    A. 20' - 10'   C. 24' - 20'
    B. 16' - 8'   D. 20' -16'

14. The maximum air pressure allowed for nailers, staplers, and other similar type equipment is _____ pressure at the tool unless the tool shall have a safety device on the muzzle to prevent the tool from ejecting fasteners.

    A. 30 psi   C. 100 psi
    B. 60 psi   D. 150 psi

    To protect employees working in excavated area from cave-ins, all excavations over 5 feet shall be protected by a slope and bench system. Unless specifically designed by qualified personnel, excavations shall not be sloped at an angle steeper than _____ to one.

    A. One   C. Two
    B. One and one-half   D. Three

ANSWERS TO PRACTICE TEST ONE

1. B	4. B	7. C	10. B	13. D
2. D	5. D	8. A	11. D	14. C
3. D	6. A	9. A	12. C	15. B

PRACTICE TEST TWO

1. All Ladder Jack scaffolds shall be limited to light duty and shall not exceed a height of _____ above the floor or ground.

   A. 10'
   B. 20'
   C. 30'
   D. 40'

2. Toe boards, where required on scaffolds, shall be a minimum of _____ in height.

   A. 2"
   B. 3-1/2"
   C. 4"
   D. 4-1/2"

Which of the following is a typical tool equipped with a constant pressure switch?

   Circular saw
   Hydraulic come-along
   Table saw
   Jig saw

4. Rungs, steps, and cleats of portable ladders and fixed ladders shall be spaced not less than _____ apart.

   A. 8"
   B. 10"
   C. 12"
   D. 14"

5. The height of handrails shall not be more than _____ nor less than _____ from the upper surface of the stairwell system to the surface of the tread, in line with the face of the riser at the forward edge of the tread.

   A. 37"...30"
   B. 37"...36"
   C. 30"...22"
   D. 36"...24"

6. The minimum rated fire extinguisher required for a 3,000 square foot building is _____ .

   A. 2A
   B. 2B
   C. 2C
   D. 2D

7. Safety belts and lanyards (ropes) should be nylon or material of equivalent strength and have a minimum diameter of _____.

   A. 1/4"
   B. 1/2"
   C. 3/4"
   D. 1"

8. The minimum acceptable clearance between a crane load and an electric service of 50 kV is?

   A. 10'
   B. 20'
   C. 15'
   D. 5'

9. The minimum number of toilet seats and urinals for 200 employees is _____ .

   A. 1   C. 3
   B. 2   D. 4

10. The minimum illumination of an indoor warehouse is _____ candles.

    A. 3'   C. 10'
    B. 5'   D. 12'

11. During demolition procedures, the maximum size opening cut in a floor for the disposal of materials shall not exceed _____ unless lateral supports of the removed flooring remain in place.

    A. 8' by 10'
    B. 10% of the total aggregate floor area
    C. 20' by 20'
    D. 25% of the total aggregate floor area

12. An interior hung scaffold is to be suspended from the beams of a ceiling. The suspension rope wire shall be capable of supporting _____ times the intended load.

    A. 4   C. 6
    B. 5   D. 7

13. The maximum weight which can be supported by a pump jack scaffold is _____ lbs.

    A. 250   C. 1,000
    B. 500   D. 2,000

14. As used in OSHA, the word "shall" means _____ .

       Recommended
       Mandatory
       Might
       Ought to

15. A stairway or ladder shall be provided at all personnel points of access where there is a break in elevation of _____ or more.

    A. 16"   C. 25"
    B. 19"   D. 36"

ANSWERS TO PRACTICE TEST TWO

1. B	4. B	7. B	10. B	13. B
2. B	5. A	8. A	11. D	14. B
3. A	6. A	9. D	12. C	15. B

PRACTICE TEST THREE

1. The proper maintenance of a carbon dioxide fire extinguisher is to _____ .

    A. Check the pressure gauge monthly.
    B. Discharge it annually and then recharge.
       Weigh semi-annually.
       Check the pressure gauge annually.

   A contractor agrees with a subcontractor to divide job site responsibilities such as providing safety programs, temporary sanitation facilities, etc. Which applies?

        Is not required
        Illegal under *OSHA* rules
        Legal: the contractor cannot be relieved of overall responsibility.
        Legal: the subcontractor and prime contractor are held liable.

3. The contents of a first aid kit should be checked _____ .

    A. Monthly   C. Bi-weekly
    B. Weekly   D. Semi-annually

4. A ladder, stairway, or ramp shall be located in trench excavations that are _____ or more in depth.

    A. 2'   C. 6'
    B. 4'   D. 10'

5. When debris is dropped through an opening in the floor without the use of a chute, the area onto which the materials are dropped shall be completely enclosed with barricades not less than _____ in height and not less than _____ from the projected edge of the opening above.

    A. 36" — 2'   C. 42" — 4'
    B. 36" — 4'   D. 42" — 6'

6. All employees using abrasive wheels shall be protected _____ .

    A. With accessory body and face guards.
    B. With flexible hooded, ventilated goggles.
    C. By the use of momentary pressure switches.
    D. By eye protection equipment.

7. When masonry blocks are stacked higher than 6 feet, the stack shall be tapered back _____ block per tier above the 6-foot level.

    A. 1/2   C. 2
    B. 1   D. 2-1/2

8. During structural steel assembly, in the final placing of solid web structural members, the load shall not be released from the hoisting line until the members are secured with bolts or the equivalent at each connection and drawn up wrench tight.

   A. All required
   B. Not less than six
   C. Not less than four
   D. Not less than two

9. Cylinders containing oxygen or acetylene shall not be _____.

   A. Taken into confined spaces.
   B. Refilled at the work site.
   C. Stored in direct sunlight.
   D. Used to troll for sharks.

10. Every open-sided floor or platform _____ above the adjacent floor or ground level shall be guarded by a standard railing, or equivalent, on all open sides except where there is an entrance to a ramp, stairs, or fixed ladder.

    A. 4'   C. 6'
    B. 5'   D. 8'

11. The proper way to hang an extension cord over a hallway ceiling during construction is _____.

    A. With wire.
    B. With staples.
    C. With rope.
    D. Under a bent nail.

13. Fixed ladders shall be used at a pitch no greater than _____ degrees from the horizontal, as measured to the back side of the ladder.

    A. 45   C. 90
    B. 60   D. 120

14. The maximum variance in riser height or tread depth shall not be over _____ in any stairway system.

    A. 1/8 inch
    B. 3/16 inch
    C. 1/4 inch
    D. 3/8 inch

ANSWERS TO PRACTICE TEST THREE

1. C	4. B	7. A	10. C	13. C
2. C	5. D	8. D	11. C	14. C
3. B	6. D	9. A	12. B	

PRACTICE TEST FOUR

1. No combustible material shall be stored outdoors within _____ of a building or structure.

    10'
    15'
    20'
    30'

2. When safety nets are required, the mesh size of the nets shall not exceed _____ by _____ .

    A. 4" — 4"   C. 8" — 8"
    B. 6" — 6"   D. 8" — 6"

3. A trench in Type B soil is 12' deep and 97' _____ long safe means of egress are required.

    A. Two   C. Four
    B. Three   D. Five

4. Safety devices on powder-actuated tools should be checked _____ .

    A. Twice daily.   C. Weekly.
    B. Daily.   D. Monthly.

5. The maximum daily exposure an employee can have to a sound level of 100 decibels is _____ .

    A. 15 minutes   C. 4 hours
    B. 2 hours   D. 8 hours

6. Overhead protective covering of 2-inch planking, _____ plywood, or other solid material of equivalent strength shall be provided on the top of every personnel hoist.

    A. ¼"   C. ½"
    B. ¾"   D. 5/8"

7. Handrails and top rails of guardrail systems shall be of such construction as to be capable of withstanding a minimum load of _____ pounds applied in any direction or point on the top rail.

    A. 100   C. 200
    B. 150   D. 250

8. The minimum diameter of hoisting and counterweight wire ropes when used for personnel hoists shall be _____ .

    A. 1/4"   C. 1/2"
    B. 3/8"   D. 5/8"

9. The side rails of portable ladders shall extend a minimum of _____ above the landing.

    A. 22"   C. 30"
    B. 24"   D. 36"

10. The factor that determines if a compressed air hose requires a pressure reduction safety device at the air source is _____.

    Length
    Inside diameter
    Pressure
    The number of fittings

11. The minimum difference between work levels without protected sides or edges that require a fall protection system is _____.

    A. 4'   C. 8'
    B. 6'   D. 10'

12. All rider-operated equipment used in site clearing operations shall be equipped with a rear canopy guard of 1/4-inch woven wire mesh with openings no greater than _____.

    A. 1"   C. 9/16"
    B. 1/2"   D. 7/8"

13. The minimum overlap for a scaffolding plank is _____, while maintaining a maximum overhang of inches beyond the supports.

    A. 16" — 12"   C. 8" — 12"
    B. 12" — 12"   D. 10" — 10"

14. The minimum number of hoisting ropes used for drum-type personnel hoists is _____.

    A. Two   C. Four
    B. Three   D. Five

ANSWERS TO PRACTICE TEST FOUR

1. A	4. B	7. C	10. B	13. B
2. B	5. B	8. C	11. B	14. A
3. A	6. B	9. D	12. A	

PRACTICE TEST FIVE

1. On a job site with a total of 275 employees, a contractor is required to have _____ portable chemical toilets.

   A. Six   C. 10
   B. Eight   D. 12

2. All of the following face and eye equipment are approved by (OSHA) Code of Federal Regulations, for protection from flying particles when using chipping tools except _____.

   A. Flexible fitting goggles.
   B. Metal-frame spectacles with side shields.
   C. Plastic-frame spectacles with side shields.
   D. Face shields.

3. No more than _____ gallons of flammable or combustible liquids shall be stored in a room outside of an approved storage cabinet.

   A. 10   C. 30
   B. 25   D. 20

4. Material stored within a building shall not be stored within _____ of a fire door opening.

   A. 3 ft.   C. 5 ft.
   B. 2 ft.   D. 1 ft.

5. When doing heavy grinding, type _____ goggles are required.

   A. 1,3,5 6, 10
   B. 2, 10
   C. 7, 8 (10 in combination with 4, 5, 6 in tinted lenses)
   D. 1, 3 7A, 8A (for severe exposure, add 10)

6. According to OSHA, a concrete block wall without supports can be constructed _____ high.

   A. 6'   C. 10'
   B. 8'   D. 12'

7. Employees should not be exposed to an impact noise on a job exceeding a peak sound pressure of _____.

   A. 100 db   C. 120 db
   B. 140 db   D. 110 db

8. Unless listed otherwise, temporary circulation-type room heaters shall have a minimum clearance on all sides to combustible materials of _____.

   A. 12"   C. 28"
   B. 22"   D. 36"

9. A scaffold having adjustable platform(s) so as to permit the raising or lowering of the platform is known as a(an) _____ scaffold.

    Mason's
    Stone setter's
    Outrigger
    Needle Beam

10. The maximum pole spacing for a light duty wood scaffold constructed with 2x10 planking is _____.

    A. 7'   C. 9'
    B. 8'   D. 10'

ANSWERS TO PRACTICE TEST FIVE

1. A	2. D	3. B	4. A	5. D
6. B	7. B	8. A	9. A	10. D

PRACTICE TEST SIX

1. The maximum loading of a heavy-duty scaffold is ___ P.S.F.

    A. 15   C. 50
    B. 25   D. 75

2. Excavation support systems shall be designed by a qualified person when the excavation is in excess of _____ in depth, is adjacent to structures or improvements, or is subject to vibration or ground water.

    A. 5'   C. 15'
    B. 20'   D. 18'

3. Whenever materials are dropped more than _____ to any point lying outside the exterior walls of the building, enclosed chute of wood or a equivalent material shall be-used.

    A. 12'   C. 18'
    B. 15'   D. 20'

4. The maximum span of 2" by 10" rough sawn lumber on a scaffold when loaded with 50 P.S.F. is _____.

    A. 6'   C. 8'
    B. 7'   D. 9'

5. A quick-closing valve on gas acetylene cylinders should not be open more than _____.

    A. One-quarter of a turn.
    B. One turn.
    C. One and one-half turns.
    D. Two turns.

6. Horse scaffolds shall not be constructed or arranged more than two tiers high or _____ in height, whichever is less.

    A. 4'   C. 8'
    B. 6'   D. 10'

7. Scaffold platforms shall extend over their center line supports at least _____.

    A. 2"   C. 6"
    B. 4"   D. 12"

8. Where platforms are overlapped to create a long platform, platforms shall be secured from movement or overlapped at least _____.

    A. 2"   C. 6"
    B. 4"   D. 12"

9. According to the (OSHA) Code of Federal Regulations, a trench is a narrow excavation in which the bottom width is not greater than _____.

    A. 5'   C. 15'
    B. 10'   D. 20'

10. Job-made wooden ladders with spliced side rails shall be used at an angle such that the horizontal distance from the top support to the foot of the ladder is _____ the working length of the ladder.

    One-third
    One-quarter
    One-fifth
    One-eighth

11. Toe boards shall be capable of withstanding at any point a force of at least _____ pounds applied in any downward or outward direction at any point.

    A. 50   C. 175
    B. 100   D. 200

12. Where oxygen deficiency or a hazardous atmosphere exists or could reasonably be expected to exist, the atmosphere in the excavations shall be tested before employees enter excavations greater than _____ deep.

    A. 4'   C. 6'
    B. 5'   D. 8'

13. The safe working load for a 1" shackle is _____ pounds.

    A. 6,400
    B. 8,600
    C. 11,200
    D. 43,400

ANSWERS TO PRACTICE TEST SIX

1. D	4. C	7. C	10. D	13. C
2. B	5. C	8. D	11. A	
3. D	6. D	9. C	12. A	

PRACTICE TEST SEVEN

1. The common drinking cup is _____ .

    A. Prohibited in hazardous areas.
    B. Prohibited in areas where more than three workmen will use the cup.
    C. Not prohibited.
    D. Always prohibited.

2. An out-of-order tag will be identified by a _____ .

    A. White tag, white letters on a red square.
    B. White tag, white letters on a red oval with a black square.
    C. Yellow tag, yellow letters on a black background.
    D. White tag, white letters on a black background.

3. A kickout _____ .

    A. Is the same as a trench jack.
    B. Prevents the fall of a scaffold.
    C. Relieves pressure from a tank.
    D. Is an accidental release or failure of a cross brace.

  Which of the following problems is not caused by asbestos?

    Lung cancer
    Gastrointestinal cancer
    Asbestosis
    Angina

5. Hallways of a construction project must be illuminated with a minimum of _____ candles.

    A. 5'
    B. 3'
    C. 7'
    D. 10'

6. Under OSHA terms, a 'competent person' is a(n) _____.

    A. Designated superintendent on the job site.
    B. Office person who is in charge of a safety program.
    C. *OSHA* official.
    D. Person who can identify a hazard in a working area and has the authorization to correct it.

7. Where skeleton steel erection is being done, a tightly planked and substantial floor shall be maintained within <u>directly below</u> and under that portion of each tier of beams on which any work is being performed.

    A. Two stories or 30 feet
    B. Four stories or 48 feet
    C. Two stories or 25 feet
    D. Eight stories or 100 feet

8. According to (OSHA) Code of Federal Regulations, a hand-held grinder with a 2-1/8" diameter wheel shall be equipped with only a _____.

    A. Constant pressure switch.
    B. Momentary contact on/off control.
    C. Positive percussion switch.
    D. Positive on/off switch.

9. Temporary stairs shall have a landing not less than _____ in the direction of travel at every 12 feet of vertical rise.

    A. 30"   C. 42"
    B. 36"   D. 48"

10. When a stack of loose bricks reaches a height of 4 feet, the stack shall be tapered back _____ for every foot of height above the 4-foot level.

    A. 1"   C. 2-1/2"
    B. 2"   D. 3"

11. The working clearance for an electrical switch panel that may likely require inspection live would be _____ if the voltage is 120.

    A. 24"   C. 36"
    B. 30"   D. 48"

13. Lifelines subjected to cutting or abrasion shall be a minimum diameter of wire core manila rope.

    A. 3/4"
    B. 7/8"

C. 1"
D. 1-1/4"

ANSWERS TO PRACTICE TEST FIVE

1. D	4. D	7. A	10. B	13. B
2. D	5. A	8. B	11. C	
3. D	6. D	9. A	12. D	

EXPLANATION OF ANSWERS

PRACTICE TEST ONE
  Ans B. 1926.301(c) Tool Handling Subpart
I: Tools - Hand and Power.
  Ans D. Subpart E: Personal ... Equipment. Sec .102 - Eye protection.(3), (i), (ii) Sec:1926.102(a)(3)
  Ans D. Subpart P: Excavations .Sec.
.651(C) (2). Access/Egress
  Ans B. Subpart C: General Safety and Health Provisions Sec .28 (a).
Ind: Personal protective equipment
  Ans. D. Sec 1926.104(b)
Subpart E: Personal Protective and Life
Saving Equipment.
6. Ans A. Sec 1926.104(d)
Subpart E: Personal Protective and Life
Saving Equipment. Sec .502(d)16(iii).
  Ans C. Subpart. F Ind: Fire Protection, Firefighting Equipment, Sec .150 (c), Pg
   See (c)(i). Note: Ans A looks possible because of the wording "each 3,000 square feet", but also says (major fraction thereof". 1,500 sq ft = major fraction of 3,000 sq ft.
  Ans A. 1926.302 Subpart I: Tools -- Hand and Power. Sec.302 - Power-operated hand tools (a).
  Ans A.1926.200(b)(2) Subpart G: Signs, Signals, and Barricades. Sec. 200 (b).
10.Ans B. Subpart H: Materials Handling, Storage, Use, and Disposal. Sec. 251 - Rigging equipment. (4)(i) pg 260.
11.Ans D. 1926 Subpart L Appendix A. 2.b
12.Ans. C Subpart D Occupational Health an Environmental Controls. Sec. 50 (2).
13.Ans D.Subpart H: Materials Handling, Storage, Use and Disposal. Sec.250 (iv).
14.Ans C. 1926.302 (b)(3) Subpart I: Tools -- Hand and Power. Sec. 302 (3).
15.Ans B. Subpart P: Excavations. Appendix B - Table B-1, pg 319.Also see Sec. 652 (1) Option.

PRACTICE TEST TWO
  Ans B. Subpart L: Scaffolds. Sec.452.(a) Ladder jack scaffolds (k).
  Ans B. Subpart L: Scaffolds. Sec. 451.(h)

Falling object protection (2) (ii).

Ans A. Subpart I: Tools -- Hand and Power. Sec. 300. (d) Switches (3).

Ans B. Subpart X: Stairways and Ladders. Sec. 1053 (3)(i).

Ans A. Subpart X: Stairways and Ladders. Sec.1052 (6). N.B. There is a difference between stair rails and hand rails

Ans A. Subpart F: Fire Protection. Sec. 150
(c) (1)(i) Portable firefighting equipment. Needs rewording: required for each 3,000 sq ft.

Ans B. Subpart E: Personal Protective and Life Saving Equipment. Sec. 104 - Safety belts, lifelines, and lanyards (d).

Ans A. Subpart N: Cranes, Derricks, Hoists, Elevators, and Conveyors. Sec. 550 (15) (ii).

Ans a Subpart D: Occupational Health and Environmental Controls. Sec 51 - Sanitation. (c) - Toilets at construction jobsites., Table D-1.

10.Ans B. Subpart D: Occupational Health and Environmental Controls. Sec. 56 - Illumination. Table D-3.

11.Ans D. Subpart T: Demolition. Sec. 853 - Removal of materials through floor openings.

12.Ans C. Subpart L: Scaffolds. Sec. 451-General requirements (4). Also see Suspension, Sec 452(t)

13.Ans. B. Subpart L: Scaffolds. Sec. 454 Training requirements (j) Pump jack scaffolds. Appendix A,, Sec 452(j)

14.Ans B. Subpart C: General Safety and Health Provisions. Sec. 32 Definitions (q). 15.Ans B. Subpart X: Stairways and Ladders. Sec. 1051 - General requirements (a).

PRACTICE TEST THREE

Ans C. Subpart F: Fire Protection. Sec. 150. Table F-1.

Ans C. Subpart B: General Interpretations. Rules of constr. Sec16 (a).

Ans B. Subpart D: Occupational Health and Environmental Controls. Sec. 50 - Medical services and first aid (2).

Ans B. Subpart P: Excavations. Sec. 651 - Specific excavation requirements (2).

Ans D. Subpart T: Demolition. Sec. 850 - Preparatory operations (h).

ALSO SUB 252 LETTER H

Ans D. Subpart I: Tools - Hand and Power. Ans A. Subpart H: Materials Handling, Storage, Use, and Disposal. Sec. 250 General requirements for storage (7).

Ans D. Subpart R: Steel Erection. Sec.750, Pg 352 Sec 756,, Beams and columns. (a)(1). "solid web structural members
...two bolts".

Ans. A Subpart J: Welding and Cutting. Sec. 350 Gas welding and cutting (b) Placing cylinders (4).

10. Ans C. Subpart M: Fall Protection. Sec.501 (b)(1).

11. Ans C. Subpart K: Electrical. Sec. 416 - Safety Related Work practices (e)(2) Extension cords...Also 405 - Wiring methods, etc. (J),

12. Ans. B. Subpart L: Scaffolds. Sec.
 - General requirements (4), (e) Access(Scaffold access) (4) Stair towers...

13. Ans C. Sec. Subpart X. Stairways and Ladders. Sec. 1053. (b) Use(5)

14. Ans C. Subpart X: Stairways and Ladders. Sec. 1052 (3).

PRACTICE TEST FOUR

Ans A. Subpart F: Fire Protection. Sec. 151(C) (5).

Ans. B. Subpart E: Personal Protective and Life Saving Equipment. Sec. 105 Safety nets (d).

Ans A. Subpart P: Excavations. Sec 651
Specific evacuation requirements(C) (2). Means of egress from trench evacuations. Not specific answer and only reference I could find.

4. Ans B. Subpart I: Tools - Hand and Power. Sec. 302- Power-operated hand tools. (e) Power-actuated tools (2).

5. Ans B. Subpart D: Occupational Health and Environment Controls. Sec. 52, Table D-2 - Permissible Noise Exposures.

6. Ans B. Subpart N: Cranes, Derricks, Hoists, Elevators, and Conveyors. Sec. 552
Material hoists...and elevators. Overhead

protection(B) (3).

   Ans C. Subpart M: Fall Protection. Sec. 502 System criteria and practices(B) (3).

   Ans C. Subpart N: Cranes, Derricks, Hoists, etc. Sec. 552 - Material hoists, personal hoists, and elevators (14)(ii).

   Ans D. Subpart X - Stairways and Ladders. Sec 1053 - Ladders. (3)(i).

10. Ans B. Subpart I: Tools -- Hand and Power. Sec. 302 - Power... hand tools(B) (7) 11. Ans B. Subpart M: Fall Protection. Sec.
   - Duty to have fall protection (b)(1). 12. Ans A. Subpart 0: Motor Vehicles, Mechanized Equipment, and Marine Operations. Sec. 604 - Site clearing (ii). 13. Ans B. Subpart L: Scaffolds. Sec. 451 - General requirements. (b) Scaffold platform construction - (7) and (5)(i).

14. Ans A. Subpart N: Crane, Derricks, Hoists...Sec. 552 (14) Ropes (i).

PRACTICE TEST FIVE

   Ans A. Subpart D: Occupational Health and Environmental Controls. Sec. 51 - Sanitation. (c) Toilets at construction jobsites,,Table D-1. 275+ 50 = 5.5. Round up to 6 toilets.

   Ans D. Subpart E: Personal Protective and LifeSaving Equipment Sec .102. See Table E-1.

   Ans. B Subpart F: Fire Protection
Sec. 152-Flammable & combustible liquids(B) Indoor Storage of...

   Ans A. Subpart F: Fire Protection. Sec. 151 Fire prevention (7)(D)..

   Ans D. Subpart E: Personal Protective and Life Saving Equipment. Sec. 102 - Eye and face protection. See Table E-1..

   Ans B. Subpart Q Concrete and Masonry Construction. Sec. 706 - Requirements for masonry construction (b).

   Ans. B. Subpart D: Occupational Health and Environmental Controls. Sec. 52 - Occupational noise exposure (e).

   Ans A. Subpart F: Fire Protection.
Sec. 154 - Temporary heating devices (b).
Plus Table F-4.

   Ans A. Subpart L: Scaffolds. Sec. 450. See Mason's adjusted supported scaffold, then

Self-contained adjustable scaffold.
10. Ans D. Subpart L: Scaffolds. Sec. 454, Appendix A, Table: Independent Wood Pole Scaffolds. See Light Duty with 2 x 10 planking. Max pole spacing = 10'.

<u>PRACTICE TEST SIX</u>
    Ans D. Subpart L: Scaffolds. Sec. 454 Training requirements. See table
    Ans B. Subpart P: Excavations,
Sec. 652, See Selection of protective systems, Appendix F,
    Ans D. Subpart H: Materials Handling, Storage, Use, & Disposal. Sec. 252 - Disposal of waste materials (a).
    Ans C. Subpart L: Scaffolds.
Appendix A, Scaffold Specifications. Table.
    Ans C. Subpart J: Welding and Cutting. Sec. 350 - Gas welding and cutting.
(d) Use of fuel gas (2).
    Ans D. Subpart L: Scaffolds. Sec .452. Additional requirements... Horse scaffolds (f)(1)..
    Ans C. Subpart L: Scaffolds . 451,
      Scaffold platform constriction (4). 8. Ans D. Subpart L: Scaffoldsi
      Scaffold platform construction (7).
. Ans C. Subpart P: Excavations Sec .650. Trench definition.
10. Ans D. Subpart X: Stairways and Ladders.
    Use. Sec.1053 Ladders (5)(i)(ii).
11. Ans A. Subpart L: Scaffolds. Sec. 451 (h) Falling object protection (4) (i)
12. Ans A. Subpart P: Excavations.
Sec. 651 - Specific excavation requirements.
    Hazardous atmospheres (i).
13. Ans C. Subpart H: Materials Handling, Storage, Use, and Disposal. Sec. 251. Table H-19, Safe Working Loads for Shackles. Page 255

PRACTICE TEST SEVEN
- Ans D. Subpart D Occupational Healths. Sec..51 Sanitation.(A) (4).
- Ans D. Subpart G: Signs, Signals, & Barricades. Sec..200. Table G-1.
- Ans D. Subpart P: Excavations Sec. 650. Definition lickout' -
- Ans D. Subpart Z: Toxic & Hazardous Appendix H. II Health Hazard Data A.B. Page 414
- Ans A. Subpart D: Occupational Health and Environmental Controls. Sec. 56 - Illumination. Table D-3.
- Ans D. Subpart C: General Safety Sec. 32. Definitions (f)
- Ans. A. Subpart R Steel Erection. Sec.760 Fall Protection, pg 3354, (b)(1). Sec. 754

s B. Subpart I: Tools -- Hand and
owlet Sec. 300 General requirements (d) Switches (2).

Ans A. Subpart X: Stairways and Ladders Sec. 1052 Stairways (1). Page 401

10.Ans B. Subpart H: Materials Handling...
Sec. 250 (6).
11.Ans C. Subpart K: Electrical. Sec. 403 Table K-1.
12.Ans D. Subpart C: Gen Safety & Health Sec 20 (b)(3).
13.Ans B. Subpart E: Personal Protective and Life Saving Equipment. Sec .104 - Safety belts, lifelines, and lanyards (c)..

BASIC MATH

NUMBERS

In nature, numbers are symbolic representations of real entities, so they are used to represent them. Different types of numbers are used depending on the nature of the quantities that must be represented; for example, using the numbers 1, 2, 3, etc .... to represent whole numbers as the number of cows in a stall or the number of documents that exist in a given file. This group of numbers is called **natural**, as the numbers in this group are used to count things that have a comprehensive nature. This group of natural numbers can be expressed as…

$$N = (1,2,3,4,5, ...)$$

There is yet another set of numbers which are called **integers**. Integers include natural numbers (explained above), zero and negative numbers. Zero is a simple concept; it is the absence of quantity. Negative numbers can be a little counterintuitive, since we are not used to thinking in terms of negatives. But, what if instead of having 20 cows in a barn, all 20 of them die, what if only 10 of them die? Then you would use negative numbers to represent their absence, meaning that you'll use -10 cows and -20 cows. This group of integral numbers can be represented as…

$$Z = (..., -5, -4, -3, -2, -1, 0, 1, 2, 3, 4, 5 ...)$$

There is another large group of numbers which represent parts of a whole, this set is called the **rational** numbers, and a very broad sense one can say that this set represents all the fractions that can be found, although this group comprises all fractions simplified. A rational rational number is one that can be written as a ratio of two whole numbers…

$$Q = \frac{a}{b} \text{ , where } b \neq 0$$

In this case there is a restriction that the number b, which is called the **denominator**; it should be different from zero, because if this takes the value of zero it generates something known as a mathematical indetermination, since dividing by zero that does not generate a result with mathematical sense. The number on top (a) is called the **numerator**. The numerator tells the number of parts that are taken from the unit, while the denominator tells the parts into which the units are divided. Analyze the chart below. Start form the 1/8 slice and work your way "up" in a counterclockwise manner. You will notice how the numerator (top number) keeps getting bigger, while the denominator (bottom number) stays the same; this is because the cake is divided into 8 equal slices, and it doesn't matter how many slices you "take", that particular cake will always be divided into 8 slices.

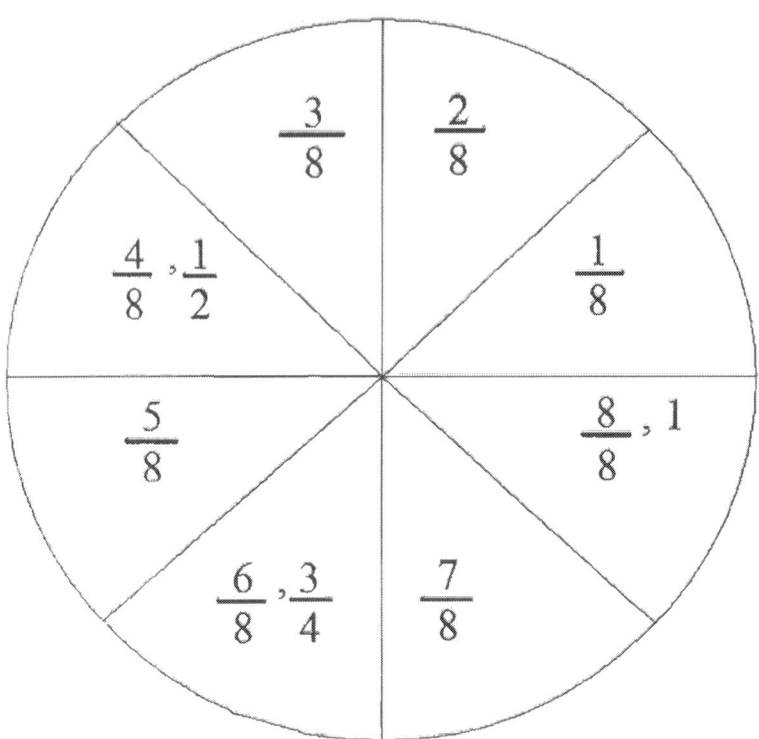

But, wait a minute! What's up with the slices that have two different fractions?, like the one that has 6/8 and 3/4, or the one that has the 8/8 and the 1. This has to do with a process called **simplification**. Anytime we have a fraction, we must try to express it in its simplest equivalent expression, meaning that we will rather say two dollars than eight quarters, even though they are the same.

If we take a fraction like 6/8, and want to simplify it, we must find a number that will divide both the numerator and the denominator (at the same time). In this case the number two will work.

6 divided by 2 = 3 ; and 8 divided by 2 = 4....That is why 6/8 and 3/4 are equivalent.

Greater than and Less than.

How do you know that a fraction is greater or less than any other fraction? Apparently is difficult because one does not know whether to look at the numerator or denominator. But it is useless to look at or compare numerator or denominator of two fractions separately, because they form a single number and therefore should be viewed as a whole. The first rule is to observe that as the denominator is bigger, it means that pieces of the pie are getting smaller. Let's compare the following numbers and determine which one is larger.

$$1/3 \text{ and } 1/8$$

What do these numbers mean? The answer is that 1 / 3 tells me that the cake is divided into three pieces, and that we take one of those 3 pieces (that's a good slice!), while 1 / 8 tells us that the cake is divided into 8 equal parts and we take one of them. In which case do you take more cake? Obviously the 1 / 3 is a much bigger slice that the 1 / 8, then we can say..

$$\frac{1}{3} > \frac{1}{8}$$

As a practice exercise draw two different pies that represent the relationship between this two fractions.

What is the relationship between rational numbers and decimal numbers?

Any decimal number is the product of the division between the components of a fraction. If you divide the number in the denominator of a fraction results in a decimal number. The issue lies in the type of decimal you get. If we speak of a rational number division will generate a decimal which can be of two forms:

A **finite decimal** $1/4 = 1 \div 4 = 0.25$

An **infinite periodic decimal** (digits repeating indefinitely) i.e. $1/3 = 1 \div 3 = 0.333 \cdots$

This is true for the case when the number is rational. However, there are special numbers that cannot be expressed as the ratio of two whole numbers. These numbers are called **irrational numbers**, and are numbers like $\sqrt{2}$, π, and e.

$\sqrt{2} = 1.4142135623731 \ldots$

$e = 2.718281828459 \ldots$

$\pi = 3.14159265358979 \ldots$

As you can see these numbers cannot be obtained by dividing two particular numbers. When this happens we say that we have an irrational number...

$$1 \neq a/b$$

OPERATIONS WITH INTEGERS: Remember that integers (whole numbers) do not include decimals or fractions.

Sum of Integers
Two numbers are added in the way the naturally join, the only difference lies in the signs of the numbers, for which there are two special cases:

a. The numbers have the same sign:

If so, add the final and usually put the sign, like this:
$$5 + 4 = 9$$

NOTE: The "+" sign is not placed before the result since it is assumed that is positive number always has an "invisible" "-" sign before it.

$$(-5) + (-4) = -9$$

NOTE: that since they have the same sign and are adding up, you must align the numbers normally and then put the sign "-" before the result. The sign "-" should always be placed before a negative number.

b. The numbers have different signs:

$$(-6) + (3) = -3$$

NOTE that the answer be the difference between the two numbers and will carry the bigger number's sign.

Subtraction of Integers:
When subtracting integers, is best to think of it as an addition with a few changes. The changes are caused by the subtraction sign "-", which changes the sing immediately in front of it...

$$7 - (-3) = ?$$

Following our little formula, we just change the subtraction sign for an addition sign and change the sign immediately after it.

$$7 + 3 = 10$$

Multiplication of Integers
Integers can be multiplied by considering the following common conventions of signs:

$(+) \times (+) = (+)$
$(+) \times (-) = (-)$
$(-) \times (+) = (-)$
$(-) \times (-) = (+)$

The first step is to carry out a simple multiplication, like we learned a long time ago with the so famous multiplication tables, and then to figure out our sign, we use the conventions mentioned above........

$$(-5) \times (-7) = (35)$$

$$(-6) \times (8) = (-48)$$

Division of Integers
To divide integers, use the same rule as for multiplication, the sign behave the same way, the only thing that changes is the actual division of the numbers.

$(+) \div (+) = (+)$
$(+) \div (-) = (-)$
$(-) \div (+) = (-)$
$(-) \div (-) = (+)$

$$(-35) \div 7 = (-5)$$
$$(-48) \div (-2) = 24$$

These rules are derived naturally from the relationship between multiplication and division.

OPERATIONS WITH RATIONAL NUMBERS (Fractions)

Sum of Fractions
The sum sound is via the following generalized expression:

$$\frac{a}{b} + \frac{c}{d} = \frac{ad + cb}{bd}$$

Note that ad, and cb actually mean a times d, and c times b.

Also note that at the end of the operation it is necessary to simplify.
Example:

$$\frac{3}{5} + \frac{1}{2} = \frac{(3)(2) + (1)(5)}{10}$$

$$\frac{6 + 5}{10} = \boxed{\frac{11}{10}}$$

Note that in this case, neither the numerator (11) nor the denominator (10) can be divided by the same number, meaning that they cannot be simplified any further. BUT, even though the answer cannot be simplified, it can be written in a different form. It can be written as a **mixed fraction** (numerator is bigger than denominator). This basically means that your pizza only has 10 slices, but you need 11 slices, so you need 1 pizza and a tenth (or slice) of another pizza. Based on this we can conclude that the answer could be written as:

$$1\tfrac{1}{10}$$

In the event that you have to add more than two fractions, then the associative property of addition can be applied. It indicates that the numbers or fractions can be added in pairs first, and then those results added until one arrives to the final answer.

Subtraction of Fractions
Subtraction is just like addition. The only thing that must be remembered is subtract instead of adding and keep all fraction and number in the same order. This last requisite is especially important, since it is not the same to have 5- 6, than 6-5 {the first one will result in negative (-) 1 and the latter will result in positive (+) 1}.

$$\frac{a}{b} - \frac{c}{d} = \frac{ad - cb}{bd}$$

Multiplication of Fractions
Multiplication is by far, the simplest of all fractions' operations. One must simply multiply numerator with numerator and denominator with denominator, or top with top and bottom with bottom.

$$\frac{a}{b} \times \frac{c}{d} = \frac{ac}{bd}$$

Division of Fractions
There are two ways to approach the division of fractions.

$$\frac{a}{b} \div \frac{c}{d} = \frac{\frac{a}{b}}{\frac{c}{d}} = \frac{ad}{bc}$$

OR,

$$\frac{a}{b} \div \frac{c}{d} = \frac{a}{b} \times \frac{d}{c} = \frac{ad}{bc}$$

Example:

$$\frac{2}{5} \div \frac{1}{3} = \frac{\frac{2}{5}}{\frac{1}{3}} = \frac{6}{5}$$

OR,

$$\frac{2}{5} \div \frac{1}{3} = \frac{2}{5} \times \frac{3}{1} = \frac{6}{5}$$

Note that the anwers can be left alone, since it cannot be simplified.

Ratios and Proportions

The **ratio** between two numbers is defined as the quotient (relation) between them, which is symbolized as

$$\frac{a}{b} \text{ or } a:b$$

Which reads as: " a is to b.."

The ratio is the number that is to relate or compare these quantities. For example, if there are 3 gallons of water per gallon of milk at a particular convenience store, then it can be said that the ratio of water to milk is....

$$\frac{3}{1} \text{ Or } 3:1 \text{ Or simply } 3$$

A Proportion is a set of two equal ratios, and it is symbolized the following way:

$$\frac{a}{b} = \frac{c}{d}$$

In order for this equality to hold true, then "ad" must equal to "bc". For example, if given the proportion

$$\frac{3}{8} = \frac{9}{24}$$

Then, it can be assumed that $(3)(24) = (8)(9)$, which in fact is true.

Solving for Unknown Variables

Now that we have so much knowledge under our belts, let's try to conquer some of the tough operations in algebra. Suppose you are a contractor running a six-men crew. If you know that each man can erect 25 yards of fence per day; how long would it take your entire crew to complete 1,500 yards of fence?

Step One: Gather data from the problem

1 man = 25 yards per day
6 men = 6 x 25 yards / day = 150 yards per day
Total Length of Fence = 1,500
Total Installation Time = Unknown ?

Step Two: Set up the equation(s)

If in 1 day, 150 yards are erected
Then,
How many days would it take to erect 1,500 yards?

$$\frac{1}{?} = \frac{150}{1500}$$

Step Three: Solve for your Unknown
This step is crucial; this is the part where most students get lost. First of all, since at this point the value we are looking for is obviously not know, we can use any "variable", it can be any letter of symbol you choose (x is commonly used). As soon as the equation is set up, we must leave it by itself on one side of the equal sign. We can accomplish this "working backwards". Lets see,
Since "?" is dividing the number one, we must send it to the other side, across from the equal sign. Anytime this is done, we must perform the "opposite" operation. For example, if the "?" was adding, we would make subtract at the other side, if it was multiplying we would make it divide, and so on. In this case, we must make it multiply on the other side o the equation.

$$1 = ? \times \frac{1}{10}$$ *notice that the fraction has been simplified*

Now, we must send the 1 / 10 to the other side (we must leave the "?" by itself), but instead of multiplying, it will be dividing (do you remember how to divide by a fraction?).

$$\frac{1}{\frac{1}{10}} = x$$

Finally, we know that the answer is 10. It will take you fencing crew 10 days to finish the job.

For some students this last problem might have been too simple, it might have been easy to do by just looking at it, than going through so many formulas and steps. That's true; but, following those steps is vital to successfully answering not-so-simple questions during a test.

Percentage

The percentage is a special proportion of any number (percentage) to a hundred. Percentages are very useful for comparing quantities. If a newspaper says that 20% (%, means percent) of all males in the U.S. use tobacco products, that actually means that 1 out of 5 males in the U.S. use tobacco products. Let examine this last example.

20% of males use tobacco products.
What if there were just 5 males in the entire U.S.?

$$5 \times 20\% = ?$$
$$5 \times \frac{20}{100} = \frac{100}{100} = \boxed{1}$$

This means that anytime you see the expression 20%, it can mean, 1 out of 5, 10 out of 50, 20 out of 100, or 200 out of 1000.

What would it mean then, to say that worker A is 25 % more productive than worker B? This would actually mean that if worker A man install 30 square feet of certain tile per hour, then worker B could only install……..? Let's try it!

If worker A is 25% more productive than worker B, then Worker B is only 75% as productive as worker A. Now, we must find out what 75% of 30 is….

We could punch it in the calculator or do it by hand (know how to do it by hand first!)

$$30 \times \frac{75}{100} = \frac{2250}{100} = \boxed{22.50}$$

This answer tells us that 75% of 20 is 22.50, meaning that worker B only installs 22.50 square feet of that certain tile in a hour.

But, what if, using this same information, we want to know how long it would take worker A to install 22.50 square feet of the same tile? That's right… you must find what the 75% of an hour is. In order to find the answer, multiply 60 (sixty minutes in an hour) times 75, and then divide everything by 100, which will equal 45. Your answer, in fact will be 45 minutes; that's how long it takes worker A to install 22.50 square feet of that particular tile.

CONSTRUCTION MATHEMATICS

In the construction industry, it is of upmost importance to quickly and accurately convert measurements from one particular unit to another. This a key factor in good construction-related communication. It wouldn't make much sense to cut a 159 inch long stud; it would definitely sound better if it was called a 13 feet and 3 inches long stud, or simply 13' 3". In the American construction industry, English units (**inch, foot, yard**) are commonly used, and due to this fact this study guide will only cover this type of units thoroughly. But, it is important to keep the standard system of units in the back of one's mind, since it will pop up frequently; this standard system is the one that use meters and centimeters (it is used in the entire world, and is easier to grasp since all units are factors of 10).

Another important concept that contractors must understand, is the difference not just in units, but in dimensions a well. There are three dimensions we'll focus on: **length, area**, and **volume** (one, two and three dimensions respectively). Each dimension is different and its quantities cannot be compare to another dimensions' quantities. For example, you would not compare 35 lineal feet with 35 square feet, or 35 cubic feet; these are like oranges and apples, they mean different things.

Length

12 Inches = 1 foot
1 Foot = 12 Inches
1 Yards = 3 Feet

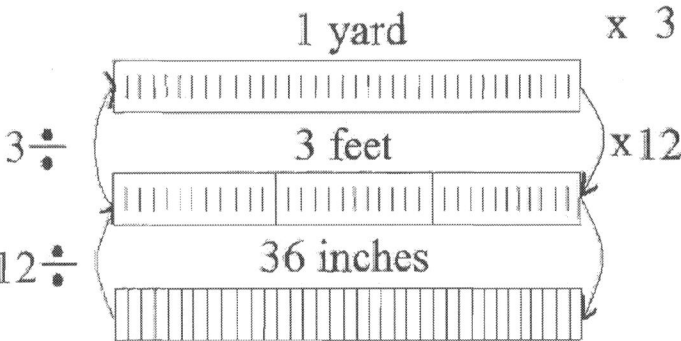

Remember that units of length only have one dimension. Units of length are the measurements from point A to point B.

Area

It is easy for all of us to understand area. This concept is drilled into our heads very often. We normally talk about the square footage of a house or building, the area affected by a particular hurricane, or simply the total area covered by carpet at a particular apartment. Just like in the measurement of length, sometimes is preferable to use smaller or larger units of area depending on the area being measure. For example, it wouldn't be wise to measure the area covered by carpet in square inches, so instead, square yards are use. But, before we jump into learning how to convert from one square unit to the other, we must fir learn how to find different areas.

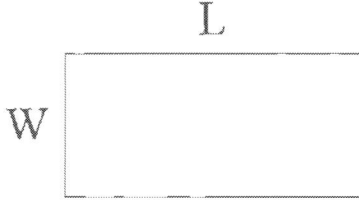

Area = L x W

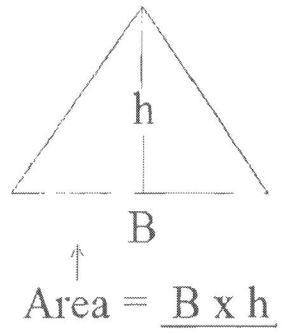

Area = $\dfrac{B \times h}{2}$

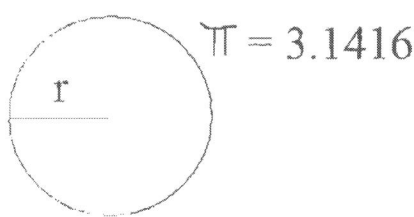

$\pi = 3.1416$

Area = $\pi \times r^2$

Circumference (C) = $2r\pi$

Special Areas

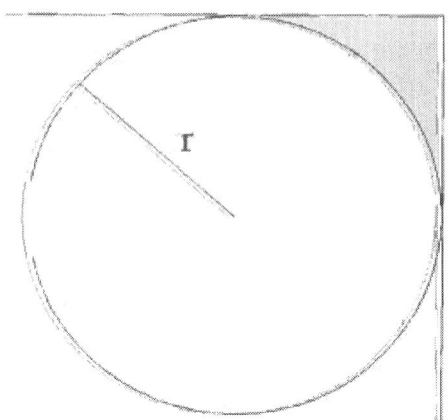

Shaded Area (A),
A = .215 x r x r

Area Conversions

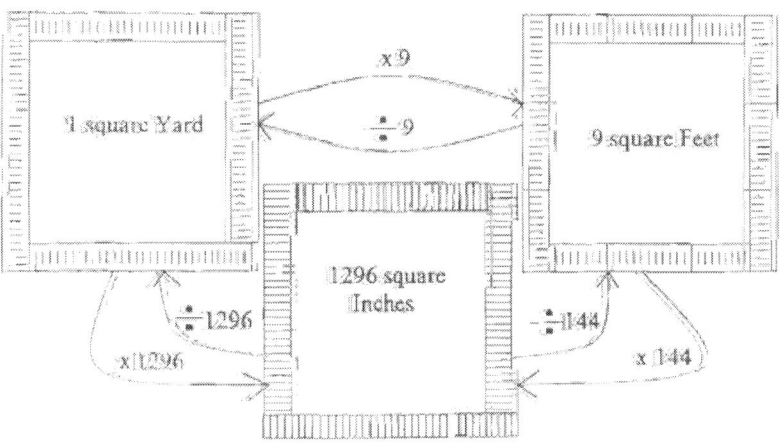

Volumes

Volume measurements are expressed in the form of cubic measurements. That's why you normally hear expression like, "315 cubic yards of concrete were poured today", or "750 cubic feet of dirt were needed to level the road". Things like boxes, concrete slabs, excavations and swimming pools have three dimensions. They all have a length, a width and a depth. When those three measurements are multiplied, the answer is cubic....something(inches, feet, yards, etc..)

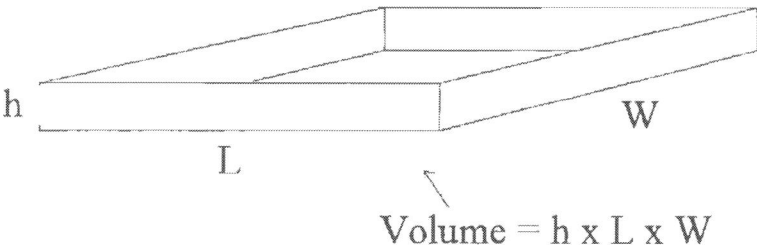

Volume = h x L x W

Note that volume could also be seen as the area times another dimension. Think about it!

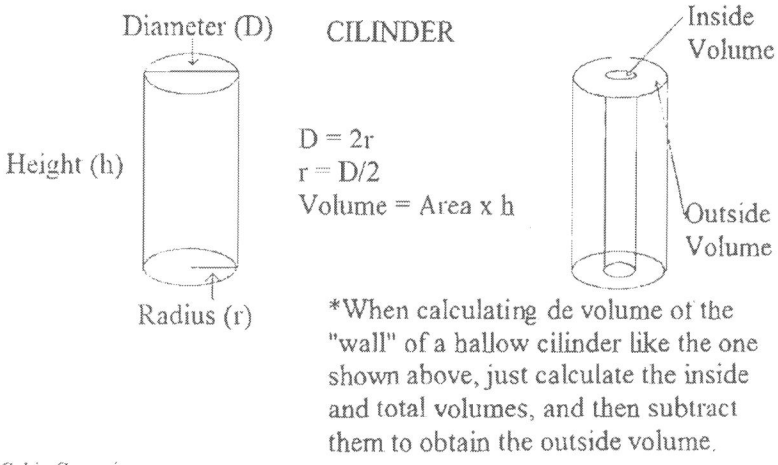

Diameter (D)   CILINDER

Height (h)

$D = 2r$
$r = D/2$
Volume = Area x h

Radius (r)

Inside Volume

Outside Volume

*When calculating de volume of the "wall" of a hallow cilinder like the one shown above, just calculate the inside and total volumes, and then subtract them to obtain the outside volume.

Cubic Cnversions

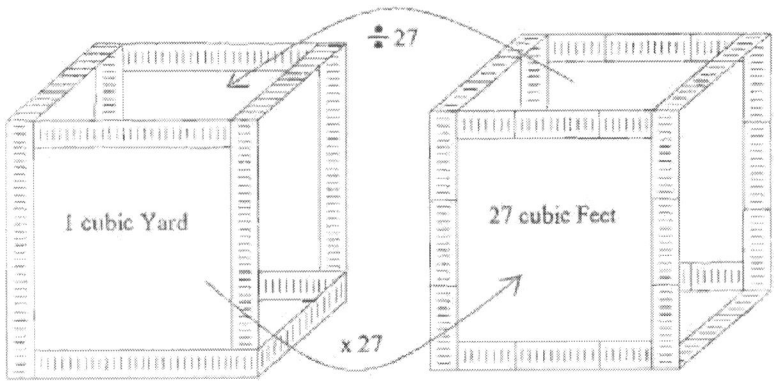

Right Triangles: *No, you're not wasting your time. This concept is key to understanding excavations, batterboards and degree measurements.*

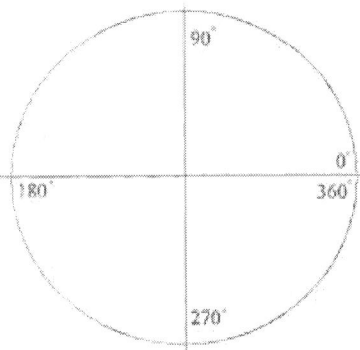

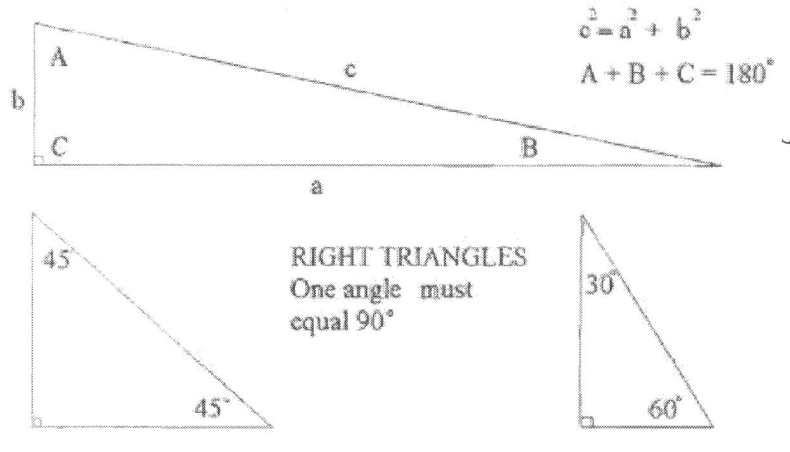

$$c^2 = a^2 + b^2$$
$$A + B + C = 180°$$

RIGHT TRIANGLES
One angle must equal 90°

Excavations

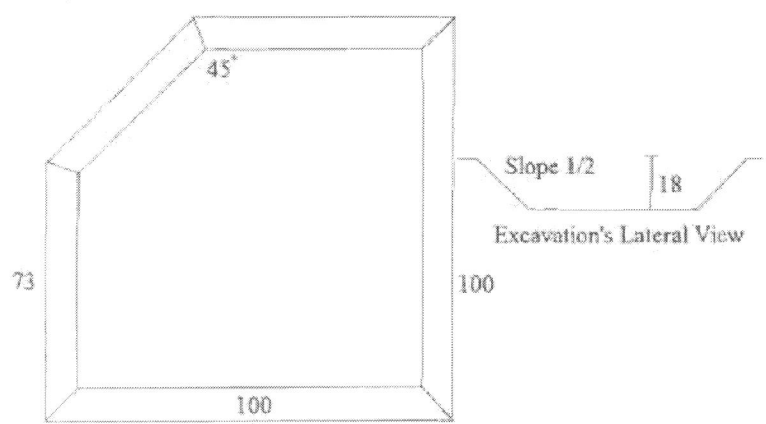

Slope 1/2

Excavation's Lateral View

Board Feet

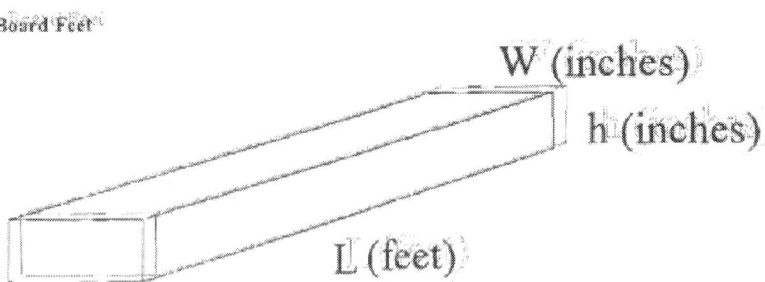

$$\text{Board Feet} = \frac{W \times h \times L}{12}$$

Piles

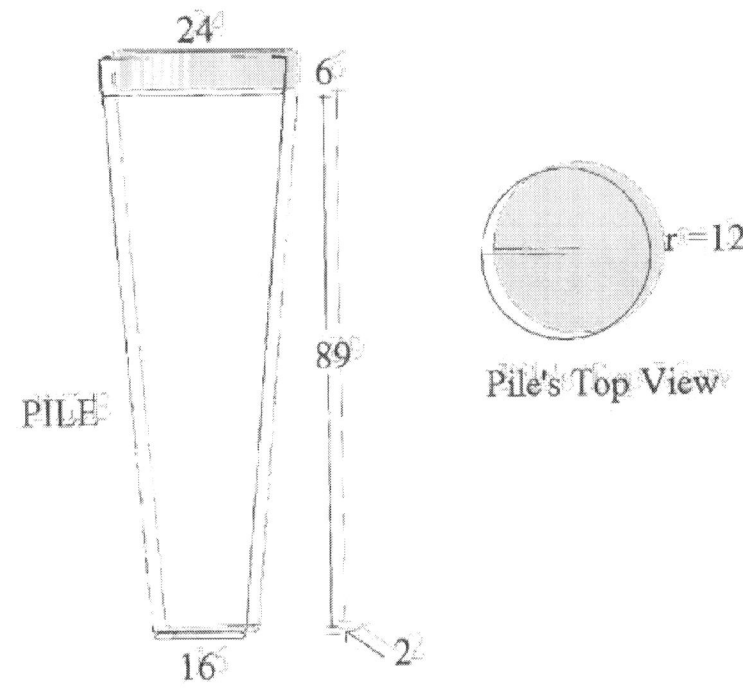

Pile's Top View

Batter Boards

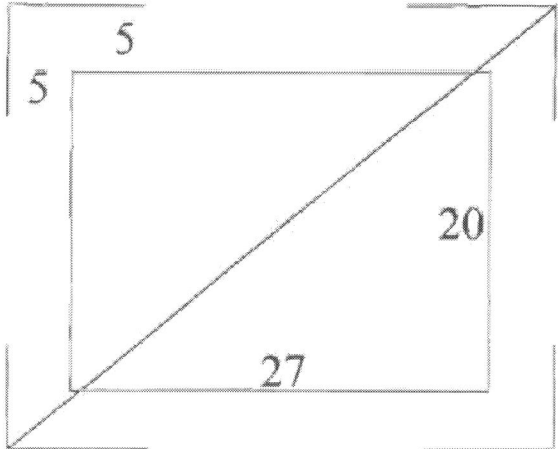

Basic "Roof" Problems: These are called "roof problems", but it does not mean that it is just for Roofing contractors. The concepts involved in solving these problems are essential for any construction field. Concepts like slope are vital for the proper functioning of almost all mechanisms, if you don't think so, ask a plumber or try to drive your truck up a vertical wall. Even though this concepts are helpful for roofers as well, they are very basic for them, and this knowledge alone will not be enough to pass a roofing exam.

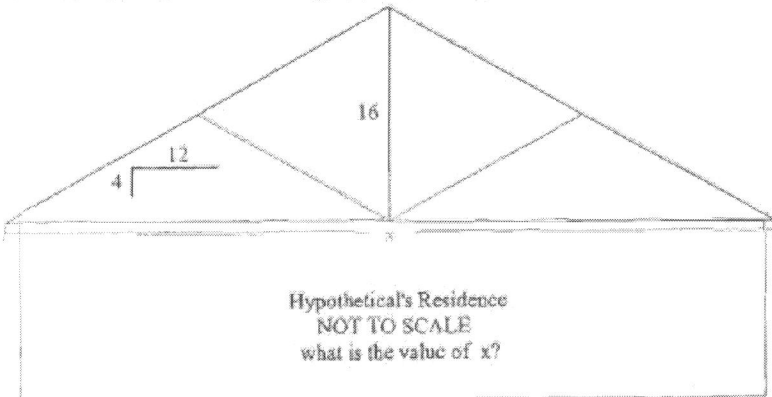

Hypothetical's Residence
NOT TO SCALE
what is the value of x?

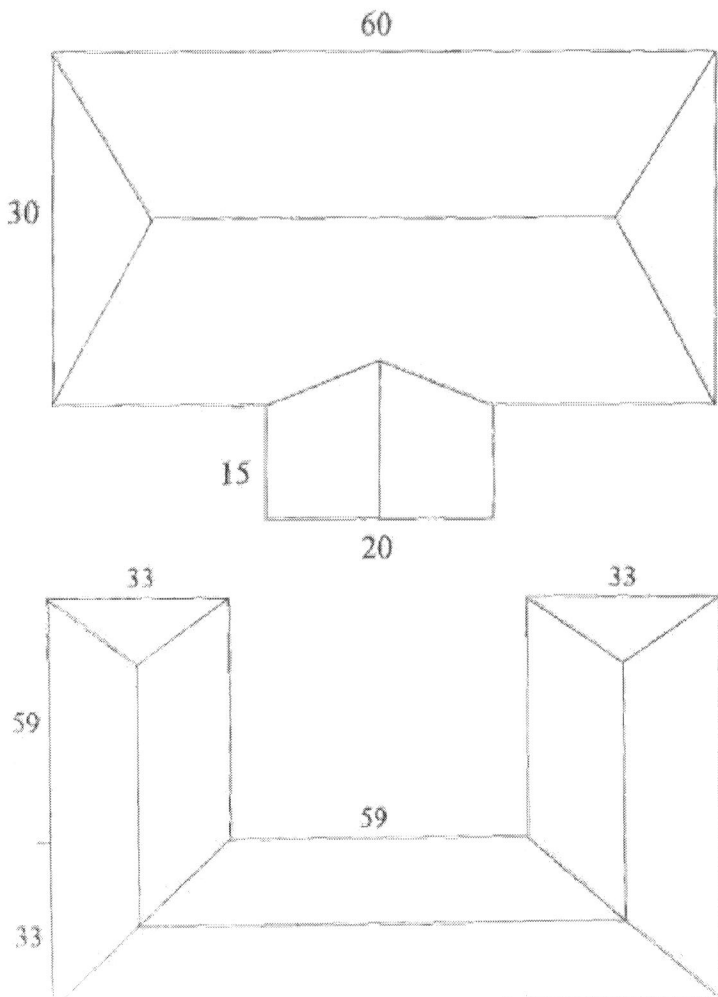

1 Exam Prep

Roofing Math Questions

1. Base flashing costs $2.83 per lineal foot. Assume a sales tax of 6.5 percent and an installation fee of $14.95 per hour per person. The total cost to complete the base flashing using a two-man crew is The crew requires three hours to complete the job.

    $391.81
    $491.51
    $487.34
    $481.51

Insulation boards measure 4' x 8'. The number of boards required for the roof deck is
Assume all measurements are to the outside.

    172
    154
    307
    287

Cap flashing is sold in galvanized sheets measuring 36" x 120". Assume the parapet wall cap to be girthed at 18". The sheets required to complete the parapet wall are
Assume all measurements are to the outside.

    16
    17
    18
    19

The built-up roof deck covering the steel deck will be 4-ply built-up. All areas with roof insulation are to be mopped at a rate of 25 pounds per ply per square. The tons of asphalt necessary to complete the roof are? Assume all measurements are to the outside.

    2
    3
    4
    5

5. Base ply fasteners are installed at a rate of 80 fasteners per square. How many fasteners are required for the built-up roof deck covering the steel deck   . Assume all measurements are to the outside.

    3,920
    3,668
    3,980
    6,240

6. Brown river gravel will be installed over the built-up deck covering the plywood deck at a rate of 400 pounds per square. How many tons are necessary to complete the job. Assume all measurements are to the outside.

    5
    6
    7
    8

7. The total number of sheets of galvanized metal, 36" x 120" needed to fabricate the gravel stop for the plywood deck is _____. Assume gravel stop to measure 12".

    5
    6
    7
    8

8. The total length of cant strip is _____. Assume all measurements are to the outside.

    210
    320
    440
    500

9. Ten sheets of 16 ounce copper 10' x 30' weigh _____ pounds.

    3,000
    4,000
    5,000
    6,000

The sheets of 18 inch by 120 inch 16-ounce copper required for fabrication of all cap and counter flashing for the Classroom is? Cap flashing and counter flashing is used on parapet walls only.

Less than 59
Between 59 and 61
Between 61 and 63
More than 63

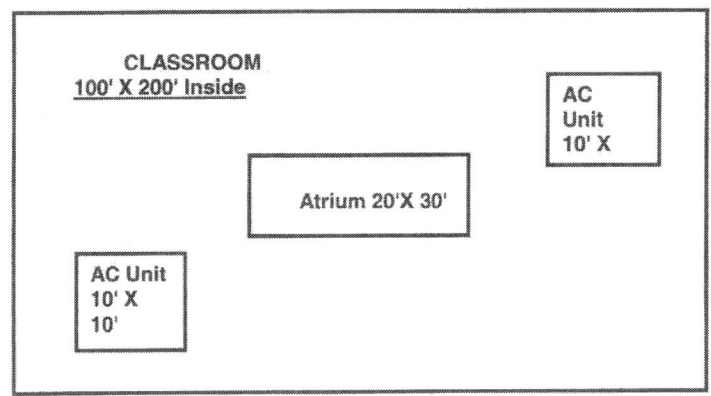

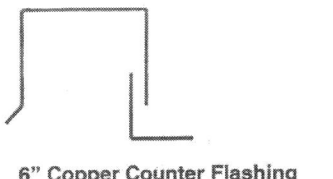

12" Girthed Copper Cap Flashing

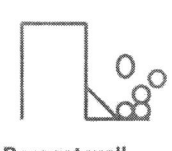

Parapet wall

6" Copper Counter Flashing

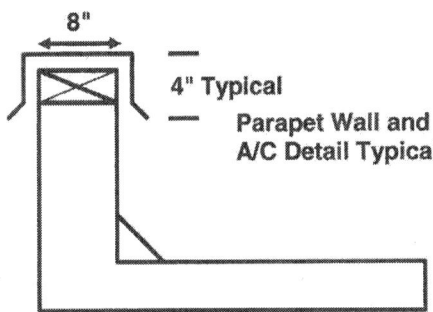

All air conditioning penetrations are curb style with 16 ounce copper sheathing coping caps. All parapet walls are covered with 16 ounce copper sheathing coping caps. All air conditioning penetrations are 12 feet by 12 feet outside measurement.

The contractor can purchase 18 inch by 120 inch 16 ounce copper sheets for $270.00 each. The total cost for the 16 ounce copper only for the air conditioning curbs and parapet walls only on the high roof of the **Community Center** is

        Less than $24,000
        Between $24,000 and $25,000
        Between $25,000 and $26,000
        More than $26,000

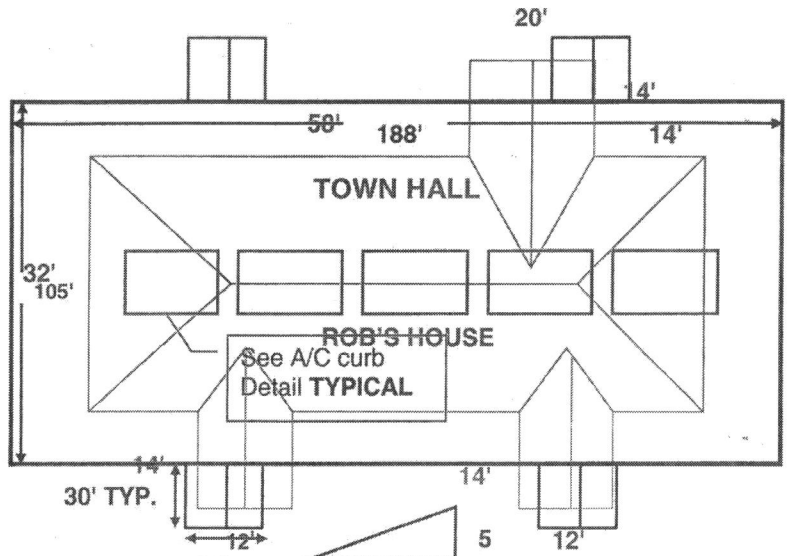

Rob's House has a rise and run of 9/12. Standard 3-tab shingles are to be applied over double layer 15 pound felt. All eave metal and flashings are 26 gage galvanized sheet metal.

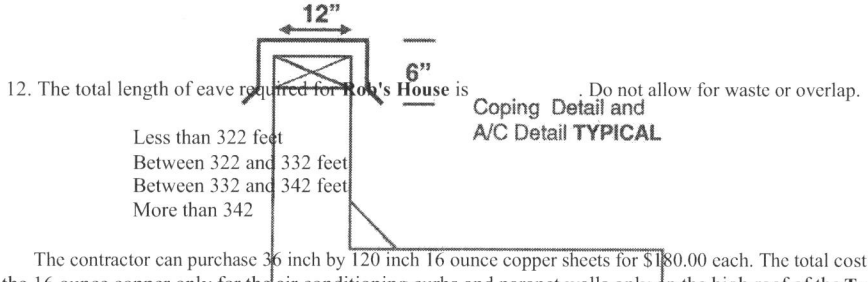

12. The total length of eave required for Rob's House is _____. Do not allow for waste or overlap.

   Less than 322 feet
   Between 322 and 332 feet
   Between 332 and 342 feet
   More than 342

The contractor can purchase 36 inch by 120 inch 16 ounce copper sheets for $180.00 each. The total cost for the 16 ounce copper only for the air conditioning curbs and parapet walls only on the high roof of the **Town Hall** is _____. (See next page for diagram.)

   Less than $ 9,500
   Between $ 9,500 and $10,000
   Between $10,000 and $10,500
   More than $10,500

All air conditioning penetrations are curb style with 16 ounce copper sheathing coping caps. All parapet walls are covered with 16 ounce copper sheathing coping caps. All air conditioning penetrations are 10 feet by 14 feet inside measurement.

Gutters are 3 inches high by 4 inches wide. The total square inches of surface area for one square foot of gutter is

        Less than 125
        Between 125 and 145
        Between 145 and 165
        More than 165

Downspouts for the house are 3 inches by 4 inches. The total square feet of surface area for one lineal foot of downspout is

        168
        14
        1.17
        1

ANSWER KEY

1. D Step 1: L x Cost PLF + Sales Tax = Material Cost
       130 x   2.83 +   6.5% =   391.81
       Step 2: Persons x Cost per Hour x Hours   = Labor Cost
               In Crew   To Complete
               2   x   14.95   x3   = 89.70
       Step 3: Step 1 + Step 2 = Total Cost
               391.81 + 89.70 = 481.51

2. D # x L x W Square Feet Per Board x Layers = Boards Step 1: 1 x 108 x 48 = 5,184
       Step 2: 3 x 20 x 10 = (600)
                        4,584 ÷ 32   x 2   = 286.5

3. A L   x   W ÷   Coverage Per Sheet   = Sheets
       110 ÷ 50 x 2- 4   x1.5   —   30   = 15.8

4. B # x L x W   x # Plies + 100 x Rate Per Square + 2000 = Tons
       Step 1: 1 x 108 x 48 = 5,184
       Step 2: 3 x 20 x 10 = (600)
                4,584 x 4 + 100 x 25 + 2000 = 2.29

5. B # x L x W ÷ 100 x # Per Square = Total Step 1: 1 x 108 x 48 = 5,184
       Step 2: 3 x 20 x 10 = (600)
                4,584 ÷ 100 x 80 = 3,667.2

6. B L x W + 100 x Pounds Per Square ÷ 2000 = Tons
       130 x 20 + 100 x   400   ÷ 2000 = 5.2

7. B L   x   W ÷   Square Feet Per Sheet =   Sheets
       170 x   1   +   30   =   5.66

8. B L   +   W   Wall Width =   Cant Length
       110 +   50 x 2   4   =   316

9. A # x   L   x   W   x   WPF =   Pounds
       10 x   10 x   30 x   1=   3,000

   B Cap Flashing: L   X W   ÷ Coverage = Sheets
                    200 + 100 X 2 + 4 X 1   M+
       Counter Flashing: 200 + 100 X 2 X .5   M+
                                    MR ÷   15 = 60.2

11. A   Centerline Length   X   W   + Coverage X Cost =   Total

   Parapets: 268 +120 X 2 — 2.67 X 1.33   M+
   A/C Curbs: 4 X 12 — 2.67 X 5   X 1.33 M+
                MR +   15   X 270 = $23,939.52

DFlat Lengths: 32 + 58 + 20 + 14 X 2 — 20 -12 — 12 + (6 X 14) = 288
   Gable: # X   Span   X   Flat Area Factor
            2 X   12 + 20   X   1.25   = 55
                                          343

13.C   Parapet: Centerline   X   W + Coverage X Cost = Total
   188 +105 X 2+4   X   2 M+
   A/C Curbs:
   14+10 X2+2 X5 X 2M+
                MR   +   30   X 180 = $10.080

 A
   Width   X   Length   =   Square Inches
   3 +3 +4   X   12   =   120
CWidthX Length +   144 = Square feet
   3 +4 X2 X   12   + 144 =   1.17

ROOFING STUDY GUIDE
ROOFING MATH PRACTICE QUESTIONS

Compute the common rafter length for a hipped roof on a building which is 30 feet wide by 60 feet long. There is a 1 foot overhang to be included and the slope of the roof is 8/12.

- 19' 2-3/4"
- 18.405'
- 18.815'
- 19' 4"

How many sheets of plywood are required to sheath the roof?

- 57
- 56
- 67
- 75

How many squares of asphalt 3 tab shingles are required, not including waste, starters, or ridge caps?

- 57
- 56
- 24
- 25

How many bundles of shingles are required, again *not* including starter or ridge cap?

- 54
- 72
- 88
- 84

How much drip edge is required?

- 184 lf
- 180 lf
- 188 lf
- None of the above

THE NEXT THREE QUESTIONS REFER TO DRAWING 1

A bag of insulation covers 22.8 sq. ft. and costs $4.00 with tax included. Labor is $.08/sq. ft. The building has flat ceilings throughout and a 12" overhang all around. The total cost of loose ceiling insulation for the entire building is

- $1,520.00
- $2,189.44
- $2,211.52
- $2,323.04

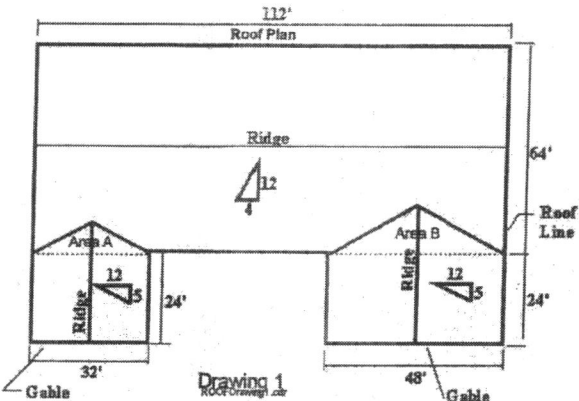

Drawing 1

The building fascia is 2" x 10" cedar costing $1,050 per thousand board feet including tax. The fascia lumber cost using a 15 percent waste factor is

Note: There are 1.66 board feet per linear foot of 2 x 10.

$558.60
$808.50
$865.38
$930.00

8. The cost of standing seam metal roofing for this building is _____. Use the bid of $415 per square, which includes waste. Refer to Drawing 1

    A. $37,700 to $37,750
    B. $39,720 to $39,770
    C. $39,960 to $40,110
    D. $40,830 to $40,880

Questions 9-19 refer to Drawing Two.

The pitch of the roof is

    4/12
    5/12
    1/4
    1/6

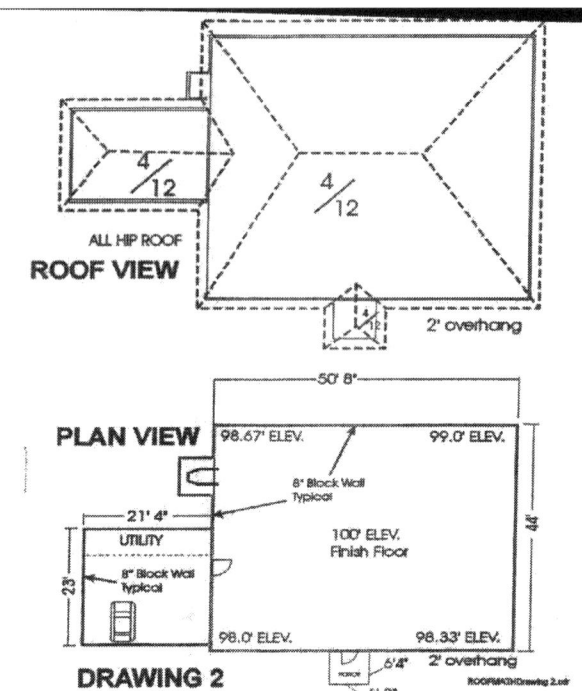

ROOF VIEW — ALL HIP ROOF

PLAN VIEW / **DRAWING 2**

10. Disregarding all starter strip and ridge caps, _____ squares of shingles are required for the building.

    34.4
    33.28
    32
    30

How many squares of starter shingles are required?

    1.09
    1.12
    2.0
    2.5

12. _____ is the length of a valley or a hip on the garage.

    19'-6"
    19' 7-3/8"
    19'
    20'

13. _____ is the length of the ridge on the garage.

    25.33
    7.83
    13.5'
    21.333'

How many hip and ridge shingles are required for the garage?

- 48
- 16
- 60
- 32

15. _____ is the length of the ridge on the main house, including the porch.

- 6.33'
- 11'
- 13'
- 18.5'

16. _____ is the total length of the hips on the main house, including the porch.

- 93'
- 102.66'
- 143.35'
- 154' - 11-3/4"

How many squares for the hip and ridge caps are required for the main house & porch?

- 1.68
- 1.28
- 1.78
- 2

18. This house and garage will require a total of _____ squares, allowing for 10% waste.

- 41.41
- 37.55
- 39.64
- 37.05

What factor would be used to calculate the roof area in this drawing?

- 1.031
- 1.054
- 1.179
- 4/12

ANSWERS TO PRACTICE QUESTIONS

1. A	5.0	9. D	13. D	17. A
2. D	6. C	10. A	14. A	18. A
3.0	7. D	11. A	15. C	19. B
4. B	8.0	12. B	16. D	

EXPLANATIONS OF ANSWERS

Ans A. Span 30 + 2(1' overhangs) = 32'. 32 ÷ 2 =16 ft. Run of rafter 16 x 1.202 = 19.232 ft or 19'-2-3/4". (.232 x 12 = 2.75")

Ans D. Round to the nearest sheet.
32' x 62' = 1,984 sq ft x 1.202 = 2,385 sq ft + 32 sq ft/sheet = 74.524 or 75 sheets.

Ans C. 32' x 62' = 1,984 sq ft. x 1.202 = 2,385 sq ft + 100 sqft/ square = 23.85 squares.

Ans B. 24 squares x 3 bundles per square = 72 bundles. RCE, Pg 108. Not in Walker's.

Ans C. Flat = 62 x 2 = 1241f. 32 x 2 = 64 lf Total 1881f.

Ans C. Area 1 = 110 x 62 = 6,820. Area 2 = 46 x 24 = 1,104. Area 3 = 30 x 24 = 720. Total Area 8,644 sq ft. #Bags = 8,644: 22.8 = 379.1 bags.
bags x $4.00/bag = $1,520. Labor = 8,644 x $.08 = $691.52. Total Cost = $1520 + $691.52 = $2,211.52.

Ans D. Flat = 112' for rear. 112' - 80' = 32' for front. Front Gable sides: 4 x 24' = 96'. Main Gables = 1.054 x (64 +64) = 135'. Front Gables (A+B): 80' x 1.083 = 87'. Total lf = 112 +32 + 96 + 135 + 87 = 462'. Convert to b/f : (T (inches) x W (inches) ÷ 12) x L(ft) = 462' x 1.666 = 770 bf. (770 15%) x $1.05/bf= $930.

Ans C. Main Roof = 112 x 64 = 7,168 sq ft - Areas A & B. Area A = 16' (Run A) x 5(Rise A) + 4 (Main Rise) x 16' = 20' x 16' = 320 sq ft. Area B 24' (Run B) x 5 (Rise B) + 4 Main Rise) x 24' =-30' x 24' = 720 sq ft. Total (Main Roof) = 7,168 - 720 = 6,128 sq ft x 1.054 = 6,459 sq ft. Front Gables = 80 x 24 =1,920 sq ft + Areas A &B = 1,920 + 322 +720 = 2,960 sq ft x 1.083 = 3,206 sq ft. Total Area = 6,459 + 3,206 = 9,665 sq ft ÷ 100 = 96.65 squares x $415/square = $40,110.

Ans D. (RCE). Pg. 77. Pitch = Slope x 1/2. Slope 4/12. Pitch = 4/12 x 1/2 = 4/24 = 1/6.

Ans A. Main house: 54.666' x 48' = 2,624 sq ft. Garage: 21.333' x 27' = 576 sq ft. Porch: 10.666' x 6.33' = 68 sq ft. Total area = 3,268 sq ft. x 1.054
3,444 sq ft. A square = 100 sq ft. 3,444 + 100 = 34.4 squares.

Ans A. Calculate perimeter. Main House: (54.666 x 2) + (48 x 2) = 205'. Garage sides: 21.333' x 2 = 43'. Porch sides: 6.333' x 2 = 13'. Total= 261' + 3(3-in-1 strip) = 87 shingles. 87 ÷ 80 (Shingles/square) = 1.09 squares. (WALK), Pg 7.46. (RCE), Pg 108.

Ans B. Length = Run x Hip Factor. Run (Garage) = 23' + 4' (Don't forget overhang) 2 = 13.5'. 13.5' x 1.453 = 19.615'. 0.615' x 12 = 7.38". 0.38" x 16 = 6/16 = 3/8". Hip Factors: (RCE), Pg 15. RunxFactor (27 ÷2)x13.5 1.453=1961 .61'x12"=7.32 .32/1"x8/8 = 3/8 Hip = Run x factor H = 13.5 x 1.453 H = 19.62 Dec' x whole' .62 x 12 = 7.44 Dec" x Whole" .44" x 16" = 7/16

Ans D. Since the slopes of both roofs are the same, the length of the Garage ridge is the same as the length of the garage: 21.333'.

Ans A. (WALK) Pg 7.45. (RCE) Pg 114. Allow
sq ft of shingles per linear foot of hip and
ridge. Hip = 13.5 x 1.453 = 19.61 x 2 hips = 39.23'. Ridge = 21.33'. Total length = 39.23 + 21.33 = 60' - 60 sq ft of shingles. Assume 5-inch exposure. Coverage of shingle = (5" (Exposure) x 36" (Length) 144 in/sqft = 1.25 sqft/shingle. #shingles = 60 sqft =1.25 sqft/shingle = 48 shingles.

Ans C. (RCE), Pg 22. Ridge = Length -Wid House = 54.666' - 48' = 6.66'. Porch: 6.33' (run). Total = 13'.

Ans D. (RCE) House: 24' (Run) x 4 hips = 96'. Porch: 5.33' x 2 hips = 10.66'. Total = 106.66 x 1.453 (Hip Factor) = 154.98'. Convert 0.98' into inches: 0.98' x 12 = 11.76" = 11-3/4".

Ans A. (RCE) Length Hips= 155' (see question 16) Hip = Total span x 1.453. (48 + 48) 96 x 1.453
139. Length of Ridges - Main House = 13' See question 15).Total Length = 155' + 13' = 168' =

sqft of shingles. # Shingles = 168 sqft =1.25 sqft/shingle = 134.4 shingles. # squares = 134.4 ÷ 80 shingles/square (Pg 108) = 1.68 squares.

Ans. A. Roof area = 34.4 (Ques. 10). Starter = 1.09 (Ques. 11). Hip & Ridge caps: Garage = 0.48 (Quest 14). House = 1.46 (Ques 17). Porch = 15.48' (Hips) + 6.33' (ridge) = 21.8' + 1.25 = 17.44 shingles ÷ 80 = 0.22. Total = 34.4 + 1.086 + 0.60

1.68 = 37.65 squares + 10% = 41.41 squares.

Ans B. For 4/12 slope, Rise = 4" and Factor = 1.054. (Walker) Div 7. (RCE) Appendix A table

Made in the USA
Monee, IL
04 April 2025

15195877R00151